OXFORD ENGLISH MONOGRAPHS

UNGOVERNED IMAGININGS

James Mill's *The History of British India* and Orientalism

JAVED MAJEED

CLARENDON PRESS · OXFORD

This book has been printed digitally and produced in a standard design in order to ensure its continuing availability

OXFORD
UNIVERSITY PRESS

Great Clarendon Street, Oxford OX2 6DP
Oxford University Press is a department of the University of Oxford.
It furthers the University's objective of excellence in research, scholarship, and education by publishing worldwide in

Oxford New York

Athens Auckland Bangkok Bogotá Buenos Aires Cape Town Chennai Dar es Salaam Delhi Florence Hong Kong Istanbul Karachi Kolkata Kuala Lumpur Madrid Melbourne Mexico City Mumbai Nairobi Paris São Paulo Singapore Taipei Tokyo Toronto Warsaw

with associated companies in Berlin Ibadan

Oxford is a registered trade mark of Oxford University Press in the UK and certain other countries

Published in the United States by Oxford University Press Inc., New York

Reprinted 2001

ISBN 0-19-811786-8

For my parents
and Zahid

Acknowledgements

I am indebted to Dr C. Bayly, Professor Marilyn Butler, and Dr T. Raychaudhuri for their constructive criticisms and help. I have had useful discussions with Dr Akbar Ahmad, Dr Neeladri Bhattacharya, Dr Raj Chandavarkar, Professor Jean-Claude Galey, Dr Tapati Guhathakurata, Dr Jonathan Katz, Dr Michael Long, Dr Farhan Nizami, Dr David Norbrook, Mr Bernard O'Donoghue, Dr Nicholas Shrimpton, Professor Romila Thapar, and Mr William Thomas. Mr M. J. Allen read the manuscript carefully and sympathetically. The staff of the Bodleian Library, Oxford, the British Library, London, the University College Library, London, and Cyprian Blackmires of the Bentham Project, the University of London, have been helpful. I am grateful to the Managers of the Smuts Memorial Fund for electing me to a post-doctoral research fellowship at the Centre of South Asian Studies, the University of Cambridge, and to the Fellows of Churchill College for electing me to a research fellowship.

Contents

INTRODUCTION

This is a study of the emergence of utilitarianism as a political language in Britain in the late eighteenth and early nineteenth centuries. It attempts to describe the relationship between the emergence of this language, as defined by Jeremy Bentham and James Mill, and the complexities of British imperial experience in India at the time. As such, it touches upon issues which have been raised by anthropologists, historians, and literary critics about the relationship between power and knowledge in the understanding and defining of non-European cultures and their histories during the age of European imperialism. In this interdisciplinary area, stress is often placed on analysing anthropological and historical material as literary texts, whose rhetoric and style are treated as clues to understanding this relationship. Indeed, the very meaning of 'literature' itself has been much debated in literary theory.[1] Talal Asad and John Dixon have described anthropological practice as 'translating' non-European cultures. They have argued that a closer examination must be made of various aspects of the style of anthropological writings in order to understand how anthropologists have 'translated' other cultures. This would also enable anthropologists to overcome their 'linguistic inertia'.[2] So, too, the analysis of literary texts, and the literary analysis of texts not usually deemed 'literary', plays an important part in the studies by Edward Said, Ranajit Guha, Ashis Nandy, and Tapan Raychaudhuri. The latter three examine not just the relation between European imperialism and the depiction of non-European cultures, but also the

[1] Terry Eagleton, *Literary Theory: An Introduction* (Oxford: Basil Blackwell, 1983), ch. 1, and Anne Jefferson and David Robey, *Modern Literary Theory: A Comparative Introduction* (London: Batsford, 1982), ch. 1.

[2] Talal Asad and John Dixon, 'Translating Europe's Others', in Francis Baker (ed.), *Europe and its Others*, 2 vols. (Colchester: University of Essex, 1985), i. 173–7. See also Brian Street, 'Orientalist Discourses in the Anthropology of Iran, Afghanistan, and Pakistan', in Richard Fardon (ed.), *Localising Strategies* (Edinburgh: Edinburgh University Press, 1989), 240–59. Street considers the problems of ethnographic style raised by Asad and Dixon, as exemplified in such debates as that between Professors Akbar Ahmed and Frederik Barth about the nature of Swat Pushtun society.

responses to that imperial expansion by indigenous literati.[3] This study is less a contribution to the polemic generated by such work, than an attempt to give the argument a detailed and specific reference, and to explore these issues by recasting some of the problems raised by them. In many ways, these issues were clearly defined in the period of this study.

The focus of this study is James Mill's *The History of British India* (1817). The work of Jeremy Bentham is treated in terms of its influence (which was considerable) upon Mill, and where there were significant differences between the two, these have been pointed out. However, this is not a study of Bentham's work in its own right. It is a study primarily of Mill's *History* and the role it played in the formation of the character of utilitarianism as a body of thought in the early nineteenth century. The target of the radical rhetoric of utilitarianism was the revitalized conservatism of this period, which was itself a response to the threat of the French Revolution. Perhaps the most strident expression of this conservatism was in Edmund Burke's *Reflections on the Revolution in France* (1791), a book which more than any other defined the main ideas underpinning the tradition of the common law as the ruling political ideology of the time. It was this tradition which was one of the prime targets of attack in Bentham's and Mill's writings. The debates about the shape which British rule in India ought to take was one arena of the struggle between this conservatism and utilitarianism. For James Mill, however, British India was not simply one issue among many around which this polemical debate took place. It was crucial in actually constituting the nature of his polemic. Aesthetic and linguistic attitudes were important components of this polemic, and indeed of British views on India generally. Furthermore, these attitudes, or what we might call 'the politics of the imagination',[4] were related to the definition and depiction of

[3] Edward Said, *Orientalism* (London: Routledge & Kegan Paul, 1978); Ranajit Guha, 'On some Aspects of the Historiography of Colonial India', *Subaltern Studies*, 1 (Delhi: Oxford University Press, 1982), 1–8, 'The Prose of Counter-Insurgency', *Subaltern Studies*, 2 (Delhi: Oxford University Press, 1983), 1–40, and *An Indian Historiography of India: A Nineteenth-Century Agenda and its Implications* (Calcutta: K. P. Bagchi, 1988); Ashis Nandy, *The Intimate Enemy: Loss and Recovery of Self under Colonialism* (Delhi: Oxford University Press, 1983); and Tapan Raychaudhuri, *Europe Reconsidered: Perceptions of the West in Nineteenth Century Bengal* (Delhi: Oxford University Press, 1988).

[4] I have taken the phrase 'the politics of the imagination' from R. F. Storch's article of that title, *Studies in Romanticism*, 21 (Autumn 1982), 448–56.

cultural identities, with which both political languages were preoccupied.

The political traditions in Britain at the end of the eighteenth and the beginning of the early nineteenth centuries were of course complex. As far as possible, these complexities have been touched upon. For example, Bentham's and Mill's attacks on other forms of political radicalism are mentioned when considering the originality of their work and the incisiveness of their methodology. The purpose here, however, is not to provide as complete a picture as possible of the traditions of British political thought in all their complexity in this period. The aim of this study is to provide an account of Mill's *History* which suggests that some of the current approaches to 'colonialist discourse' are misguided when they deal with texts such as this. The question of whether or not the work of a figure is representative of larger currents of thought is always a vexed one. To an important extent, Bentham and Mill were establishing a body of thought which it is fruitful to see less as a culmination of a larger intellectual tradition, than the foundation of one radically departing from the traditions it contended with. Dealing with this body of ideas as symptomatic of wider currents of thought tends to neglect the challenging aspects of its rhetoric. Furthermore, the relationship of an author's work to its context is problematic and ambiguous. Some texts are important precisely because they cannot be reduced to being merely reflections of their contexts. Indeed, by focusing on the texts and issues they grapple with they are partly responsible for actually creating their own contexts. The traditions texts contend with can be traditions which they have defined for their own purposes.[5] Thus, while there is ample evidence to suggest that as a Supreme Court judge in Calcutta and in his projected digest of Indian law Sir William Jones both shaped and reflected the prevailing ethos of the East India Company in the late eighteenth century, it was Mill who first clearly defined Jones's body of ideas as conservative and as a reflection of that ethos. But even before Mill had done so, Jones's work had become part of the conservative ideology articulated by Burke. Any study of Jones has to take into account this complex of interpretations of his ideas in this period, which simplified the conflicting strands in his work.

[5] For an extended discussion of these issues, see Dominick La Capra, *Rethinking Intellectual History: Texts, Contexts, Language* (Ithaca, NY: Cornell University Press, 1983) and *History and Criticism* (Ithaca, NY: Cornell University Press, 1985).

The influence of his work was in some ways at odds with its strand of political radicalism, but it would be naïve to assume that the influence of a corpus of texts was always in keeping with the author's intentions, even where these can be reliably ascertained. Nor is it clear what role knowledge of an author's intentions can play in the interpretation of a text, let alone in the assessment of its influence.

This study tries to uncover the complexity of each author's work, while also paying heed to its relationship with the way different strands of thought define each other. So, for example, the contradictions and ambiguities in Mill's *History* are stressed. Such tensions are to be expected in a text like the *History*, which sought to undertake the formidable task of criticizing the ideology of the British establishment in its entirety. By neglecting these tensions in Mill's work, commentators have been able to characterize it as an unproblematic reflection of a systematic body of thought, rather than as a text whose contradictions are indicative of a body of thought struggling to articulate itself. But while this reading of the *History* emphasizes its gaps and inconsistencies, the type of process involved in the defining of intellectual traditions is exemplified by H. H. Wilson's edition of Mill's *History*. This edition was composed of three strands, Jones's orientalism as formulated and attacked by Mill's philosophic radicalism, which in turn was countered by Wilson's defence of Jones. Wilson's defence of Jones points both to the way in which a set of ideas can be rearticulated in response to a critique, and to the way in which one set of ideas can be relocated within another context.

In his powerful study of the epistemological ventures which were integral to European imperialism, Edward Said has argued that the Orient was in a very real sense the creation of a whole apparatus of intellectual practices which were a part of such ventures. In the oriental works of Robert Southey and Thomas Moore studied here, it is clear that the Orient was a creation which played a vital role in constituting their differing religious, political, and aesthetic positions. Furthermore, the intimate and complex relationship between popular and scholarly orientalism in their works can also be interpreted in the light of Said's conception of the orientalist venture. But whilst Said remains an indispensable starting point for any study of this kind, the shortcomings of his argument also have to be kept clearly in view. The thinkers and poets examined here had a much more sophisticated awareness of the issues which Said has argued constituted orientalism than he and others have allowed. For example, that at one level contemporaries recognized the Orient was a creation of some kind is evident in some of the reviews of Moore's *Lalla Rookh*, which attacked the Orient in it as a convenient and enabling fiction for Moore's 'licentious' imagination. Indeed, this was at the heart of Mill's critique of Jones, when he argued not only that Jones's Orient was the product of an undisciplined imagination, but that the Orient as Jones and others had conceived it underpinned notions of the imagination which were dangerous on epistemological and political grounds. Furthermore, the attention paid to the conflicting strands in the works of the authors analysed here, and the problematic relationship of these texts to the contexts which they were in part structured by, and which they in part created, runs counter to Said's rather monolithic and ahistorical conception of orientalism. Moore's orientalism, at least in *Lalla Rookh*, was part of a larger anti-imperialist strategy which reflected his ambiguous position as an Anglo-Irish poet in London society, whilst the interpretation (and defence) offered here of Mill's critique of orientalism in his *History* suggests ways in which a liberating critique of some sort was being sketched out in a text whose self-reflexivity has often been ignored.

The general nature of James Mill's *History* and the utilitarianism it embodied was shaped by the series of problems which it addressed in its engagement with its historical context. The late eighteenth and early nineteenth centuries saw both the rise of Britain as the dominant power in the world, and the growth of a revitalized conservatism in Britain itself, which was mirrored in the institutions of the British empire abroad.[6] This conservatism was a reaction against the threat of the French revolution, which appeared to threaten the European social order as a whole.[7] The reaction was evident in the extension of the powers of the state to suppress political radicalism during the early part of the war, and in the immediate post-war period.[8] It was also evident in increased propaganda drives to ensure the loyalty of the lower orders of society.

[6] C. A. Bayly, *Imperial Meridian: The British Empire and the World, 1780–1830* (London: Longman, 1989), 2, 11.

[7] Clive Emsley, *British Society and the French Wars 1793–1815* (London: Macmillan, 1979), 22.

[8] J. Ann Hone, *For the Cause of Truth: Radicalism in London 1796–1821* (Oxford: Clarendon Press, 1982), 11–20, 266–70, 305.

Radicals were aware of the propagandist uses to which public ceremonies and rituals were being put by the government; in his 'Essay on Colonies', written for the 1817 *Supplement to the Encyclopaedia Britannica*, James Mill described how 'splendour and parade . . . captivate and subdue the imagination, and make men contented, one would almost say happy, to be slaves'.[9] Jeremy Bentham in his Introduction (written in 1809) to *Plan of Parliamentary Reform* (1817) listed the 'Splendor [*sic*] of the crown' as one of the strategies used by the ruling élite to 'increase the respect, and with it the submission, and with it the happiness of the people'.[10] Indeed, the period of the reign of George III saw the increasing manipulation of public ceremonies to enhance the public presentation and reputation of the monarchy as part of an attempt to consolidate loyalty in the face of the French threat.[11] So, too, the earlier aversion to standing armies was no longer in evidence in this period, and military processions were generally well received by the populace.[12] It has been estimated that by 1809 roughly one in every nine or ten men of military age in Great Britain and Ireland was serving in the forces of the army, navy, or regular militia; and if we are to include volunteers and local militias in this calculation, the proportion rises to about one in six men.[13] These forces were sometimes used to suppress disorder within Britain itself; thus, during the Luddite disturbances, 12,000 soldiers were deployed in the counties suffering disorder during the summer and autumn of 1812. This was a greater number of troops than had landed with Wellesley in Portugal in 1808.[14] It was for this reason that Jeremy Bentham was to describe the British government as military, and to declare 'by a standing army is it that we are governed'.[15] Furthermore, the period of the French wars also saw the introduction of such measures as the income tax in December 1798, in order to help finance the war effort. Measures such as these necessitated an increased professionalism of central government, the reform and

[9] 'Essay on Colonies' (n.d.), 32.

[10] Jeremy Bentham, *Plan of Parliamentary Reform, in the Form of a Catechism, with Reasons for Each Article, with an Introduction, Shewing the Necessity of Radical, and the Inadequacy of Moderate, Reform* (London: R. Hunter, 1817), p. xv.

[11] Linda Colley, 'The Apotheosis of George III: Loyalty, Royalty, and the British Nation 1760–1820', *Past and Present*, 102 (1984), 94–129.

[12] Ibid. 118–19. [13] Emsley, *The French Wars*, 133. [14] Ibid. 158.

[15] Bentham, *Plan of Parliamentary Reform*, pp. xxxii–xxxv.

expansion of departments such as the Treasury, and a changing view as to the responsibility and powers of government itself.[16]

These changes were a response to the need to preserve order at home while sustaining the conflict with France. Christopher Bayly has stressed the global character of this conflict; from 1806 onwards, for example, British troops and fleets were engaged in Holland and Spain, the Mediterranean, and from the Baltic to South America.[17] Some contemporary British commentators argued that the only way to counteract the French threat was to extend and 'perpetuate our empire'.[18] It was in fact the period of the French wars which saw the greatest expansion of British imperial domination. It has been estimated that by 1820 the total population of British territories was 26 per cent of the world population.[19] India played a major part in this imperial system. By 1815, the East India Company's army was one of the largest European-style standing armies in the world; it had been used after 1790 to forward British interests in southern and eastern Asia and the Middle East, and it opened up a second Front against the other great European land powers of Russia, the Ottomans, France, and Austria.[20] During the first two decades of the nineteenth century, India also provided the base from which to build up informal empires of trade and influence in the Middle East and East Africa, and along the China Coast.[21]

There are three features of the character of the British empire in this period which are of relevance to the general thrust of Mill's thought. First, it is clear that economic motives were less important in the British imperial expansion of the late eighteenth and early nineteenth centuries than fear of social disorder at home and abroad. It is for this reason that a recognition of ideological and institutional change is important for our understanding of this period. In 1808 G. F. Leckie complained that 'there is no uniform spirit that pervades our distant provinces, and stamps them as much as circumstances will permit with an homogeneous character'.[22] The competing ideologies of the period sought to provide this uniform spirit for the empire. James Mill's *The History of British*

[16] Emsley, *The French Wars*, 179.
[17] Bayly, *Imperial Meridian*, 3–4.
[18] G. F. Leckie, *An Historical Survey of the Foreign Affairs of Great Britain* (London: J. Bell, 1808), 10.
[19] Bayly, *Imperial Meridian*, 3.
[20] C. A. Bayly, *Indian Society and the Making of the British Empire* (Cambridge: Cambridge University Press, 1988), 1.
[21] Ibid. 1.
[22] Leckie, *Foreign Affairs of Great Britain*, 16.

India (1817) was an attempt to define an idiom for the British empire as a whole which would replace the dominant conservative one.

Secondly, the global conflict with France, and the expansion of the British empire in reaction to the French threat, meant that colonial and domestic issues could not be separated in this period. To a certain extent, the interest which Parliament took from the 1780s onwards in the affairs of the East India Company had already established a framework in which to consider the political and constitutional implications of East India Company rule for Britain itself. Edmund Burke, who more than any other public figure was responsible for this interest in the Company's affairs, firmly believed that India should not be considered in isolation. During the parliamentary session of 1781, he was appointed to the Select Committee of the House of Commons, whose purpose was to investigate the administration of justice in Bengal. In 1772 the Company had assumed direct responsibility for the administration of civil justice in Bengal, but the Select Committee was to inquire mainly into petitions directed against the Supreme Court in Calcutta, which had been established in 1773 under the Regulating Act. These petitions accused the court of exceeding its powers and acting in a manner oppressive to British subjects and the Indian population of Bengal as a whole. Burke's investigations only ended with the acquittal of Warren Hastings in 1795. At the beginning of the 1782 session the Select Committee was reconvened with the wider remit to consider 'the British Possessions' in India as a whole, and to report, in Burke's words, on 'how the British Possessions in the East Indies may be held and governed with the greatest security and Advantage to this Country, and by what Means the Happiness of the Native Inhabitants may be best promoted'.[23] This Committee produced eleven reports between 1782 and 1783 on various aspects of Company rule; its Ninth Report of June 1783 described the period of British rule from 1773 to 1782 as one in which 'Disorders and Abuses of every Kind multiplied', and it feared that India 'instead of a Resource to the Public, may itself come, in no great Length of Time, to be reckoned amongst the Public Burthens'.[24] It was for this reason that Parliament considered itself bound to make the investigations it was pursuing. For Burke himself, the com-

[23] *The Writings and Speeches of Edmund Burke: India: Madras and Bengal 1774–1785*, ed. P. J. Marshall (Oxford: Clarendon Press, 1981), v. 145.
[24] Ibid. 220–1.

placency he had shown about the Company's administration had been shaken earlier with the arrival of the news in the spring of 1777 that Lord Pigot, the governor of Madras, had been arrested and deposed by the majority of his council, after he had tried to restore Tanjore, conquered by Company troops in 1773, to its erstwhile raja.[25] The importance of the Select Committee's reports of 1782–3 lay not only in their clear definition of a number of issues relating to British India, which Mill was later to address in his *History*. What was particularly interesting was the attempt to understand the alien and complex cultures of India in order to prescribe the character of British rule there. Burke had already depicted Tanjore as a self-sufficient society with a benevolent despotism, and the depiction of Indian cultures in the reports followed this trend. It was for this reason that the reports were unsympathetic to what was regarded as the imposition of alien law on these societies, and denied that 'Parliament ever intended to act upon a Supposition of the Utter Extinction of all the original Laws and Rights of the Natives'.[26] Indian cultures were depicted and defended in the same terms as Burke was later to defend the French *ancien régime* in his *Reflections on the Revolution in France* (1790). Thus, although the French Revolution raised questions about the nature of cultural identity, these questions had already been raised by British involvement in India. With the threat of the French Revolution these questions became more urgent than ever before. The debate about what form British rule in India should take, and the character of reform in Britain itself, depended ultimately on how cultures were to be understood and defined, and for both conservatism and utilitarianism, the question of reform in Britain and of reform in India could not be separated. As G. F. Leckie observed in 1808, after the French revolution, 'the defenders of established government held it equally dangerous to deride the absurdity and tyranny of an Asiatic despotism, as to question or cavil at the perfections of the British constitution'.[27] Jeremy Bentham and James Mill were to deride both these despotisms, and indeed, to show that to cavil at the perfections of one meant cavilling at the perfections of the other.

[25] Ibid. 5.

[26] Ibid., First Report of the Select Committee, 5 Feb. 1782, 178.

[27] Leckie, *Foreign Affairs of Great Britain*, 8.

Finally, as P. J. Marshall has stressed, the British empire of the late eighteenth century no longer consisted of communities of British origin. It now included numerous peoples not British in origin, incorporated into the empire by conquest, and ruled without representation.[28] This presented a host of novel problems, not least of which was the extent to which a system of laws derived from another society could be applicable to very different cultures, and the possibility that government overseas might assume a different form from government at home. Furthermore, this empire provided a testing ground for the various legal, social, and educational theories of the period. It is only by examining how India was a testing ground for such theories that we can understand the emergence of utilitarianism as a new political language in this period. Jeremy Bentham and James Mill were to provide a set of answers to the novel problems raised by the heterogeneous character of the empire, and in doing so they were to give an entirely different character to the earlier liberal imperialism of such figures as Sir William Jones. Indeed, much of James Mill's *History of British India* was an attack upon Sir William Jones and the body of ideas which Mill believed he had defined. In order to understand the force of these criticisms, the first chapter considers the work of Sir William Jones, and how it defined a series of positions which James Mill was to attack in his attempt to articulate a new idiom which would place thinking on British India on a different footing.

[28] P. J. Marshall, 'Empire and Authority in the Later Eighteenth Century', *Journal of Imperial and Commonwealth History*, 15 (Jan. 1987), 115.

CHAPTER 1

SIR WILLIAM JONES

Introduction

Much has been written on Sir William Jones, the linguist, scholar, and lawyer, who arrived in Bengal in 1783 as a Supreme Court judge, and on his influence on the thought and literature of the late eighteenth and the nineteenth centuries.[1] R. M. Hewitt has stressed the wide extent of his influence: 'If we were compiling a thesis on the influence of Jones, we could collect most of our material from footnotes, ranging from Gibbon (1776) to Tennyson (1827) and including *Vathek* and *The Curse of Kehama*.'[2] Garland Cannon has traced Jones's influence on Romantic literature,[3] which has also been documented in detail by other scholars.[4] In the study of languages particular emphasis has been placed on Jones's role in the break from the philosophical, a priori method of the eighteenth century, to the historical, a posteriori method of the nineteenth century.[5] The importance of Jones's work for the historical and comparative linguistics of the nineteenth century is also well documented.[6]

[1] The two standard biographies of Jones are Garland Cannon's *Oriental Jones: A Biography of Sir William Jones (1746–1794)* (New York: Asia Publishing House, 1964) and S. N. Mukherjee, *Sir William Jones: A Study in Eighteenth-Century British Attitudes to India* (Cambridge: Cambridge University Press, 1968).

[2] R. M. Hewitt, 'Harmonious Jones', *Essays and Studies*, 28 (1942), 42–59.

[3] G. Cannon, 'The Literary Place of Sir William Jones, 1746–94', *Journal of the Asiatic Society*, 11 (1960), 47–61, and 'The Construction of the European Image of the Orient: A Bicentenary Appraisal of Sir William Jones as Poet and Translator', *Comparative Criticism*, 8 (1986), 167–88.

[4] V. de Sola Pinto, 'Sir William Jones and English Literature', *Bulletin of the School of Oriental and African Studies*, 11 (1943–6), 686–98.

[5] H. Aarsleff, *The Study of Language in England, 1780–1860* (1967: Minneapolis: University of Minnesota Press, 1983), 127.

[6] R. H. Robins, *A Short History of Linguistics* (London: Longman, 1979), ch. 6. See also Alfred Masters, 'The Influence of Sir William Jones upon Sanskrit Studies,' *Bulletin of the School of Oriental and African Studies*, 11 (1943–6), 798–806; Giuliano Bonfante, 'Ideas on the Kinship of the European Languages from 1200 to 1800', *Journal of World History*, 1 (July 1953), 679–99.

This chapter defines and considers the four dominant themes to Sir William Jones's work: his study of Sanskrit and his formulation of the Indo-European family of languages; his project for a digest of Indian law; its relation to discussions of land revenue systems; and his formulation of a methodology for the study of Indian history. The purpose here is not to reiterate the many accounts of the importance of various aspects of Jones's work, but to show how his work shaped certain issues which scholars on Jones have on the whole neglected. Thus, it is argued that what was important about the Indo-European thesis of languages in the context of the late eighteenth and early nineteenth centuries was that it enabled comparisons to be made between cultures on a firmer foundation than before. Jones's legal work is examined in terms of the problems which it posed for Bentham and Mill, whilst his hymns to Hindu deities are examined in the context of his legal work and his attempt to define the cultural identity of a rejuvenated Hinduism. Whilst Jones stressed the need for an accurate history when he defined his methodology for the study of Indian history, the distinction he drew between such a history and 'poetical fables' collapsed in his own work. This points to the different notions of history which were contested in this period. Mill was to respond to these themes in Jones's work when he addressed similar problems in his *History*. In doing so, he was to put what has been called 'liberal imperialism' on an altogether different footing from Jones. Indeed, it is not clear how useful it is to characterize Jones as a liberal imperialist at all. Rather than explaining the ambiguities in his position in terms of his supposed liberal imperialism, it seems more fruitful to see these ambiguities as stemming from a confusion about how to arrive at an understanding of cultures which would both respect their uniqueness, and compare and contrast them to other cultures in a neutral idiom.

The Indo-European Family of Languages and Nations

R. H. Robins writes that towards the end of the eighteenth century, 'thinkers in different countries and with diverse backgrounds were drawn towards the history of language on the eve of a century wherein the history of languages, enlivened by a flash of light from the east, was to make unprecedented advances'.[7] The 'flash of light

7 Robins, *A Short History of Linguistics*, 159.

from the east' was Sir William Jones's declaration of the affinity of Sanskrit and Greek and Latin in his 'Third Anniversary Discourse' to the Asiatic Society of Bengal, of 2 February 1786:

The Sanscrit language, whatever be its antiquity, is of a wonderful structure; more perfect than the *Greek*, more copious than the *Latin*, and more exquisitely refined than either, yet bearing to both of them a stronger affinity both in the roots of verbs and in the forms of grammar, than could possibly have been produced by accident; so strong indeed, that no philologer could examine them all three, without believing them to have sprung from some common source, which, perhaps, no longer exists . . .[8]

The comparison of Sanskrit with European languages formed the first stage in the growth of historical and comparative linguistics. Although the affinity between Sanskrit and Greek and Latin had been noticed as early as the sixteenth century by Filippo Sassetti, an Italian merchant who visited India in 1583,[9] his observations and those of others, remained isolated and forgotten until Jones appeared. As president of the Asiatic Society of Bengal, which he established in 1784, Jones's announcement had more significance than previous observations.

What was particularly innovatory in Jones's linguistic work was his methodology. He shunned the etymological method of antiquarians like Jacob Bryant and thought Bryant's etymology the weakest part of the *Analysis of Ancient Mythology* (1775):

Etymology has, no doubt, some use in historical researches; but it is a medium of proof so very fallacious, that, where it elucidates one fact, it observes a thousand, and more frequently borders on the ridiculous, than leads to any solid conclusion . . .[10]

He reiterates these criticisms of 'etymological conjectures' as a weak 'mode of reasoning', and goes on:

I beg leave, as a philologer, to enter my protest against conjectural etymology in historical researches, and principally against the licentiousness of etymologists in transposing and inserting letters, in substituting at pleasure any consonant for another of the same order, and in totally disregarding the vowels . . .[11]

[8] 'On the Hindu's [*sic*]' *Asiatick Researches* (hereafter *As. Res.*), 1 (1788), 422–3.

[9] Masters, 'The Influence of Sir William Jones upon Sanskrit Studies', 799; Bonfante, 'Ideas on the Kinship of the European Languages', 686–7.

[10] 'On the Hindu's', 416.

[11] 'On the Origin and Families of Nations', *As. Res.* 3 (1792), 489.

In contrast to Bryant, Jones stressed the importance of the empirical study of languages, and especially of grammatical structure when investigating relationships of kinship. It was this, more than anything else, which paved the way for the historical method of nineteenth-century linguistics.[12] Jeremy Bentham and James Mill were to have very different views on the study of language, views which were to impede the development of historical and comparative linguistics in Britain in the early part of the nineteenth century, and which were also an important factor in their approach to Indian affairs.

However, the character of Jones's work is more accurately represented by such comparativist essays as 'On the Gods of Greece, Italy, and India', 'On the Mystical Poetry of the Persians and Hindus', and 'On the Philosophy of the Asiaticks',[13] than by the 'Third Anniversary Discourse'. Jones had already made frequent intercultural comparisons in his earlier writings on literature and language. In his essay 'On the Poetry of the Eastern nations', which appeared in *Poems Consisting Chiefly of Translations from the Asiatick Languages* (1772), he had drawn comparisons between ancient Greek, Persian, and English literature.[14] Later, in his 1789 translation of Kalidasa's *Sakuntala*, he compared Kalidasa to Shakespeare.[15] To a certain extent, Jones's syncretistic treatises were part of a long tradition, which included such works as Athanasius Kircher's *China Illustra* (1667), and Bernard Picart's *Cérémonies et coutumes religieuses des tous les peuples du monde* (1723); this latter work reproduced the major works of ethnographers and travellers, with their illustrations.[16] It is possible to see eighteenth-century syncretism as a revival of interpretations made by Hellenistic and Roman authors of late antiquity, which blended the distinct features of gods of different religions to render them indistinguishable. For example, Mathurin Veyssière de la Croze's *History of Christianity in the Indies* (1724) argued that linga worship was essentially the worship of Osiris and Bacchus. As far back as the fifth century BC Herodotus had presented these two

[12] Aarsleff, *The Study of Language*, 124, 132.

[13] These appeared in *As. Res.* 1 (1788), 221–75; 3 (1792), 165–83; and 4 (1794), 165–80.

[14] *The Works of Sir William Jones*, ed. A. M. Jones, 6 vols. (London: G. G. and J. Robinson, R. H. Evens, 1799), iv. 405, 542.

[15] *Works*, vi. 205.

[16] Partha Mitter, *Much Maligned Monsters: The History of European Reactions to Indian Art* (Oxford: Clarendon Press, 1977), 55, 59–60.

chthonic gods as identical, and by the time of Plutarch, Osiris had been fully assimilated into the classical pantheon. La Croze was therefore reviving a late antique syncretizing tradition, and extending its scope to include Indian gods such as Siva, identifying Siva with Osiris.[17]

Clearly, what was important about Jones's thesis of the Indo-European family of languages was that it enabled comparisons to be made between cultures on a much firmer foundation than before. The relations of kinship which he traced between languages of the Indo-European family also reinforced what Roy Harris has described as the 'remarkable proposition that languages are translatable', a view which makes a fundamental difference to the European notion of language, which 'intrinsically accommodates the principle of translatability'.[18] In his first contribution to the *Asiatick Researches*, Jones described languages as the 'mere instruments of learning' and argued that they should not be 'improperly confounded with learning itself'.[19] He expressed this sense of the superficiality of linguistic differences when he discusses the doctrines of Vedanta and Sufism: 'From [their] principles flow a thousand metaphors and other poetical figures, which abound in the sacred poems of the *Persians* and *Hindus*, who seem to mean the same thing in substance, and differ only in expression, as their languages differ only in idiom!'[20] Jones used his Indo-European thesis to substantiate the Mosaic story of the monogenesis of mankind. In 1784, from the detailed parallels he drew between Greek, Roman, and Indian mythology, he inferred a 'general union or affinity between the most distinguished inhabitants of the primitive world, at the time when they deviated, as they did too early deviate, from the rational adoration of the only true God'.[21] Later he designated Iran as the centre from which the 'whole race of man proceeded'.[22]

17 Mitter, *Much Maligned Monsters*, 79.

18 Roy Harris, *The Language Makers* (London: Duckworth, 1980), 5–6.

19 'A Discourse on the Institution of a Society, for Inquiring into the History, Civil and Natural, the Antiquities, Arts, Sciences, and Literature of Asia', *As. Res.* 1 (1788), p. xiv.

20 'On the Mystical Poetry of the Persians and Hindus', 171. For a discussion on the extent to which Jones may have conceived of Indian classical philosophy and poetry in Neoplatonic terms, see John Drew, *India and the Romantic Imagination* (Delhi: Oxford University Press, 1987), ch. 2.

21 'On the Gods of Greece', 221.

22 'On the Origin and Families of Nations', 487.

What has been ignored is the fact that Jones's attempt to define an idiom in which cultures could be compared and contrasted was in part a response to the need for such an idiom in the late eighteenth century. It was only through the use of such an idiom that the cultures of the heterogeneous British empire could be compared, the nature of British rule overseas determined, and the empire unified by the same ethos. For Jeremy Bentham and James Mill, the comparison and contrast of cultures was essential for their formulation of a programme of reform which would be relevant to both Indian and British society, but their approach to this issue was to be very different from Jones's.

The Digest of Indian Laws

Jones's work was not only important for the development of comparative and historical linguistics. His work on law had an important bearing on historical and comparative legal studies. Jones himself considered his most important work in India to be his project for a digest of Hindu and Muslim laws, and not his discovery of the affinity of Sanskrit and Greek and Latin. In a letter of 1791, he described this projected digest as 'a noble legacy from me to three & twenty millions of black British subjects'.[23] As early as 1786, he described himself as the 'Justinian of India', and declared, 'my great object, at which I have long been labouring, is to give our country a complete digest of Hindu and Mussulman law'.[24] The fruition of this project, which established his reputation as a jurist, was the publication of *Al Sirajiyyah: or the Mohamedan Law of Inheritance* in 1792, and the *Institutes of Hindu Law, or the ordinances of Menu* in 1796, which remain the basis on which all juridical interpretation of this branch of law in India has been built.[25] These works, together with the earlier *The Speeches of Isaeus* (1779) and *An Essay on the Law of Bailments* (1782), made Jones a forerunner of the historical and comparative school of legal philosophy. The work of Sir Henry Maine and his successors might have lacked some of its most distinctive features if Jones's *Institutes*

[23] Sir William Jones, 'To the second Earl Spencer', 19 Oct. 1791, letter 565 of *The Letters of Sir William Jones*, ed. Garland Cannon, 2 vols. (Oxford: Clarendon Press, 1970), ii. 898–9; hereafter *Letters*.

[24] Jones, 'To Sir John Macpherson', 6 May 1786, letter 453 of *Letters*, ii. 699.

[25] S. G. Vesey-Fitzgerald, 'Sir William Jones, the Jurist', *Bulletin of the School of Oriental and African Studies*, 11 (1943–6), 813–14.

of Hindu Law had not been available to Maine when he was writing his *Ancient Law* (1883).[26]

In his *Institutes of Hindu Law*, Jones had been preceded by Nathaniel Brassey Halhed's *Code of Gentoo Laws* of 1776, which had been commissioned by Warren Hastings, and which he had been asked to review.[27] In 1772 the East India Company had assumed direct responsibility for the administration of civil justice in Bengal. This meant that Europeans were frequently called upon to act as judges in cases to be decided according to Hindu law. For this reason, Hastings hoped to provide a corpus of law which would replace conflicting sources and rival interpretations of pandits. His *Plan for the Administration of Justice* of 1772 listed the civil cases which would fall under Muslim and Hindu law, and provided for the necessity to consult Indian legal experts on these subjects.[28] This plan was later enacted as the Administration of Justice Regulation of 5 July 1781, with the addition of 'succession' as a topic.[29] Eleven pandits were instructed to draw on the best authorities, and lay down the law on certain disputed points. The Sanskrit code they produced was translated into Persian, and rendered from Persian into English by Halhed, who added his own preface. But the code was never accepted as a final authority.[30] Jones's knowledge of Sanskrit was superior to Halhed's, and his work was used at the East India Company's college at Haileybury (founded in 1805), which enormously influenced British attitudes to the subject of Hindu law. It was H. T. Colebrooke's rigorous work, however, starting with his *Digest of Hindu Law* (1798), which commanded the development of Hindu law as we know it.[31]

In 1773, Lord North's Regulation Act had established the King's Court in Calcutta, but its authority was not clearly defined. Its jurisdiction was revised by an Act of Parliament in 1781, which recognized the customs and usages of Hindus and Muslims in inheritance and contract. There were already pandits and maulvis

26 Ibid. 807.

27 Jones, 'To Ralph Griffiths', May 1777, letter 137 of *Letters*, i. 235.

28 *A Plan for the Administration of Justice, Extracted from the Proceedings of the Committee of Circuit, 15th August, 1772*, in *Selections from the State Papers of the Governors-General of India*, ed. G. W. Forrest (1910), ii. 295–6.

29 J. D. M. Derrett, *Religion, Law and the State in India* (London: Faber & Faber, 1968), 289.

30 P. J. Marshall, *The British Discovery of Hinduism in the Eighteenth Century* (Cambridge: Cambridge University Press, 1970), 10–11.

31 J. D. M. Derrett, private communication.

attached to the Supreme Court to interpret Indian laws, as there were in the Company's courts, so this act gave old practice a new authority,[32] but it was not until 1797 that Parliament gave full legislative powers to the East India Company.[33] Jones was very much behind the spirit of the 1781 Act. In a letter of June, 1781, he wrote, 'I should hardly think of instructing the Gentoos in the maxims of the Athenians.'[34] In fact, Jones was consulted about the Indian judicature by the Select Committee of the House of Commons established in 1781 for the purpose of collecting evidence on the whole Indian situation. In 1782 he produced *The Mahomedan Law of Succession* for the use of the Bengal government; in the preface he described a knowledge of Muslim jurisprudence as 'essential to a complete administration of justice in our *Asiatick* territories'.[35] From 1781 until the unsuccessful defence of Fox's India Bill in 1783, Edmund Burke was in frequent conference with Jones on the question of Indian legislation.[36] In a letter to Viscount Althorp in 1781, Jones mentions that he had been asked to 'draw up a report or opinion of the *Bengal judicature* from its first establishment, with my observations on the defects of it and the means of correcting them'.[37] The central principle in this 'Best Practicable System of Judicature for India', which he sent to Burke in 1784, was, 'A system forced upon a people invincibly attached to opposite habits would in truth be a system of cruel tyranny.'[38]

Jones thus had very clear ideas about Indian legislation before he arrived in India, which were strengthened upon his arrival. In his 1783 'Charge to the Grand Jury', soon after his arrival, he declared the purpose of the Supreme Court to be the protection and government of British subjects in India by British laws, and to ensure 'that the natives of these important provinces be indulged in their own prejudices, civil and religious, and suffered to enjoy their own customs unmolested'.[39] In a letter of 1788, he writes that British law is 'fully sufficient to punish every temporal evil, that can injure the public or individuals', but would be 'offensive' and 'oppressive'

[32] Mukherjee, *Jones*, 128.

[33] Jorg Fisch, *Cheap Lives and Dear Limbs: The British Transformation of the Bengal Criminal Law 1769–1817* (Wiesbaden: Franz Steiner Verlag, 1983), 3.

[34] Jones, 'To Edward Gibbon', 30 June 1781, letter 278 of *Letters*, ii. 482.

[35] *Works*, iii. 470.

[36] Garland Cannon, 'Sir William Jones and Edmund Burke', *Modern Philology*, 54 (1956–7), 174.

[37] Jones, 'To the Viscount Althorp', 4 Aug. 1781, letter 283 of *Letters*, ii. 486.

[38] Mukherjee, *Jones*, 142.

[39] *Works*, iii. 3.

if used for 'the punishment of religious offences by Hindus or Mussulmans'.[40] In this, his views reflected the division in English law between the Bishops' Courts, which dealt with matters of marriage and divorce, questions of testaments and distribution of goods, and issues of religious worship and discipline under ecclesiastical law, and the Crown Courts which dealt with other matters. The Supreme Court established in Calcutta was a combination of both a temporal and spiritual court.[41] Jones's philosophy is reiterated in the prefaces to *Al Sirajiyyah* and *Institutes of Hindu Law*. In the latter, he writes:

> It is a maxim in the science of legislation and government, that *Laws are of no avail without manners*, or, to explain the sentence more fully, that the best intended legislative provisions would have no beneficial effect even at first, and none at all in a short course of time, unless they were congenial to the disposition and habits, to the religious prejudices, and approved immemorial usages, of the people, for whom they were enacted . . .[42]

Thus, the main reason why Jones learnt Sanskrit was to compose a reliable digest of Indian laws. The purpose of such a digest was to check the power of pandits in the court. This was made clear in a letter of 1785: 'I have left orders at Benares and Gaya, both holy cities, for the oldest book on the *Hindu* laws to be translated from the *Shanscrit*; which I am almost tempted to learn, that I may be a check on the Pundits of the court.'[43] In another letter during the same period, he wrote, 'It is of the utmost importance, that the stream of Hindu law should be pure; for we are entirely at the power of the native lawyers, through our ignorance of Shanscrit.'[44] Again, in his famous letter to Cornwallis in 1788, Jones argued for 'a complete Digest of Hindu and Mohammedan laws, after the model of Justinian's inestimable Pandects' which would ensure that the pandits and maulvis 'would hardly venture to impose on us when their impositions might so easily be detected'.[45] It was Jones's detection of a forgery in 1789 which confirmed his fears; had this been undetected, other productions would have increased the number of texts pandits cited in support of their determinations.[46]

[40] Jones, 'To John Shore', 7 Feb. 1788, letter 481 in *Letters*, ii. 787.

[41] Derrett, *Religion, Law and the State in India*, 223–4.

[42] *Works*, iii. 53.

[43] Jones, 'To William Pitt the Younger', 5 Feb. 1785, letter 396 of *Letters*, ii. 661.

[44] Jones, 'To Charles Wilkins', Mar. 1785, letter 398 of *Letters*, ii. 666.

[45] Jones, 'To the First Marquis of Cornwallis', 19 Mar. 1788, letter 485 of *Letters*, ii. 794.

[46] Derrett, *Religion, Law and the State in India*, 245.

Jones expressed again and again the need to learn Sanskrit in order to curb the legal power of the pandits and maulvis.[47] His main purpose was to undermine what he perceived to be the legal authority of the sacerdotal classes of Bengal. British power could only be safely secured in the administration of justice if the power of the pandits and maulvis was curbed. Ranajit Guha has discussed the British fear of the power of indigenous knowledge, which was seen as a possible threat to imperial authority.[48] The British definition of Muslim and Hindu codes of law did much to reduce the power of pandits and maulvis. By the third decade of the nineteenth century works by European authors, such as Francis W. Macnaghten's *Principles and Precedents of Hindu Law* (1828–9), were of more practical use. Courts used recent miscellaneous works less, and relied more on translated ancient works. This tendency was encouraged by an inability to tell whether the pandits' references were genuine or not.[49] The position of Muslim law officers remained intact until Regulation 17 of 1817 empowered the Nizamat Adalat, the central criminal court at Calcutta, to overrule the fatwas of the law officers in all cases.[50] With this Muslim law lost its status as the criminal law of the land, although it was not until 1864, after the Indian penal code was promulgated in 1862, that the institution of law officers and their fatwas was abolished.[51]

So for Jones the apparent monopoly of a form of indigenous knowledge by certain classes could only be broken through translation. This would mean that the British would be as conversant in their traditions as they were, and that their idioms would be desacralized by the very act of translation. The imagery of Jones's writings on this subject suggests a breaking into sacred precincts, or an unlocking of hitherto unopened riches. In his early *A Grammar of the Persian Language* (1771), intended for East India Company employees in India, where Persian was the diplomatic language

[47] See e.g. his letters to Charles Chapman and Arthur Pritchard in 1785, *Letters*, ii. 683 and 686.

[48] Guha, *An Indian Historiography of India: A Nineteenth Century Agenda and its Implications* (Calcutta: K. P. Bagchi, 1988), 6. Both Ernest Gellner and Benedict Anderson have discussed how the definition of communities in modern nationalism has been dependent on the demise of such sacerdotal classes; see Ernest Gellner, *Nations and Nationalism* (1983; Oxford: Basil Blackwell, 1984), esp. 141–2; and Benedict Anderson, *Imagined Communities: Reflections on the Origin and Spread of Nationalism* (London: Verso, 1983), 47.

[49] Derrett, *Religion, Law and the State in India*, 254–5.

[50] Fisch, *Cheap Lives and Dear Limbs*, 82.

[51] Ibid. 111.

until 1835, he wrote that 'the man of taste will undoubtedly be pleased *to unlock* the stores of native genius, and to gather the flowers of unrestrained and luxuriant fancy'.[52] In his letter to Cornwallis of 1788, Jones again writes of Muslim and Hindu law as '*locked up* for the most part in two very difficult languages, Sanscrit and Arabick'.[53] This imagery corresponds to Jones's frequent assertion of the commercial value of India for Britain:

> Whatever opinion in short may be formed of MENU and his laws . . . it must be remembered, that those laws are actually revered, as the word of the Most High, by nations of great importance to the political and commercial interests of *Europe*, and particularly by many millions of *Hindu* subjects, whose well directed industry would add largely to the wealth of *Britain* . . .[54]

The cultural and commercial riches of India were to be made available through Jones's linguistic work. His breaking into these sacred codes also made the idioms of these cultures available for comparison and contrast with other cultures.

Jones's linguistic and legal work were thus intertwined. This was also a matter of personal satisfaction for him. Before he arrived in India, Jones was forced to abandon his interest in Arabic and Persian literature, because it was not profitable. In *A Grammar of the Persian Language*, he described his life as a scholar as 'attended with peculiar hardships', mainly because the nobility were not interested in patronizing letters.[55] He dedicated himself to the Law, and enrolled at the Middle Temple in 1770, and was called to the Bar in 1774. Edward Gibbon was one of many who regretted Jones's abandonment of literature when in his *History* he wrote, 'The public must lament that Mr. Jones has suspended the pursuit of Oriental learning.'[56] India therefore provided Jones with an opportunity to unite his interest in literature and law. Jones saw this opportunity as early as 1778 when he wrote to Lady Spencer,

[52] *Works*, ii. 133; my emphases.

[53] Jones, 'To the First Marquis of Cornwallis', 19 Mar. 1788, letter 485 of *Letters*, ii. 795; my emphases.

[54] 'Institutes of Hindu Law', *Works*, iii. 62. The reference to Menu's laws alludes to the manavadharmasastra, on which Jones based his digest.

[55] *Works*, ii. 124–5.

[56] Edward Gibbon, *The History of the Decline and Fall of the Roman Empire* (1776–88), ed. William Smith, 8 vols. (London: John Murray, 1862), iii. 304. Gibbon was a member of the Club, of which Dr Johnson and Edmund Burke were also members. Jones was elected a member in 1773 and was president in 1780. (Cannon, 'Sir William Jones and Edmund Burke', 166–7.)

'my desire to unite Persian and Law make me eager for the appointment' of a judgeship in India.[57] In his letters he expressed satisfaction at being able to combine duty and pleasure:

I enjoy those advantages, which you mention, of discharging my laborious duty with some benefit, I trust, both to my countrymen and to the natives, and of satisfying my early passion for Asiatick literature by the very studies, which are intimately connected with my duty, I mean those of Indian or Arabian Laws.[58]

It was in this way that Jones's digest of Indian laws in the form of *Al Sirajiyyah* and *Institutes of Hindu Law* represented a synthesis of his interest in law and 'Asiatick' literature.

What interests us here are three important features of Jones's legal work and the nature of British legal administration in India which were to be of paramount interest to James Mill. First, Jones's concern to define and administer indigenous codes of law reflected the larger concern of British rule to legitimize itself in an Indian idiom. Mill was to severely criticize this in his attempt to define a new idiom for British rule in India. The concern to legitimize British rule in an Indian idiom is also evident in some of Jones's literary writings, such as the revised plan of 1787 for his epic *Britain Discovered*, and his nine hymns to Hindu deities, the first six of which appeared in *The Asiatick Miscellany* of 1785.[59] In the revised plan of *Britain Discovered*, as in the earlier plan of 1770, Prince Britanus of Tyre journeys to Britain where he marries the nymph Albion. Their marriage, symbolizing the marriage of Royalty and Liberty, is meant to illustrate 'the excellence of our Constitution, and the character of a perfect king of England'.[60] In the later version, however, Indian gods try to prevent Tyre from reaching Britain because the goddess Ganga expresses:

her apprehensions of his ultimate success, but advises the most vehement opposition to him; declaring, that his victory will prove the origin of a wonderful nation, who will possess themselves of her banks, profane her waters, mock the temples of the *Indian* divinities, appropriate the wealth of

[57] Jones, 'To Lady Spencer', 24 May 1778, letter 157 of *Letters*, i. 271.

[58] Jones, 'To Arthur Lee', 1 Oct. 1786, letter 443 of *Letters*, ii. 712. See also letter 463, 'To the Second Earl Spencer', ii. 742, and letter 465, 'To John Shore', ii. 762.

[59] All nine, with prose prefaces, were printed in the 1810, 1816, and 1818 editions of Jones's poetry. (De Sola Pinto, 'Sir William Jones and English Literature', 692.)

[60] Lord Teignmouth, *Memoirs of the Life, Writings, and Correspondence of Sir William Jones* (London: J. Brettell and J. Hatchard, 1804), 476.

their adorers, introduce new laws, a new religion, a new government, insult the *Brahmens*, and disregard the sacred ordinances of *Brihma*.[61]

However, the plan ends with Britanus' attendant spirit, a druid, predicting the future glories of Britain, and recommending 'the government of the *Indians* by their own laws'.[62] The attempt to legitimize British rule in an Indian idiom is even more apparent in the hymns to the Hindu deities. These hymns were favourably reviewed.[63] Their main importance lies in their introduction to what Jones conceived to be the mythology of Hinduism. They also contain the gist of some of Jones's important work for the *Asiatick Researches*; for example, the prose prefaces to the hymns are a version of his 1784 syncretistic essay, 'On the Gods of Greece, Italy, and India'. The hymn to Lakshmi ends with a picture of a priest-ridden Hinduism, which it is suggested the British will undermine:

Oh! bid the patient *Hindu* rise and live.
His erring mind, that wizard lore beguiles
Clouded by priestly wiles,
To senseless nature bows for nature's GOD.
Now, stretch'd o'er ocean's vast from happier isles,
He sees the wand of empire, not the rod:
Ah, may those beams, that western skies illume,
Disperse th'unholy gloom![64]

Jones seems to be hinting here at some sort of project to redeem India, and so looks forward to what has been called the 'liberal commitment to India's emancipation'.[65] In a letter of 1786, he also claims that the Indians 'are happier under us than they were or could have been under the Sultans of Delhi or petty Rajas'.[66] None the less, he still makes a plea for the Indians to be governed according to their own laws:

Meanwhile may laws, by myriads long rever'd,
Their strife appease, their gentler claims decide.[67]

61 Ibid. 484.
62 Ibid. 487.
63 See e.g. *Monthly Review*, 76 (May and June 1787), 414–23 and 480–4; and *Critical Review*, 59 (1785), 19–21, and 63 (1787), 266–9.
64 *Works*, vi. 365.
65 Francis G. Hutchins, *The Illusion of Permanence: British Imperialism in India* (Princeton, NJ: Princeton University Press, 1967), p. x.
66 Jones, 'To Arthur Lee', 1 Oct. 1786, letter 443 of *Letters*, ii. 713.
67 *Works*, vi. 365.

Since Lakshmi is the goddess of good fortune and prosperity, the bountiful effects of British rule are appropriately described in a hymn to her. 'A Hymn to Ganga' is 'feigned to have been the work of a BRAHMEN, in an early age of HINDU antiquity, who, by a prophetical spirit, discerns the toleration and equity of the BRITISH government, and concludes with a prayer *for its peaceful duration under good laws well administered*'.[68] The hymn ends with a plea to the goddess to look on the British with favour:

> Nor frown, dread Goddess, on a peerless race
> With lib'ral heart and martial grace,
> Wafted from colder isles remote:
> As they preserve our laws, and bid our terror cease,
> So be their darling laws preserv'd in wealth, in joy, in peace![69]

The desire to legitimize British rule in an Indian idiom is paralleled by Jones's posture in the hymns as a Hindu poet. For example, in 'A Hymn to Surya', Jones depicts himself as a poet who is Surya's devotee:

> Then roves thy poet free,
> Who with no borrow'd art
> Dares hymn thy pow'r, and durst provoke thy blaze,
> But felt thy thrilling dart . . .[70]

In his letters, Jones expresses the same desire to naturalize himself as an Indian. He not only declares it his ambition 'to know *India* better than any other European ever knew it',[71] but claims that the Brahmins 'consider me as a Pandit', and 'many millions of Indians' look up to him 'not as their judge only, but as their legislator'.[72]

The concern to legitimize British rule in an Indian idiom also reflected the persistence of Mughal culture in eighteenth-century India. The Mughal emperor continued to be the source of authority long after his power had declined and all groups seeking to establish their rule needed to acquire imperial titles and rights. The British,

[68] *Works*, vi. 383.

[69] Ibid. vi. 392.

[70] Ibid. vi. 353. Surya is the sun god who, along with Indra and Agni, forms the Vedic triad of deities; hence the reference to 'thy blaze'.

[71] Jones, 'To the Second Earl Spencer', 4–30 Aug. 1787, letter 764 of *Letters*, ii. 751.

[72] Jones, 'To the Second Earl Spencer', 19 Sept. 1788, letter 494, and 25 Sept.–24 Nov. 1793, letter 588 of *Letters*, ii. 813, 920.

too, showed regard for Mughal authority.[73] They took over some of the functions of their Mughal predecessors in the administration of justice, the collection of taxation, and the maintenance of a police force.[74] They continued the supervision of some temples and shrines as well, and their sensitivity to the religious sensibilities of the communities under their rule was reflected in the prohibition of missionary activity until 1813. They also acted as patrons of learning when they established such centres as the Calcutta Madrasa for the study of Persian and Arabic in 1781, and the Sanskrit college at Benares in 1794. Persian remained the language of diplomacy and the higher courts until 1835, when a series of enactments were begun which were to replace Persian as the language of record and legal proceedings with English and the Indian vernaculars. So there were important threads of continuity between the successor states to Mughal power in the eighteenth century and British rule in this period. It was for these reasons that Bentham was to call East India Company rule a 'sort of local monarchy',[75] and it was the status of the Company as a 'local monarchy' which Mill was to attack in his *History*.

The second feature of the legal administration in British India which was of interest to Mill was the confusion of codes and courts. There was a dual system of the Crown's and Company's courts in Calcutta, Bombay, and Madras, which lasted until 1862 when the Indian penal code was promulgated. In addition different codes of law were used: British law for British subjects, and Hindu and Muslim law for civil cases, and Muslim law for criminal law, except in Bombay where Hindu criminal law was used for Hindus.[76] Furthermore, these codes could be supplemented by local laws and usages where appropriate. However, it has to be stressed that what passed as Hindu or Muslim law was often a patchwork of indigenous and European elements.[77] Thus, the topics, their order of appearance, and the relative weight given to each in Halhed's *A Code of Gentoo Laws* (1776), did not correspond to anything known to the usual sastric works.[78] This was because the *Code* was

[73] Bayly, *Indian Society and the Making of the British Empire* (Cambridge: Cambridge University Press, 1988), 14–16.

[74] P. J. Marshall, *Bengal: The British Bridgehead: Eastern India 1740–1828* (Cambridge: Cambridge University Press, 1987), 131.

[75] Bentham, *Plan of Parliamentary Reform in the Form of a Catechism, with Reasons for Each Article* . . . (R. Hunter, 1817), p. xciv.

[76] Fisch, *Cheap Lives and Dear Limbs*, 4–5.

[77] Derrett, *Religion, Law and the State in India*, 274.

[78] Ibid. 240–1.

compiled for what Warren Hastings believed would be needed by the courts, and also the whole scheme to make Hindu and Islamic laws known to European judges was based on the need for a consistent and steady administration. This introduced new elements, such as the principle of *stare decisis*, into the administration of Hindu law, especially after the jurisdiction of the Supreme Court at Calcutta was revised by Parliament in 1781; from now on the laws and usages of Hindus were applicable in 'inheritance and succession to land rent and goods and all matters of contract and dealing between party and party'.[79] Jones's attempt to compile a digest of Indian law reflects the mistaken view that it was possible to obtain a single code of Hindu law. His pandit Jagannatha Tarkapancanana's assistants were mainly Bengalis, and so there was a preponderance of ideas belonging to that school. Furthermore, the digest consisted of a continuous running treatment of Inheritance and Contracts, these being the topics prescribed for the Supreme Court.[80] It was not until the 1820s that it became clear that the pandits attached to the court were interpreting a changing legal culture. Works of Hindu law produced during the period from 1772 to the 1850s had little practical influence, and after 1864 the whole process of restating Hindu law came to be abandoned.[81] So although the British depicted themselves as preserving indigenous law, there were inevitable changes simply because of the framework in which this law was defined and employed. Central to British law was the notion of a decision, and an insistence on finality. These were foreign to the indigenous codes, which reflected various types of decision-making and of decision enforcement.[82] Mill's arguments for a single comprehensive code of law based on clear and rational principles were defined both in opposition to the common law tradition in Britain, and the legal situation in India. Jones had spoken with great admiration of Blackstone's *Commentaries on the Laws of England* (1767)[83] and he had also spoken highly of common law:

. . . the constitutional or public law is partly unwritten, and grounded upon immemorial usage, and partly written or enacted by the legislative

[79] Ibid. 236–7.
[80] Ibid. 246–8. [81] Ibid. 269. [82] Ibid. 277–8.
[83] Jones, 'To Lady Spencer', 26 Feb. 1773, and 'To Viscount Althorp', 18 Feb. 1780, letters 69 and 196 of *Letters*, i. 121 and 345.

power; but the written, or common law, contains the true spirit of our Constitution: the written one has often most unjustifiably altered the form of it; the common law is the collected wisdom of many centuries, having been used and approved by successive generations; but the statutes frequently contain the whims of a few leading men, and sometimes of the mere individuals employed to draw them; lastly, the unwritten law is eminently favourable, and the written law generally hostile, to the absolute rights of persons.[84]

It is certainly possible that Jones's attitude to indigenous codes of law was influenced by this notion of common law.[85] It seems likely that many of the assumptions on which the common law tradition was based influenced British attitudes to indigenous legal traditions in India. The common law tradition was seen by Bentham as the ideology of the ruling class in Britain,[86] and the criticisms directed against it were just as relevant to the legal administration in British India as they were to that in Britain.

This brings us to the third feature of interest to Mill. The attempt to codify and administer indigenous law in British India raised questions about the nature of legal traditions and the role that they played in defining and characterizing communities and cultures. These were questions which Bentham and Mill also had to address in their work if they were to succeed in their attacks on the common law tradition and its apparent influence on the British Indian legal administration. The conservative thrust of British rule in India was not only evident in the attempt to legitimize British rule in an Indian idiom and to continue the administration of indigenous codes of law. In fact, the insistence on certainty and uniformity, and the attempt to codify traditions, actually meant that sometimes Anglo-Hindu law was more orthodox than the sastras.[87] Similarly, in many ways, courts now followed the sharia more closely than before, so that one of the results of the conquest by a non-Muslim power was that the administration of criminal justice was actually nearer to Islamic law than under the Mughal rulers.[88] This is because the British interfered much less than their predecessors, who had exercised considerable influence in attempts to counterbalance the mildness of the religious law. Also, because of the

[84] Jones, 'To Thomas Yeates', 7 June 1782, letter 322 of *Letters*, i. 553.

[85] Mukherjee, *Jones*, 59–60.

[86] Gerald J. Postema, *Bentham and the Common Law Tradition* (1986; Oxford: Clarendon Press, 1989), 311.

[87] Ibid. 310–11.

[88] Fisch, *Cheap Lives and Dear Limbs*, 119–20.

concern for centralization the British had decided to choose the sharia as the point of reference for legality; that is, the point of reference was now ideal, and not actual, practice.[89] The general effect of defining legal tradition in this way was to reinforce the hierarchical nature of the societies of the subcontinent and to consolidate traditional India. The scene was set for the emergence of a more stratified and rigid system of castes, and a more homogeneous religious practice within all the main communities. This was especially because scholars like Jones and his colleague H. T. Colebrooke, who completed Jones's *Institutes of Hindu Law*, derived their material from the Brahminical centres of learning in Tanjore, Benares, and Nadia. It was this tradition emphasizing rigid caste distinctions which influenced the law dispensed to castes and communities by the British.[90] Furthermore, the British themselves ranked and graded Indian social orders in an attempt to understand them.[91] The problem Mill had to consider was to what extent, if at all, it would be possible to use indigenous idioms to further reforms, without reinforcing the conservative bias in the way the British had defined cultural communities for their purposes in India.

The Permanent Settlement of 1793

For James Mill the conservative bias in British rule was also evident in the land revenue system instituted by Cornwallis in March 1793. This was the Permanent Settlement which, as its title suggests, allowed the proprietors of land and their successors 'to hold their estates at such assessment for ever'.[92] Warren Hastings's rural administration had been based on the auctioning of estates at the end of each term of settlement. These estates were then farmed out to the highest bidders for leases not extending beyond five years. This 'farming system' was seen to subvert the security of property, and the Permanent Settlement was defined in opposition to this system.[93] The basis of the latter was a belief that sound administration must be based on security of landownership, and that this

89 Ibid. 22–3.

90 Bayly, *Indian Society and the Making of the British Empire*, 156–8.

91 Ibid. 158.

92 Ranajit Guha, *A Rule of Property for Bengal: An Essay on the Idea of Permanent Settlement* (1963; New Delhi: Orient Longman, 1982), 11.

93 Ibid. 16–17.

involved consolidating a rural landowning class modelled on the improving landlords of the Whig aristocracy in England.[94] This would ensure the loyalty of a class who would also guarantee stability in the countryside. Jones considered one of the purposes of his digest of laws to be the re-establishment in India of 'that security of descendable property, a want of which . . . has prevented the people of Asia from improving their agriculture and mechanical arts'.[95] He wrote that if his digest 'gave stability to their property, real and personal, and security to their persons, it will be the greatest benefit they ever received from us'.[96] In this way, Jones's work complemented the Permanent Settlement.[97] In *Al Sirajiyyah*, Jones argued that in Muslim law the ruler has no right to the property and goods of the people. He also argued, '*Indian* princes never had, nor pretended to have, an unlimited legislative authority, but were always under the control of laws believed to be divine, with which they never claimed any power of dispensing.'[98] In arguing for the existence of property rights in the soil, Jones was going against the notion of 'oriental despotism' based on the belief that there was no private property in pre-British India. This notion had already been attacked by Anquétil-Duperron in his *Legislation orientale* (1778), and after him, by Charles William Boughton Rous in his *Dissertation Concerning the Landed Property of Bengal* (1791).[99]

Jones clearly held another notion of despotism. In a letter of 1784, he writes that the democratic system in his *Principles of Government* is 'wholly inapplicable' to India, 'where millions of men are so wedded to inveterate prejudices and habits, that if liberty could be forced upon them by Britain, it would make them as miserable as the cruelest despotism'.[100] Later he writes that Indians are 'incapable of civil liberty; few of them have any idea of

[94] Ibid. 17–18.

[95] Jones, 'To Arthur Lee', 1 Oct. 1785, letter 443 of *Letters*, ii. 712.

[96] Jones, 'To Lady Spencer', 24 Oct. 1791, letter 567 of *Letters*, ii. 902.

[97] Mukherjee, *Jones*, 132.

[98] *Works*, iii. 513.

[99] Franco Venturi, 'Oriental Despotism', *Journal of the History of Ideas*, 24 (Jan.–Mar. 1963), 137–41. Mukherjee has also shown that Jones had little sympathy for the idea of oriental despotism as developed by Montesquieu in his *Esprit des lois* (1748). In *The History of the Life of Nader Shah* (1773), Jones played down the cruelties of the Shah. He was nearer to Voltaire and other admirers of Asia, who believed that the oriental system of state and society was similar to the European feudal system. (Mukherjee, *Jones*, 40.)

[100] Jones, recipient unknown, 13 Apr. 1784, letter 386 of *Letters*, ii. 642.

it; and those, who have, do not wish it'. As a result, they 'must be ruled by absolute power'.[101] In this, Jones was looking back to a notion of 'legal despotism' as defined by the physiocrats, for whom despotism was a conscious and energetic form of absolutism, which attempted to re-establish and enforce the natural legal code, and the laws of nature which rightfully should regulate economic and social existence.[102] For Jones, 'legal despotism' involved a despotic British rule reconstituting the ancient polity of India, based on his Indian digest of laws. This was in keeping with the model of benevolent despotism which seemed to underpin the Permanent Settlement as a whole.[103]

Ranajit Guha has traced the influence of physiocratic ideas on Philip Francis's 'Plan for a Settlement of the Revenues of Bengal, Bihar, and Orissa', which helped to shape some of the salient features of the Permanent Settlement.[104] Christopher Bayly, however, has argued that another important influence was 'agrarian patriotism' in Britain. This was a form of patriotism which tried to integrate great landowners, yeomen farmers, and the professional classes into a moral community, and was based on a faith in agrarian improvement.[105] It was this patriotism which was transformed by the Board of Agriculture, established in 1793, into a scientific and statistical method for the integration of state and empire.[106] The systematic compilation of facts and figures which the board commissioned from seven districts of England and Scotland, which was published as the *General Report on the Agricultural State and Political Circumstances of Scotland* (1814), was paralleled in India by Colebrooke's and Lambert's *Account of the Husbandry and Internal Commerce of Bengal*, and the statistical surveys of North and South India carried out by Francis Buchanan between 1798 and 1815.[107] It was this form of patriotism which was the dominant discourse of the second British empire. It was not until the 1840s that India became a significant market for British manufactured goods, and that the industrial revolution could be said to have some significant effect on the relationship between India and Britain. Much more important in this period was the favouring of direct alienable property tenures in the colonies, which in effect led to a

[101] Jones, 'To Arthur Lee', 1 Oct. 1786, letter 443 of *Letters*, ii. 712–13.
[102] Venturi, 'Oriental Despotism', 135.
[103] Guha, *A Rule of Property*, 151.
[104] Ibid. 97–159.
[105] Bayly, *Imperial Meridian*, 80–1.
[106] Ibid. 121–5.
[107] Ibid. 124–5.

revolution in the concept of property in South Asia.[108] Both Bentham and Mill were suspicious of various forms of patriotism which were seen by them as a threat to their attempt to formulate universal principles as the basis of their legal and political creeds. Thus, Bentham was to make it clear in the *Constitutional Code* that although the context of the constitution necessarily limits the perspective of the legislator, the universalistic character of the greatest happiness principle impels him to look beyond this in his calculations. He should not only constrain himself from acting in a way that causes expense to other states, but ought to promote the happiness of every foreign state as well.[109] Indeed, Frederick Rosen has suggested that the spirit of reform embodied in the *Constitutional Code* might have served to replace earlier notions of civic virtue and patriotism.[110] Mill was especially interested in agrarian patriotism, because he also believed that security of property was the only basis on which improvements could be made in British India, but he was to argue for another form of land revenue system which was defined in opposition to the Permanent Settlement. More importantly, he agreed with Bentham that 'in the language of the Aristocratic School, *property* and *virtue* are synonymous terms'.[111] Mill's attack on this language influenced his attitude to the role of property in the functioning of societies.

The Study of Indian History

The major contribution of Jones and his colleagues to modern historiography was to draw attention to the early period of Indian history and to Indian historical traditions, so as to evolve a methodology which was to be improved by later scholars.[112] In his 'Third Anniversary Discourse' of 1786, Jones lists the four 'general media of satisfying our curiosity' about ancient India: 'namely, first, their *Languages* and *Letters*; secondly, their *Philosophy* and *Religion*; thirdly, the actual remains of their old *Sculpture* and *Architecture*; and fourthly, the written memorials of their *Science* and *Arts*'.[113] William Chambers's essay, 'Some Account of the Sculptures and Ruins of Mavalipuram', in the *Asiatick Researches*

[108] Ibid. 6.

[109] Frederick Rosen, *Jeremy Bentham and Representative Democracy: A Study of the Constitutional Code* (Oxford: Clarendon Press, 1983), 205–6.

[110] Ibid. 23.

[111] Bentham, *Plan of Parliamentary Reform*, p. xix.

[112] Mukherjee, *Jones*, 110.

[113] 'On the Hindu's', 421.

of 1788, summed up this methodology when he suggested that Indian history should be reconstructed by 'comparing names and great events recorded by them [Indians] with those interspersed in the memories of other nations and by calling in the assistance of ancient monuments, coins and inscriptions as occasion shall offer'.[114] Mukherjee has emphasized the importance of Jones's identification of Sandracottas and Palibothra as a landmark in the history of Indian studies. The identification of at least one figure from hundreds of Indian gods and heroes with a historical character could now be used to reconstruct a history of ancient India.[115]

This contribution to historiography involved a strong stress on the empirical in historical research. In *An Introduction to the History of the Life of Nader Shah* (1773), Jones writes: 'The very soul and essence of History, is *Truth* . . . the most interesting circumstances in a barren chronicle are more interesting to a sensible reader, than the greatest events, how copiously or elegantly soever they may be described, in a romance or legend . . .'[116] He later refers to '*plain truth as the beauty of historical composition*'.[117] Jones was also careful to draw a distinction between 'fables' and history; in *A Prefatory Discourse to an Essay on the History of the Turks* he makes this distinction. In historical writings, '*nothing should be written that is fabulous, nor any thing, how true so ever it may be, but what deserves to be read*'.[118] The historian should always check his sources and authorities in order not to 'obtrude upon his reader a set of fables, which the factious or envious invent in all ages, and which the ignorant or malevolent are always ready to circulate'.[119] Jones also distinguishes between history, philosophy, and art: 'my present address to the society shall be confined to history, civil and natural, or the observation and remembrance of *mere facts*, independently of *ratiocination*, which belongs to philosophy, or of *imitations* and *substitutions*, which are the province of art.'[120] Jones's emphasis on the empirical is close to James Mill's criterion for writing history in *The History of British India*. Where Jones differed from Mill was in his conviction that some sort of historical narrative could be recovered from Indian legends. In 'On the Gods of Greece, Italy, and India', Jones

[114] Mukherjee, *Jones*, 110–11. [115] Mukherjee, *Jones*, 108.
[116] *Works*, v. 539.
[117] 'On Asiatick History, Civil and Natural', *As. Res.* 4 (1794), 7.
[118] Teignmouth, *Memoirs*, 512. [119] *Nader Shah*, in *Works*, v. 546.
[120] 'On Asiatick History', 2.

asserted that one of the four sources of mythology is 'Historical, or natural, truth perverted into fable by ignorance, imagination, flattery, or stupidity';[121] in 'Asiatick' history 'truth and fiction are so blended as to be scarcely distinguishable'.[122] It is because 'authentic history' is so 'marked and bedecked in the fantastic robes of mythology and metaphor' that a knowledge of Sanskrit and 'a confidential intercourse with learned *Brahmens*, are the only means of separating truth from fable'.[123] Nonetheless, it is possible to 'collect some rays of historical truth' from Sanskrit literature; and from the Puranas 'we may recover some disfigured, but valuable, pictures of ancient manners and governments; while the popular *tales* of the *Hindus*, in prose and in verse, contain fragments of history; and even in their *dramas* we may find as many real characters and events.'[124]

However, Jones's apparent commitment to this criterion for writing history needs to be qualified. He sometimes expressed scepticism as to whether his ideals of historical composition could be fulfilled, and pointed to the disjunction between a personal knowledge of events, and those events as they are recorded by others:

> His [the historian's] caution must be still greater, when he records the events of very distant nations; since we have no small difficulty to learn the true state of those occurrences, which pass around us every day; and it generally happens, that, the more intimately we are concerned in any transactions, the more mistakes we find in the publick accounts of it.[125]

He stresses the difficulty of an accurate history of distant events: 'The History . . . of those events, which happen in remote countries, can hardly fail of being erroneous; for, in general, we are forced to depend upon reports of reports, echoed from the ignorant natives to inquisitive travellers, and brought by them to *Europe* decorated with a thousand ornaments.'[126] Jones even suggests that historiography generally, and not just 'Asiatick history', is in some ways close to the writing of fiction: 'while the abstract *sciences* are all the truth, and the fine *arts* all fiction, we cannot but own, that, in the *details of history*, truth and fiction are so blended as to be scarce distinguishable'.[127] Lionel Gossman has pointed out that

[121] 'On the Gods of Greece', 222.
[122] 'On Asiatick History', 7.
[123] Ibid. 9.
[124] Ibid. 5–6.
[125] *Nader Shah*, in *Works*, v. 546.
[126] Ibid. v. 547.
[127] 'On Asiatick History', 7.

during the eighteenth century historiography was a literary genre. History was always distinguishable from 'mere' scholarship and antiquarianism, on the grounds that the historian was a writer, whereas the scholar and antiquarian were not.[128] In his *History*, James Mill grappled with these problems of writing history, and was to arrive at different conclusions, both about the writing of history, and especially the writing of the histories of other cultures.

Furthermore, Jones's distinction between accurate history and 'poetical fables' sometimes collapses. This is the case with his adherence to the Mosaic chronology. In 'On the Gods of Greece, Italy, and India', Jones sees the validity of the Mosaic chronology at stake in any researches on ancient history:

> Disquisitions concerning the manners and conduct of our species in early times, or indeed at any time, are of solid importance in an age, when some intelligent and virtuous persons are inclined to doubt the authenticity of the accounts, delivered by Moses, concerning the primitive world; since no modes or sources of reasoning can be unimportant, which have a tendency to remove such doubts . . . Either the first eleven chapters of Genesis, all due allowances being made for an Eastern style, are true, or the whole fabrick of our national religion is false; a conclusion, which none of us, I trust, would wish to be drawn.[129]

He goes on to conclude that if 'a connexion subsisted between the old idolatrous nations of Egypt, India, Greece, and Italy, long before they migrated to their several settlements, and consequently before the birth of Moses', this does not affect 'the truth and sanctity of the Mosaick History, which, if confirmation were necessary, it would rather tend to confirm'.[130] In the 'Ninth Anniversary Discourse' of 1792, Jones is more confident about the validity of the Mosaic chronology and the theopneusty of the Old Testament; he asserts that the first eleven chapters of Genesis 'are merely a Preface to the oldest civil history now extant', and he argues that

> we see the truth of them confirmed by antecedent reasoning, and by evidence in part highly probable, and in part certain; but the *connexion* of the *Mosaick* history with that of the Gospel by a chain of sublime

[128] Lionel Gossman, 'History and Literature: Reproduction or Signification', in Robert H. Canary and Henry Kozicki (eds.), *The Writing of History: Literary Form and Historical Understanding* (Madison, Wis.: University of Wisconsin Press, 1978).

[129] 'On the Gods of Greece', 224–5.

[130] Ibid. 271.

predictions unquestionably ancient and apparently fulfilled, must induce us to think the *Hebrew* narrative more than human in its origin . . .[131]

On the basis of this, he regards it as not just probable, but 'absolutely certain', that 'the whole race of man proceeded from *Iran*, as from a centre'.[132] The method Jones uses here is similar to that in *An Essay on the Laws of Bailments*, namely the arrival at an hypothesis through 'antecedent reasoning', which is then confirmed by evidence. Jones also deciphers Indian histories in terms of the Mosaic chronology. He declares, 'we might produce the same account of the *creation* and the *fall*, expressed by symbols very nearly similar, from the *Puranas* themselves, and even from the *Veda*, which appears to stand next in antiquity to the five books of Moses.'[133] Similarly, the deluge is 'an historical fact admitted as true by every nation, to whose literature we have access'.[134]

Thus, in his attitude to the Mosaic chronology Jones ignored the distinction he made between fable and history. In a page and a half, with a sweeping panoramic command, Jones traces the initial migration of three families from one region to the British conquest of Bengal.[135] Whilst elsewhere he condemns 'a phantom of our imagination instead of reality' in history,[136] here he calls for the aid of the imagination to help envisage the early events of the human race and its migrations from one region in the postdiluvian period.[137] Jones's emphasis on the use of the imagination to reconstruct distant events which could be called mythical was close to the notion of mythological history as articulated in the biblical criticism of the late eighteenth and early nineteenth centuries, which entailed the view that myth was not mere fable or unworthy fiction, but 'the oldest history and the oldest philosophy'.[138] Events in the Bible are in a mythic mode and miracles become the paradigm of reported historical events.[139] Inspiration was seen as the capacity to recreate imaginatively the experience of faith, and to reconstruct events which could not be known in any other way.[140]

These ambiguities in Jones's views on history point to the way in which different notions of history were articulated and contested in

131 'Ninth Anniversary Discourse', 486–7.
132 Ibid. 487.
133 Ibid. 484.
134 Ibid. 484.
135 'On Asiatick History', 3–5.
136 *Nader Shah*, in *Works*, v. 548.
137 'On Asiatick History', 3–4.
138 E. S. Shaffer, *'Kubla Khan' and the Fall of Jerusalem: The Mythological School in Biblical Criticism and Secular Literature 1770–1880* (Cambridge: Cambridge University Press, 1975), 125.
139 Ibid. 47.
140 Ibid. 85–6.

this period. Mill's *History of British India* was to define what can be described as a 'documentary' concept of history in opposition to what Robert Southey called 'mythological' history. None the less, in spite of some of the ambiguities in Jones's views on history, it is clear that the activities of the Asiatic Society from 1784 to 1838 marked the emergence of a knowledge about India's past. This past was now given the shape of a coherent history.[141] Kejariwal has shown how the Society pioneered new techniques in such areas as epigraphy and numismatics, which helped to bring to light some of the ruling dynasties of ancient India.[142] The Society was also involved in studying the contemporary cultures of India, defining their languages and customs, and also their evolution.[143] Mukherjee and others have emphasized the importance of Jones for Indian nationalism.[144] The rediscovery of an Indian past by Jones and his colleagues provided the foundations for the nationalist interest in and glorification of the past.[145] In some ways, the Asiatic Society initiated the integration of the vast collection of myths, beliefs, rituals, and laws into a coherent religion, and shaped an amorphous heritage into the faith now known as Hinduism.[146]

The preoccupation with the definition of a Hindu identity is evident in Jones's hymns to the Hindu deities. Most of the hymns celebrate some aspect of the creative process. 'The Hymn to Bhavani' opens with a description of the 'forms of animated nature' being brought forth by love from the 'wild abyss' before the beginning of time.[147] Similarly, in 'The Hymn to Narayena', it is through 'mystick love' that 'Things unexisting to existence sprung, | And grateful descant sung.'[148] The world the hymns celebrate is a sensuous, fertile and jocund world of nature; 'gay creation laugh'd, and procreant Nature rang' when the Almighty

[141] O. P. Kejariwal, *The Asiatic Society of Bengal and the Discovery of India's Past, 1784–1838* (Delhi: Oxford University Press, 1988), 222.

[142] Ibid. 57, 158, 167–218.

[143] Ibid. 79, 83–5.

[144] Mukherjee, *Jones*, 140–1.

[145] Romila Thapar, 'Communalism and the Writing of Ancient Indian History', in Romila Thapar, Harbans Mukhia, and Bipan Chandra (eds.), *Communalism and the Writing of Indian History* (New Delhi: People's Publishing House, 1977), 5. In 'On the Philosophy of the Asiaticks', Jones goes so far as to claim that Newton's theology and part of his philosophy are to be found in the Vedas and in the works of the Sufis (176).

[146] David Kopf, 'Hermeneutics versus History', *Journal of Asian Studies*, 39 (May 1980), 502. See also Romila Thapar, 'Imagined Religious Communities? Ancient History and the Modern Search for a Hindu Identity', *Modern Asian Studies*, 23 (1989), 218.

[147] *Works*, vi. 333.

[148] Ibid. vi. 369.

framed 'this gorgeous Universe'.[149] The first hymn of the nine hymns is 'A Hymn to Camdeo', or more properly, Kama, the god of love, whose consort is Rati, or sexual desire. In the Vedas, Desire is said to have been the first thing that stirred in the Deep at the dawn of creation, and in the *Atharva-veda*, Kama is exalted as a creator. It is in this role that Jones invokes him in the first stanza of his hymn:

Hail, pow'r unknown! for at thy beck
Vales and groves their bosoms deck,
And ev'ry laughing blossom dresses
With gems of dew his musky tresses.
I feel, I feel thy genial flame divine.
And hallow thee and kiss thy shrine.[150]

So the hymns open with a celebration of the fertility of the creative process and the natural world, which reflects Jones's own creativity in bringing into being a newly defined Hinduism. Invoking the Hindu deities, Jones calls into being a newly defined Hindu world, a cultural vision which can be compared and contrasted on equal terms with any other. The sense of creativity and fecundity is reinforced by the imagery scattered throughout the hymns of the issuing of springs. In 'A Hymn to Narayena' the issuing of the primeval spring forms part of the first stage of the Creation:

First an all-potent all-pervading sound
Bade flow the waters—and the waters flow'd,
Exulting in their measureless abode,
Diffusive, multitudinous, profound,
Above, beneath, around . . .[151]

In 'The Hymn to Durga' and 'A Hymn to Lacshmi', the Himalayas are depicted as the source 'whence holy rivers gush, | Bright from their secret fountains'.[152] The probing of sources from whence so much flows also reflects Jones's concern to draw 'orient knowledge from its fountains pure'.[153] In 'On Asiatick History, Civil and Natural', Jones advises, 'in history, as in law, we must not follow streams, when we may investigate fountains'.[154] In 'On the Musical Modes of the Hindus', Jones writes of the 'pure fountain of *Hindu*

149 Ibid. vi. 370.
150 Ibid. vi. 314.
151 Ibid. vi. 370.
152 Ibid. vi. 323, 357–8.
153 'A Hymn to Surya', *Works*, vi. 353.
154 'On Asiatick History', 5.

learning',[155] and in a letter of 1785 he asserts, 'It is of the utmost importance, that the stream of Hindu law should be pure; for we are entirely at the devotion of the native lawyers, through our ignorance of Shanscrit.'[156] Thus, the imagery of springs and fountains in the hymns to Hindu deities points to Jones's own desire to tap the sources of a pure 'orient knowledge', both to undermine the authority of the sacerdotal classes and to redefine the ancient constitution of India, which he believed had been fragmented and dispersed for centuries.

There are also hints in these hymns of a renascent, aggressive Hinduism. In the argument to 'Two Hymns to Pracriti', Jones writes that 'The Hymn to Durga' is based on Kalidasa's *Kumārasaṁbhava*, 'The Birth of the War-god', which relates how Parvati won the love of Siva in order to bring into the world Kumara, that is, Karttikeya, the god of war, to destroy the demon Taraka.[157] Durga herself is closely related to Kali, and is the slayer of asuras or demons. Jones writes of her 'battle with a demon in the shape of a buffalo', that is, the buffalo-demon Mahishi, and speaks of 'her martial character as the patroness of *Virtue*'.[158] The hymn ends depicting Durga as deigning 'to shield | Man's feeble virtue with celestial might'.[159] This stridency of tone is also evident in 'A Hymn to Indra'. Indra is the most celebrated god of the Rig-veda, and was first the god of the atmosphere and weather, thunder and lightning, dew and rain, and later the god of war. In subsequent myths, especially those of brahminical and later Hindu periods, Indra is relegated to the background and suffers a slow but progressive attenuation of his powers. He is defeated by Vishnu and Siva again and again, and is discomfited by Krishna. In the hymn, the poet playfully sings of the latter episode, and of another incident when Indra had to be rescued by genii, after which his swaggering is slightly comic.[160] None the less, the poet ends by evoking his martial virility, 'When through the waves of war thy charger sprang, | Each rock rebellow'd and each forest rang, | Till vanquish'd *Asurs* felt avenging pains.' He asks him to 'Send o'er their seats the snake, that never dies, | But waft the virtuous to the skies.'[161] To some extent, this hymn tries to rehabilitate Indra as the god of war.

155 *As. Res.* 3 (1792), 65.
156 Jones, 'To Charles Wilkins', letter 398 of *Letters*, ii. 666.
157 *Works*, vi. 317.
158 Ibid. vi. 321.
159 Ibid. vi. 332.
160 Ibid. vi. 343.
161 Ibid. vi. 344.

These hymns, and some of Jones's other writings, must also be placed in the context of eighteenth-century English literature. In *The Pleasures of Imagination* (1744), for example, Akenside had described the 'source of ever-flowing love' as making nature 'music to his [man's] ear'.[162] In his essay 'On the Musical Modes of the Hindus', Jones writes of music 'speaking, as it were, the language of beautiful nature'.[163] Akenside also described the 'finer organs of the mind' as attuned to 'sweet sound' which 'Thrills thro' imagination's tender frame, | From nerve to nerve'.[164] Jones seems to echo this in his essay on Indian music, when he considers the 'human frame as the noblest and sweetest of musical instruments, endued with a natural disposition to resonance and sympathy, alternately affecting and affected by the soul, which pervades it'.[165] The world which the hymns to the Hindu deities celebrates is often a world of music. In a 'Hymn to Narayena' when 'Things unexisting to existence sprung', they sang 'grateful descant'.[166] Similarly, in 'A Hymn to Sereswaty', Narada, the chief of the Gandharvas or heavenly musicians, who was the patron of music and the inventor of the lute, 'Creative spreads around | The mighty world of sound'.[167] The natural world is also depicted in terms of music:

> Then, rising gay in many a waving rank,
> The stalks redundant into laughter burst;
> The rivers broad, like busy should'ring bands,
> Clap their applauding hands;
> The marish dances and the forest sings . . .[168]

There are also some parallels to be drawn between Collins's 'Ode on the Poetical Character' and some of Jones's hymns. Collins depicted the creative Fancy as feminine and, although an attribute of God, as separate from him. He also touches on the notion of a

[162] Mark Akenside, *The Pleasures of Imagination: A Poem* (London: R. Dodsley, 1744), 118.

[163] p. 55. Jonathan Katz has discussed this essay as 'one of the first and one of the most remarkable of early European contributions to the study of Indian musicology'. ('Indian Musicological Literature and its Context,' *Purusartha*, 7 (1983), 65.)

[164] Akenside, *Pleasures of Imagination*, 15.

[165] 'On the Musical Modes of the Hindus', *As. Res.* 3, 57.

[166] *Works*, vi. 369.

[167] Ibid. vi. p. 378.

[168] Ibid. vi. 297. Schopenhauer, whose interest in Vedic literature is well known, also saw the world as 'embodied music' and as 'an expression of the world'. (*The World as Will and Representation*, 2 vols. trans. E. F. J. Payne (New York: Dover Publications, 1969), i. 262–3. I am indebted to Jonathan Katz for pointing this out to me.

musical world, when he describes how Fancy 'from out the veiling cloud, | Breathed her magic notes aloud; | And thou, thou rich-haired youth of morn, | And all thy subject life was born!'[169] In 'On the Gods of Greece, Italy, and India', and in the argument to 'Two Hymns to Pracriti', Jones discusses the concept of sakti. This term applies to the wife of a god, and signifies the power of the deity manifested in and through his consort, or, as Jones puts it, the '*female* divinity, in the mythological systems of the East, represents the active *power* of the *male*'.[170] In a 'A Hymn to Sereswaty' the idea of sakti has full play. Seresvati is the chief wife of the creator, Brahma, and is the goddess of wisdom and science, of speech and music, and the deviser of the Sanskrit script, and so she 'possesses the powers of Imagination and Invention'.[171] The characterization of the powers of the imagination in terms of an active feminine principle of a masculine god recalls Collins's 'Ode', and suggests that in some ways Jones was developing in a different guise an already existing set of images. This was in general keeping with the comparative nature of his work; as already discussed, he often drew parallels between the literatures of different cultures. However, placing these hymns in their English literary context must not obscure their general import; their martial note, and the creativity and fecundity which they celebrate, reflect the rejuvenated Hinduism which Jones tried to bring into being. This potent mixture of fertility, femininity, and a redefined and revitalized Hinduism was to play an important part in Mill's attack on Jones in the *The History of British India*.[172]

Jones's Liberal Imperialism

Mukherjee has described Jones as 'undoubtedly a precursor of the authoritarian liberal statesmen in India', who 'preached liberalism at home, but upheld the authoritarian rule in India'.[173] It is clear that Jones expressed radical political views whilst he was in England. He was an honorary member of the Society for Constitu-

169 *The Poems of Thomas Gray, William Collins, and Oliver Goldsmith*, ed. Roger Lonsdale (1969; London: Longman, 1980), 432.

170 *Works*, vi. 318.

171 Ibid. vi. 375.

172 For a stimulating discussion of notions of masculinity and femininity in British India, see Ashis Nandy's *The Intimate Enemy: Loss and Recovery of Self under Colonialism* (Delhi: Oxford University Press, 1988), 7–9, 37.

173 Mukherjee, *Jones*, 141.

tional Information, which was established in April 1780 to fight for parliamentary reform. In a letter of 1782 to the secretary of the Society, thanking him for the 'flattering' honour of his election, he made his political views clear:

On the people depend the welfare, the security, and the permanence of every legal government; in the people must reside all substantial power; and to the People must all those, in whose ability and knowledge we sometimes wisely, often imprudently, confide, be always accountable for the due exercise of that power, with which they are for a time intrusted.[174]

In *The Principles of Government* (1782) Jones argued that the governor of a nation should be chosen by an assembly representing the nation, and this assembly should be the legislature, since 'the *whole* nation or people' should make laws.[175] It echoed many of the ideas of the Society for Constitutional Information, who published 10,000 copies of it and distributed it gratis. Mukherjee concludes that this pamphlet was one of the most influential in the movement for parliamentary reform in the late eighteenth and early nineteenth centuries, and gave Jones a prominent position in the history of the reform movement.[176] This pamphlet became the centre of a case when the Sheriff of Flintshire prosecuted the dean of St Asaph, Jones's brother-in-law, for publishing an edition of the *Dialogue* in Flintshire in 1783. He was acquitted in November 1784 and this was celebrated throughout the country with bonfires and illuminations. Not least, the pamphlet was important because it believed that the principles of government were 'so plain and intelligible, that a clown of common understanding might apprehend them'.[177] It was written in clear and simple language, in an age when the vulgar were considered incapable of serious political thought because of the inadequacy of their spoken language.[178]

In his letters, Jones's radicalism comes across clearly. At a time when patronage was so important, Jones took an almost foolishly independent stance. His letters to members of the Spencer family, who had appointed him as a tutor to their son, Viscount Althorp,

174 Jones, 'To Thomas Yeates', 25 Apr. 1782, letter 312 of *Letters*, ii. 533.

175 *Works*, iii. 573.

176 Mukherjee, *Jones*, 53.

177 Jones, 'To Lloyd Kenyon', 28 Mar. 1783, letter 356 of *Letters*, ii. 147. See also letter 386, recipient unknown, 13 Apr. 1784, ii. 642.

178 Olivia Smith, *The Politics of Language, 1791–1819* (Oxford: Clarendon Press, 1984) discusses the relationship between politics and attitudes to language in this period.

in 1765, and his resignation from the post, are indicative of this sense of independence. He sometimes expresses views verging on republicanism. In a letter of 1781 he wrote that a '*pure republick*' was the only 'rational and manly form of government',[179] but he did not think that such a form of government would be appropriate for England, where only a mixed form of government was suitable.[180] Like many other radicals, Jones considered emigrating to America, because of his increasing disillusionment with English politics, and especially with what he saw as the growing power of the Crown. This disillusionment was particularly bitter after his defeat in the Oxford election of 1780.[181] Like his friend Richard Price in the *Observations on Civil Liberty and the Justice and Policy of the War with America* (1776), Jones also condemned the war with America.[182] In his religious views, too, Jones was close to Price's Unitarianism. He agreed with Price's *Sermons on the Christian Doctrine*, and commented that the '*Church of England*, as it is called, would inevitably fall, and the Religion of the Gospel be substituted in its place, if it were not for the interest of so many thousands to profess a belief in riddles for the sake of rectories, prebends, and lawn-sleeves'.[183] In a letter of 1780 Jones actually drew a comparison between himself and dissenters.[184] So Jones's removal to India was a form of self-exile. His appointment there gave him the independence he needed, and also the opportunity to fulfil his political, literary, and legal ambitions which had been thwarted in Britain. His sense of alienation in Britain was overcome by the possibilities which India provided for self-rejuvenation.[185]

However, it is misleading to cast Jones as a 'liberal imperialist' in the way Mukherjee has done. Jones's role in legitimizing British rule in an Indian idiom has been discussed, as have the threads of

[179] Jones, 'To Viscount Althorp', 31 Mar. 1781, letter 264 of *Letters*, ii. 463.

[180] Jones, 'To Viscount Althorp', 28 Sept. 1781, letter 290 of *Letters*, ii. 499, and 'To Joseph Emin', 10 Aug. 1788, letter 490 of *Letters*, ii. 807.

[181] Jones, 'To Viscount Althorp', 25 Jan. 1781, letter 260 of *Letters*, ii. 458.

[182] Jones, 'To Lady Spencer', 26 May 1780, letter 221 of *Letters*, i. 388.

[183] Jones, 'To the Second Earl Spencer', 4–30 Aug. 1787, letter 764 of *Letters*, ii. 758.

[184] Jones, 'To Viscount Althorp', 4 Sept. 1780, letter 243 of *Letters*, i. 430.

[185] For Jones's idealization of the Middle East and India in particular, as providing solace for his political disillusionment in Britain, see 'To Edmund Cartwright', 12 Nov. 1780, letter 252 of *Letters*, i. 444; also 'To Lady Spencer', 8 Oct. 1787, letter 476, ii. 783, 'To Thomas Caldecott', 27 Sept. 1787, letter 472, and 'To the Second Earl Spencer', 25 Sept.–24 Nov. 1793, letter 588, ii. 921.

continuity between Company rule and its predecessors. The concern to define and administer indigenous codes of law is in sharp contrast to what Francis Hutchins has called the 'liberal commitment to India's emancipation' from her own cultures.[186] In fact, Sir William Jones was to be one of the prime targets of criticism in James Mill's *The History of British India* precisely because he was seen to be committed to actually preserving indigenous Indian cultures. It is also difficult to argue for a tension between Jones's political views at home and his views on India unless the criterion of consistency is made clear. James Mill was to try to formulate an idiom in which cultures could be compared and contrasted, as well as criticized. This helped to define what constituted consistency between one's views on Britain and one's views on India. It seems more useful to see the apparent tensions in Jones's position as stemming from an attempt both to understand cultures in their own terms, and to measure and define them according to some culturally neutral standards. The ambivalences which this could lead to are evident in Jones's remarks on the manavadharmasastra, which served as the basis for his *Institutes of Hindu Law*. He criticizes it as a 'system of despotism and priestcraft', and as 'filled with strange conceits' and 'idle superstitions', with a 'scheme of theology most obscurely figurative'. He continues in this vein by describing it as full of 'minute and childish formalities', with 'absurd' and 'ridiculous' ceremonies, and with punishments both 'partial and fanciful'. But he then praises it for 'its spirit of sublime devotion, of benevolence to mankind, and of amiable tenderness to all sentient creatures'. Its style has 'a certain austere majesty, that sounds like the language of legislation and extorts a respectful awe'.[187] The sudden change from denigration to praise does not strike one as ironic; rather, it reflects the dilemma implicit in the attempt both to respect the uniqueness of cultures, and to define a neutral idiom in which cultures could be compared and contrasted. Bentham and Mill were to make this dilemma explicit, and to suggest ways of solving it.

Ernest Gellner's description of anthropologists as 'liberals in their own society and Tories on behalf of the society they were investigating'[188] could apply to Jones as well, and seems closer to

[186] Francis G. Hutchins, *The Illusion of Permanence*, p. x.

[187] *Works*, iii. 62.

[188] Ernest Gellner, 'Concepts and Society', in Bryan R. Wilson (ed.), *Rationality* (1970; Oxford: Basil Blackwell, 1985), 31.

the nature of Jones's views than the description of him as a liberal imperialist. It also points to the way his views on India became part of the conservatism of the time. It has been pointed out that Burke had been in frequent conference with Jones on the question of Indian legislation, and that Jones sent his 'Best Practicable System of Judicature for India' to Burke in 1784. Jones later described Burke's principles as 'too aristocratical'. He also had grave misgivings about Burke's *Reflections on the Revolution in France* (1790). He admitted to not reading it, but 'grave unprejudiced men' had assured him that it was 'the wickedest, the silliest, and the worst written book in our language', and he added 'if you love that man, you will ever find me your rival'.[189] However, it seems likely that these remarks were influenced more by Warren Hastings's trial and Burke's prominent role in this, than a careful consideration of Burke's political ideas. Burke's *Reflections on the Revolution in France* defined the ideological and polemical basis of conservatism[190] and marked the emergence of the author as 'one of the principal champions of the counter-revolution throughout the world'.[191] It defined the ideology of the *ancien régime* and the central ideas of the common law tradition, with its emphasis on a respect for the uniqueness of cultures, for the way they had evolved, for their differing degrees of rank, their ways of life, and above all for the past and its importance for cultural identities of the present. Jones's description of the common law as the 'collected wisdom of many centuries, having been used and approved by successive generations', is very much in keeping with Burke's emphasis on a constitution as '*an inheritance from our forefathers*', and as '*an entailed inheritance*'.[192] Also, when Jones stressed the importance of protecting or indulging 'native' prejudices, his use of the word prejudice seems to prefigure Burke's definition of it. Burke argued that there was often a 'latent wisdom' in prejudices, and more specifically, prejudice rendered 'a man's virtue his habit; and not a series of unconnected acts'.[193] Furthermore, Burke's definition of the 'science of jurisprudence' as 'the collected reason

[189] Jones, 'To the Second Earl Spencer', 19 Oct. 1791, letter 565 of *Letters*, ii. 898.

[190] Robert Nisbet, *Conservatism: Dream and Reality* (Milton Keynes: Open University Press, 1986), 1.

[191] Jacques Godechot, *The Counter-Revolution: Doctrine and Action, 1789–1804* (London: Routledge & Kegan Paul, 1961), 66.

[192] Edmund Burke, *Reflections on the Revolution in France* (1790; London: Penguin, 1984), 117–19.

[193] Burke, *Reflections*, 183.

of ages, combining the principles of original justice with the infinite variety of human concerns'[194] is close to Jones's own conception of jurisprudence. In *The Speeches of Isaeus* (1779), Jones had expressed a similar view:

In the course of his [the legal scholar's] enquiries he will constantly observe a striking similarity among all nations, whatever seas or mountains may separate them, or how many ages soever may have elapsed between the periods of their existence, in those great and fundamental principles, which being clearly deduced from natural reason, are equally diffused over all mankind, and are not subject to alteration by any change of place or time; nor will he fail to remark as striking a diversity in those laws, which proceeding merely from positive institution, are consequently as various as the wills and fancies of those who enact them.[195]

What gave Jones's views even more currency was the revitalized conservatism of British institutions at home and abroad to deal with the Jacobin threat of the French Revolution. For example, Fort William College was established at Calcutta in 1800 to embody Wellesley's ideal of an élite civil service, thoroughly versed in the languages of the subcontinent. It was also established to counteract the spread of French revolutionary ideas in India, a fear reinforced by the success of the French in the Middle East in 1799.[196] Raymond Schwab has argued that the 'oriental renaissance' of the late eighteenth and early nineteenth centuries was associated with the threat of the French Revolution to Europe.[197] This chapter has suggested that it is more accurate to see Sir William Jones's work, which was of immense importance to this 'renaissance', as acquiring shape as part of the revitalized conservatism of this period, a shape which ignored the politically radical strands evident in his writings before his arrival in India. The next chapter considers the character of the 'oriental renaissance' and its influence on the poetry of Robert Southey. Jones's work was important, if not central, to this renaissance, since it was the arrival of Sanskrit texts in Europe in the late eighteenth and early nineteenth centuries which had an effect similar to that produced in the fifteenth century by the arrival of

[194] Ibid. 193.

[195] *Works*, iv. 9–10.

[196] David Kopf, *British Orientalism and the Bengal Renaissance: The Dynamics of Indian Modernization 1773–1835* (Berkeley, Calif.: University of California Press, 1969), 46–7.

[197] Raymond Schwab, *The Oriental Renaissance: Europe's Rediscovery of India and the East, 1680–1880* (1950), trans. Gene Patterson-Black and Victor Reinking (New York: Columbia University Press, 1984), 23.

Greek manuscripts and Byzantine commentators after the fall of Constantinople.[198] Southey's work reflects not only the important influence of this renaissance, but also the conflicting and contradictory nature of thinking about India at the time, which James Mill was to try to break away from in his *History*. More importantly, both Southey and Thomas Moore's works on the Orient demonstrate not just how the variety of possible responses to oriental subject matter was determined by the political and religious views from which it was approached, but how the very creation of an Orient in these works played an important part in the actual constitution of their political positions.

[198] Ibid. 11.

CHAPTER 2

ROBERT SOUTHEY AND THE ORIENTAL RENAISSANCE

A New Set of Images and Similitudes

Raymond Schwab has argued that the oriental renaissance was inaugurated in 1771 by Anquétil-Duperron's *Zend-Avesta, ouvrage de Zorastre.* This was the first approach to an Asian text totally independent of biblical and classical traditions.[1] Robert Southey's two epics *Thalaba the Destroyer* (1801) and *The Curse of Kehama* (1810) reflect this revival of interest in the history, literature, and antiquities of non-European cultures. Southey was certainly aware of the importance of Duperron's work. In 1800 he commented that it was 'rather disgraceful that the most important acquisition of Oriental learning should have been given us by a Frenchman', and he described Duperron as 'certainly a far more useful and meritorious orientalist than Sir Wm. Jones'.[2] When he received a copy of the *Zend-Avesta* in 1799 from his friend John May, he declared, 'Something I shall one day build upon the base of Zoroaster, but what I know not.'[3] In 1801 he claimed to have 'fixed the ground-plan' of a Persian epic based on the *Zend-Avesta*.[4] As late as 1814 he was confident that his next 'mythological poem . . . would be founded upon the system of Zoroaster',[5] but Thomas Moore's 'The Fire-Worshippers' in *Lalla Rookh* (1817) pre-empted his plans.

[1] Raymond Schwab, *The Oriental Renaissance: Europe's Rediscovery of India and the East, 1680–1880,* trans. Gene Patterson-Black and Victor Reinking (New York: Columbia University Press, 1984), 17.

[2] Robert Southey, 'To C. W. W. Wynn', 23 July 1800, in *The Life and Correspondence of Robert Southey*, ed. Revd Charles Cuthbert Southey, 6 vols. (London: Longman, Brown, Green, and Longmans, 1849), ii. 96; hereafter *Life.*

[3] Southey, 'To John May', 3 Sept. 1799, in *Selections from the Letters of Robert Southey*, ed. John Wood Warter, 4 vols. (London: Longman, Brown, Green, and Longmans, 1856), i. 82; hereafter *Selections.*

[4] Southey, 'To G. C. Bedford', June 1801, in *Selections*, i. 163.

[5] Southey, 'To the Rev. John Martyn Longmire', 4 Nov. 1812, in *Life*, iii. 352.

Southey had even suggested a plot which was similar to that of Moore's 'The Fire-Worshippers'.[6]

Southey was correct in his estimation of the true importance of Duperron's work, which was eclipsed for a time by Jones's reputation. There was an element of truth in his criticism of Jones for 'enviously abusing' Duperron.[7] Jones had considered Duperron's work as an unreliable translation of modern forgeries, and it was not until Rasmus Rask demonstrated that the Zend was not a corrupt form of Sanskrit, but a pre-third-century BC predecessor of Persian, that this misconception was rectified.[8] However, despite Southey's other negative remarks about Jones,[9] he advised his brother to read the *Institutes of Hindu Law* and the *Asiatick Researches*, if he wanted to form an accurate conception of Indian cultures.[10] When he received a gift of Jones's complete works, he thanked the sender, even though 'I had long ago gone through those works of Sir William, and made from them such extracts as were necessary for my purpose.' Since he was working on what was to become *Kehama*, Jones's works were of 'immediate use'. Jones would have been interested in the poem, 'because it has the system of Hindoo mythology for its basis'.[11] He mentions he had read Jones's hymns to Hindu deities, and believed that those who have read the hymns 'can be expected to have . . . heard of my Divinities' in *Kehama*.[12]

Southey's notes to *Thalaba the Destroyer* (1801) and *The Curse of Kehama* (1810) show the extent of his reading in Jones's works. His epics were also in part a response to Jones's plea in his essay 'On the Poetry of the Eastern Nations' (1772) to revivify European literature through 'a new set of images and similitudes' drawn from the 'principal writings of the *Asiaticks*' and the 'language of the Eastern nations'.[13] This plea was made with even more vigour by

[6] Southey, 'To C. W. W. Wynn', 23 July 1800, in *Life*, ii. 97.

[7] Ibid. ii. 96.

[8] G. Cannon, 'The Construction of the European Image of the Orient: A Bicentenary Reappraisal of Sir William Jones as Poet and Translator', *Comparative Criticism*, 8 (1986), 172.

[9] Southey, 'To Miss Barker', 22 June 1808, in *Selections*, ii. 75, and Southey, 'To Dr. H. H. Southey', 16 Oct. 1808, in *Selections*, ii. 96.

[10] Southey, 'To H. H. Southey', 1804, in *Selections*, i. 301.

[11] Southey, 'To Mr. Neville White', 20 June 1808, in *Life*, iii. 153.

[12] Southey, 'To Walter Savage Landor', 20 May 1808, in *Life*, iii. 147.

[13] *The Works of Sir William Jones*, ed. A. M. Jones, 6 vols. (London: G. G. and J. Robinson, R. H. Evens, 1799), iv. 548.

Friedrich Schlegel in 1808 in 'On the Language and Learning of the Indians'.[14] Southey also shared Jones's interest in comparative mythology. In the preface to *Kehama*, Southey writes that while he was still at school in Westminster, he 'formed an intention of exhibiting the most remarkable forms of Mythology which have at any time obtained among mankind, by making each the groundwork of a narrative poem'.[15] When Southey was fifteen, he had read Picart's work on comparative mythology, *Cérémonies et coutumes religieuses des tous les peuples du monde* (1723), and 'soon became as well acquainted with the gods of Asia and America, as with those of Greece and Rome'. It was Picart who led him to 'conceive a design of rendering every mythology, which had ever extended itself widely, and powerfully influenced the human mind, [as] the basis of a narrative poem'.[16] To a certain extent, *Thalaba* and *Kehama*, as well as *Madoc* (1805), all of which Southey mentions in his letters in or before 1800, are a partial fulfilment of this plan. Southey also complained that there is no 'English story for a poem', and no 'worthier hero' than Robin Hood, 'and that lowers the key too much; so I shall go on with Kehama.'[17] For Southey the oriental renaissance gave English literature both a 'new set of images and similitudes' and a novel heroic idiom.

The concern to tap new sources of creativity made available by the oriental renaissance is evident in the preoccupation with the plumbing and probing of depths in Southey's epics. In *Thalaba*, the hero comes across a spring:

> The spring was clear, the water deep;
> A venturous man were he, and rash,
> That should have probed its depths;
> For all its loosen'd bed below,
> Heaved strangely up and down,
> And to and fro, from side to side,
> It heaved, and waved, and toss'd,
> And yet the depths were clear . . .[18]

[14] Schwab, *Oriental Renaissance*, 13.

[15] *The Curse of Kehama*, in *The Poetical Works of Robert Southey, Collected by Himself*, 10 vols. (London: Longman, Orme, Brown, Green, and Longmans, 1840), viii, p. xiii.

[16] Southey, 'To the Rev. John Martyn Longmire', 4 Nov. 1812, in *Life*, iii. 351.

[17] Southey, 'To C. W. W. Wynn', 30 Dec. 1804, *Selections*, i. 295–6.

[18] *Thalaba the Destroyer*, in *Works*, iv. 404.

Ladurlad in *Kehama* 'treads the river-depths in transport wild'.[19] As he approaches the submarine city, a sense of chiaroscuro and refraction is evoked:

> The dark green waves with emerald hue,
> Imbue the beams of day,
> And on the wrinkled sand below,
> Rolling their mazy network to and fro,
> Light shadows shift and play.[20]

The preoccupation with echoes in these epics is part of this plumbing of depths. Sometimes the echoes are muffled, as when Mohareb and Thalaba explore the 'cave of punishment', and come across 'a spacious vault, | Where the black river-fountains burst their way'. The 'deaden'd roar | Echoed beneath, collapsing as it sunk | Within a dark abyss'.[21] Generally the echoes are clear and ringing. Before the entrance of the cavern, the cries of the sea birds 'rung in wild discordance round the rock'.[22] Strong echoes are also evident in *Kehama*; when the crowd chant Arvalan's name, 'The overpowering sound, | From house to house repeated rings about, | From tower to tower rolls around.'[23] When the Brahmin strikes the hour at the palaces, 'For leagues and leagues around, the brazen sound | Rolls through the stillness of departing day.'[24] The mighty cataract rushes from Meru Mountain, its 'incessant roar' resounding around its summit.[25] When the Glendoveer strikes 'the Bell, which self-suspended hung | Before the Mystic Rose', then 'From side to side the silver tongue | Melodious swung, and far and wide | Soul-thrilling tones of heavenly music rung'.[26] In Padalon the 'mutinous uproar' of the inmates rings over 'all the echoing vaults of Padalon'.[27] They call upon Kehama as their saviour, and 'Thundering the dreadful echo rolls about, | And Hell's whole vault repeats Kehama's name'.[28] As Padalon awaits Kehama's advent there are 'dread storms' in 'that infernal sky', and the sound of thunder 'vollied round the vault of Hell'.[29] Jeffrey criticizes *Thalaba* for being 'composed of scraps' from travel and oriental literature,[30] and to a certain extent the echoes in *Thalaba* and *Kehama* are indicative of their composition from scraps and echoes of other material. More importantly, however, the sounding of depths suggests a tentative

19 *Kehama*, 19.
20 Ibid. 131.
21 Ibid. 193.
22 *Thalaba*, 425.
23 *Kehama*, 3.
24 Ibid. 29.
25 Ibid. 75.
26 Ibid. 164.
27 Ibid. 179.
28 Ibid. 190.
29 Ibid. 193.
30 *Edinburgh Review*, 1 (Oct. 1802), 77.

exploration and probing of new sources of creativity and material made available by the oriental renaissance for the purposes of poetry. It also suggests an attempt to penetrate a resistant environment in order to elicit friendly echoes; Southey was experimenting with a new form of poetry, whose alien subject matter had to be domesticated, and whose readership was uncertain.

Schwab's characterization of the oriental renaissance in terms of the 'rediscovery' of India and 'the East' by European scholars and its influence on European literature and philosophy is useful for casting light on some aspects of Southey's epics. However, Schwab does not comment on some of the other, and perhaps deeper, problems which were raised by this renaissance in the late eighteenth and early nineteenth centuries. In particular, he does not consider the questions it raised about the nature and viability of cultural identities, questions evident in the preoccupation with the definition of cultures on the basis of historical, mythological, and literary material in the work of Jones and the Asiatic Society. It was because of this preoccupation with authenticity that Jones was so anxious to distance himself from the eighteenth-century tradition of pseudo-translations, such as Collins's 'Persian Eclogues', and the genre of pseudo-letters, such as Montesquieu's *Lettres persanes* (1721), Lord Lyttleton's *Persian Letters* (1735), Horace Walpole's *Letter from Xo-Ho* (1757), and Goldsmith's *Citizen of the World* (1762). In his preface to *Poems Consisting Chiefly of Translations from the Asiatick Languages* (1772) Jones stressed that his translations were of 'genuine compositions of *Arabia* and *Persia*'.[31] He wanted to clear his publication 'from the slightest suspicion of imposture', since 'so many productions, invented in *France*, have been offered to the publick as genuine translations from the languages of *Asia*'.[32] This concern with accuracy was reinforced after his arrival in British India, particularly by the East India Company's attempt to define a Hindu and Muslim code of law in accordance with carefully selected texts deemed to be representative of the cultures which they were to rule over. It was also evident in his hymns to Hindu deities, the prefaces of which stressed the fidelity of the hymns to Hindu mythologies.[33]

Southey was likewise anxious to stress that his epics, although fictional, were none the less accurately based on the mythologies which were their subject matters. In his review of *Thalaba*, Jeffrey

[31] *Works*, iv. 405. [32] Ibid. iv. 401. [33] See ch. 1.

criticized the display of learning in the notes to the poem. He pointed out that Southey has been 'scrupulously correct in the citation of his authorities, as if he were the compiler of a true history, and thought his reputation would be ruined by the imputation of a single fiction'. He goes on to comment, 'There is no prodigy, accordingly, or a deception, for which he does not produce his vouchers, and generally lays before the readers the whole original passage from which his imitation has been taken.'[34] In the original preface to *Kehama*, to the objection that Hinduism was 'not generally known enough to supply fit machinery for an English poem', Southey answers 'if every allusion to it throughout the work is not sufficiently explained to render the passage intelligible, there is a want of skill in the poet'.[35] Thus Southey presented his mythological poems as self-contained wholes which were faithful to their originals. Hence his insistence that *Kehama* is 'consistent with the superstition upon which it is built', and that its 'startling' fictions 'might almost be called credible when compared with the genuine tales of Hindoo mythology'.[36] This rhetoric of authenticity and fidelity in Southey's epics was in part indicative of the anxiety in the oriental renaissance in this period to draw 'orient knowledge from its fountains pure',[37] for purposes of legal codification and works of fiction, purposes which were simultaneously diverse and intimately related.

Southey's epics can also be interpreted in the light of another aspect of the oriental renaissance which has been neglected by Schwab: namely the attempt by Jones to formulate an idiom in which to compare and contrast cultures in response to the demands made on administrator scholars by the heterogeneous character of the British empire in the late eighteenth and early nineteenth centuries.[38] It was this attempt which was an integral part of Jones's thesis of the Indo-European family of languages and his notion of translation. Southey's work is often imbued with the exhilaration of frequent intercultural comparisons. It reflects the empowering nature of the oriental renaissance, which granted its scholars the ability to define and constitute cultures. In the Preface to *The Byrth, Lyf, and Actes of King Arthur* (1817), he argues that 'in similar stages of civilisation, or states of society, the fictions of

[34] *Edinburgh Review*, 1 (Oct. 1802), 77.
[35] *Kehama*, p. xxiv.
[36] Ibid. p. xxiii.
[37] See ch. 1.
[38] See introduction.

different people will bear a corresponding resemblance, notwithstanding the differences of time and scene'. He considers the possibility of a common origin to explain 'particular resemblances'.[39] In a letter of 1805 to William Taylor he expressed his exhilaration at his imaginative journeys between cultures when he wrote, 'You will see my Hippogryff touch at Hindostan, fly back to Scandinavia, and then carry me among the fire-worshippers of Istakhar.'[40] The comparisons and contrasts in his reviews of travel literature suggest the command of a panoramic view encompassing a variety of cultures. For example, in the *Quarterly Review* of March 1812 he compared Christian missionaries in Iceland to the 'Moors in India', who also upheld their religion 'as more honourable than that of the idolaters', and he unfavourably contrasted the 'earthly paradises of the South Sea' with 'this ravaged island of Iceland'.[41]

Southey acted as though he were in a laboratory of cultures, experimenting with and constructing different cultural identities. Just as he posed as a Welsh Bard in *Madoc*, so he adopted similar positions as a spokesman for other cultures. This is clear in his *History of Brazil* (1810–19). This was part of an unfinished *magnum opus*, which was to be a history of Portugal, on which Southey worked for most of his life. As early as 1799, Southey had declared his intention to 'undertake one great historical work, the History of Portugal'.[42] Soon afterwards he felt that he had 'the general facts already in my memory', and 'a fair and accurate opinion of the chief personages, differing very considerably from their received characters'.[43] In 1804 he laid down his general plans for his historical work:

> My whole historical labours will . . . consist of three separate works. 1. Hist. of Portugal,—the European part, 3 vols. 2. Hist. of the Portuguese Empire in Asia, 2 or 3 vols. 3. Hist. of Brazil. 4. Hist. of the Jesuits in

[39] *The Byrth, Lyf, and Actes of King Arthur; of His Noble Knyghtes of the Rounde Table, Theyr Merveyllous Conquestes and Aduentures*, 2 vols. (London: Longman, Hurst, Rees, Orme, Brown, 1817), i, pp. ii–iii. This was printed from Caxton's 1485 edition. Southey was responsible for the introduction and notes to the text only; the text was prepared by William Upcott, sublibrarian of the London Institution. See Barry Gaines, 'The Editions of Malory in the Early Nineteenth Century', *Papers of the Bibliographical Society of America*, 68 (1974), 1–17.

[40] Cited by Herbert G. Wright, 'Southey's Relations with Finland and Scandinavia', *Modern Language Review*, 27 (Jan. 1932), 149.

[41] *Quarterly Review*, 7 (Mar. 1812), 54, 84.

[42] Southey, 'To Joseph Cottle', 22 Sept. 1799, in *Life*, ii. 25.

[43] Southey, 'To John Rickman', 22 Aug. 1800, in *Life*, ii. 103.

Japan. 5. Literary History of Spain and Portugal, 2 vols. 6. Hist. of Monachism. In all, ten, eleven, or twelve quarto volumes; and you cannot easily imagine with what pleasure I look to all the labour before me.[44]

There were a number of reasons why Southey decided to make the *History of Brazil* the first in his series. In the summer of 1806 the British had occupied Buenos Aires, the capital of the Spanish viceroyalty of the Rio de la Plata. The town was recaptured less than seven weeks later, but it was not until the New Year that news of this reached England. It was because of 'the times being South American mad' that Southey decided to write his *History*.[45] His uncle, Herbert Hill, who was chaplain to the British factory in Lisbon, wrote urging him to take this opportunity to bring forward the Brazilian part of his history.[46] Southey began to write his history in February, 1807, only ten months before the royal family of Portugal sought safety in Brazil from Napoleon;[47] and the first volume of his *History* appeared while the Peninsular War was raging. Southey's enthusiasm was aroused by the Iberian resistance to the invader, adding his old admiration for Portugal to hatred for Bonaparte.[48] In 1818 he wrote that 'when Brazil shall become the great and prosperous country which one day it must be, I shall be regarded the first person who ever attempted to give a consistent form to its crude, unconnected, and neglected history'.[49] Southey's *History* was in fact the first comprehensive treatment of Brazil's colonial history and was not superseded until 1854, when the first edition of Varnhagen's work appeared.[50]

Thus, like Jones, Southey presented himself as giving a narrative form to the disparate materials of a hitherto undefined nation. Furthermore, in the process of composing his history of Portugal, Southey felt that 'the long attention I have given to their history and the whole of their literature has given me a sort of intellectual naturalization among them'.[51] As early as 1806, he thought he knew more about Portugal than any foreigner, and as much 'as any native', and he describes himself as 'the Portuguese histori-

[44] Southey, 'To Thomas Southey', 12 Sept. 1804, in *Life*, ii. 305–6.

[45] Southey, 'To John Rickman', 23 Dec. 1806, in *Life*, iii. 55.

[46] R. A. Humphreys, *Robert Southey and His History of Brazil* (London: The Hispanic and Luso-Brazilian Council, 1978), 7. [47] Ibid. 11.

[48] J. de Sousa-Leao, 'Southey and Brazil', *Modern Language Review*, 38 (1943), 190.

[49] Cited by Humphreys, *Robert Southey and His History of Brazil*, 17.

[50] Sousa-Leao, 'Southey and Brazil', 188–9. [51] Ibid. 189.

ographer'.[52] The *Letters from England by Don Manuel Alvarez Espriella* (1807), in which Southey wanted to give 'a complete picture of the actual state of England, such as it would appear to a foreigner',[53] is indicative of this apparent ability to move from one cultural perspective to another. It also recalls Jones's own concern to portray himself as a native Indian poet in his attempt to legitimize British rule in an Indian idiom.[54]

This ability to move from one cultural perspective to another is further evident in Southey's journal of his trip to Scotland in 1819 with Thomas Telford and John Rickman, but here, rather than being compared and contrasted, cultures are viewed and depicted through the assumed spectacles of another culture. For example, Southey often used terms such as 'remansos', 'plaza', and 'quintas' to describe the towns and villages in the region.[55] He described seeing a flock of goats at Contin, and went on to write: 'This was not the only circumstance which gave a foreign character to the scene, and reminded me of the Leon; the women with their white caps looked at a little distance more like Spaniards or Portugueze than Englishwomen.'[56] Cultures are not just viewed through the assumed spectacles of other cultures; their landscapes are also duplicated within other landscapes. For example, in the Highlands Southey comes across a gentleman's carriage 'with an Asiatic on the dickey, whiskered and wearing a turban'.[57] A room in an inn at Grantown 'has some prints in true Portsmouth taste, of Marquis Cornwallis receiving the sons of Tippoo Saib'.[58] Southey also describes the estates of Sir Hector Munro, on which there were 'some odd edifices . . . which he is said to have designed as imitations of the hill-forts in India'.[59] In *Thalaba*, Thalaba comes across a garden in a region of snow, 'whose delightful air | Was mild and fragrant as the evening wind | Passing in summer o'er the coffee-groves'.[60] Within this garden a 'fount of Fire that in the centre play'd | Roll'd all around its wondrous rivulets, | And fed the garden with the heat of life'. Southey's work reflects not just the

[52] Southey, 'To G. C. Bedford', 6 Mar. 1806, in *Life*, iii. 32–3.

[53] Southey, 'To Miss Barker', 26 Jan. 1805, in *Selections*, i. 314.

[54] See ch. 1.

[55] *Journal of a Tour in Scotland in 1819*, ed. C. H. Herford (London: John Murray, 1929), 40, 61, 258.

[56] Ibid. 147–8.

[57] Ibid. 105.

[58] Ibid. 99. Tipu Sultan was defeated by Lord Mornington (Marquis Wellesley), who successfully stormed Seringapatam on 6 May 1799.

[59] Ibid. 120. Sir Hector Munro was the governor of Madras from 1820 to 1824.

[60] *Thalaba*, 354.

search for an idiom in which to compare and contrast cultures; the replication of landscapes within contrary landscapes hints at the way in which cultures in some sense actually constitute each other, and inhabit each other's centres in the process of defining their 'Others' and so themselves.

The exhilaration of moving beyond and confounding boundaries also imbues the epics, but here the sense of expansive movement outwards is balanced by a sense of the containment of energy within circles of confinement. When Ladurlad, Kailyal, and Ereenia travel to Yamen, they reach 'The Earth's remotest bound, | Where outer Ocean girds it round'.[61] They travel over this ocean until they reach their 'destined shores', where 'A level belt of ice' binds the 'waters of the sleeping Ocean round'.[62] The cosmic map in the poem is of 'This world, that in the centre, | Within its salt-sea girdle, lies confined; | Yea the Seven Earths that, each with its own ocean, | Ring clasping ring, compose the mighty round.'[63] The general impression created is of bounded infinitudes; the poem continually discovers apparent infinitudes to be bounded. Similarly, a 'fiery flood' surrounds Padalon, 'A sea of flame it seem'd to be, | Sea without bound', but this sea is spanned by 'A single rib of steel, | Keen as the cage of keenest scymitar'.[64] This sense of bounded infinitude is also apparent in *Thalaba*, which opens with a description of a moonlit night: 'Beneath her steady ray | The desert-circle spreads, | Like the round ocean, girdled with the sky.'[65] Zeinab contemplates the desert scene: 'The dark blue sky, closed round, | And rested like a dome, | Upon the circling waste.'[66] In *Madoc* the hero relates the fears he felt on his journey across the ocean: 'Did the Waters | Here on their outmost circle meet the Void, | The verge and brink of Chaos?'[67] It is not long, however, before Madoc and his crew stand 'triumphant on another world'.[68] As in *Thalaba* and *Kehama*, apparently insuperable boundaries are continually being pierced; in *Kehama* the poet asks:

> What power of motion,
> In less than endless years shall bear him there,
> Along the limitless extent,
> To the utmost bound of the remotest spheres?
> What strength of wing

[61] *Kehama*, 168. [62] Ibid. 172. [63] Ibid. 160–1.
[64] Ibid. 187. [65] *Thalaba*, 398. [66] Ibid. 6.
[67] *Madoc* (1805), in *Works*, v. 34. [68] Ibid. v. 35.

Suffice to pierce the Golden Firmament
That closes all within?
Yet he hath pass'd the measureless extent,
And pierc'd the Golden Firmament;
For Faith hath given him power, and Space and Time
Vanish before that energy sublime.[69]

To a certain extent, a similar set of images is to be found in Jones's hymns. In 'The Hymn to Durga', God 'Sat in a crystal cave new worlds designing'.[70] The sky is described as a 'blue vault' in both 'A Hymn to Indra' and 'A Hymn to Narayena'.[71] Ganga is depicted as gracing 'the caverns of the west' in 'The Hymn to Ganga.'[72] An attempt to pierce these vaults is also dramatized in these hymns. 'A Hymn to Narayena' opens with the invocation:

Spirit of Spirits, who, through ev'ry part
Of space expanded and of endless time,
Beyond the stretch of lab'ring thought sublime,
Badst uproar into beauteous order start.[73]

In 'A Hymn to Surya', there is a sense of piercing the vaults and filling them with an all-pervading power. The hymn opens invoking the 'Fountain of living light, | That o'er all nature streams, | Of this vast microcosm both nerve and soul'.[74] As Surya is the manifestation of the divine energy of heaven, this light is all pervading and all sustaining. Southey may have been influenced by the characterization of light in Jones's translation of *Sakuntala*, as 'that subtil fluid which was created before its reservoir, the sun, as water was created before the sea', and of Kasyapa, or Surya, as the personification of 'infinite space, comprehending different worlds'.[75] The imagery of piercing vaults to the heroic energy beyond them in Jones's hymns and Southey's epics is suggestive of their attempt to break into a new sort of poetry with an enhanced fertility of imagery. The violation of boundaries also dramatizes the attempt to break open the insulated idioms of cultures in order to display and contrast them with other idioms. But Southey's epics were not only partly shaped by the Jones role in defining some of the concerns of the oriental renaissance. The sense of outward

[69] *Kehama*, 161. [70] *Works*, vi. 324. [71] Ibid. vi. 339, 372.

[72] Ibid. vi. 338. Garland Cannon has plausibly argued that this hymn influenced 'Kubla Khan'. (Garland H. Cannon, 'A New, Probable Source for "Kubla Khan"', *College English*, 17 (Dec. 1955), 136–42.)

[73] *Works*, vi. 369. [74] Ibid. vi. 347. [75] Ibid. vi. 207.

expansion and inward confinement reflects the two axes around which Jones's work and the oriental renaissance in this period revolved; namely, a heroic universe of imaginative expansion thrilled with the prospects of untried possibilities, and the equally heroic but disciplined world of legal codification, both of them underpinned by a rhetoric of fidelity to presumed originals.

Mythological Histories and the Reanimation of Cultures

The tension between and fusion of the roles of the visionary and of the scholar in the oriental renaissance revolved around these two axes. This tension and fusion is also evident in the notion of history which was sometimes used to redefine cultures in this period. Southey explored the relationship between fact and fiction in this form of history, as Jones had done before him.[76] *Madoc* (1805) was a playful rendering of this complex relationship. Southey had worked on *Madoc* for a considerable period of time. He began it in prose in 1789, 'then it slept' until 1794, and after another interval was taken up again in 1797 and 1798.[77] It was finally completed and published in 1805. In 1803 he declared that 'not one line in five stands as originally written'.[78] He hoped *Madoc* would be 'the pillar of my reputation',[79] and said it 'must be my monument'.[80] However, the details of the plot in *Madoc* are of less importance for our purposes than its subject matter, the Welsh legend of the discovery of America by Madoc, and its major concern with the nature of cultures and their rejuvenation.

Madoc was a playful fantasy in which what Matthew Arnold was to call the 'colossal, impetuous, adventurous wanderer, the Titan of the early world',[81] regained his heroic place in history. The subject matter of *Madoc* is the Welsh legend of the discovery of America by Madoc, the son of Owain Gwynedd, a prince of Gwynedd in North-West Wales in the twelfth century.[82] This legend

[76] See ch. 1.

[77] Southey, 'To Charles Danver', in *New Letters of Robert Southey*, ed. K. Curry, 2 vols. (New York: Columbia University Press, 1965), i. 332.

[78] Southey, 'To Thomas Southey', 29 Oct. 1803, in *Life*, ii. 230.

[79] Southey, 'To G. C. Bedford', 1 Oct. 1795, in *Life*, i. 248.

[80] Southey, 'To C. W. W. Wynn', 30 Apr. 1801, in *Selections*, i. 147.

[81] Matthew Arnold, *On the Study of Celtic Literature* (1867), in *The Complete Prose Works of Matthew Arnold*, ed. R. H. Super, 11 vols. (Ann Arbor, Mich.: University of Michigan Press, 1962), iii. 346.

[82] Gwyn A. Williams, 'Welsh Indians: The Madoc Legend and the First Welsh Radicalism', *History Workshop*, 1 (Spring 1976), 140.

was revived in the 1790s, when Welsh Jacobins looked to Ohio and Missouri for the establishment of a republic of Wales. Edward Williams, one of the leaders of a coterie of London-Welsh intellectuals, was busy drafting schemes for the wholesale transfer of the Welsh to a new homeland. He drew up an eighteen-point plan for this transatlantic Cambria, in which the French revolutionary calendar coexisted with the revived Order of the Druids, and in which the official language was to be Welsh.[83] In the late eighteenth century the London Welsh radicals sponsored an exploratory expedition west of the Mississippi, whose aim was to find the Madoc Indians. This expedition was part of the Jacobin campaign to plant a new Wales in America. The Madoc myth in the 1790s was thus an integral component of the new and radical 'collective mentality' forming among a minority of Welsh intellectuals, who foreshadowed the populist radicalism of nineteenth-century Wales.[84] Furthermore, the myth can be seen as prefiguring the emergence of a 'nation' in nineteenth-century Wales. With the demise of the aristocracy, only a few gentry houses patronized Welsh, with the result that Welsh was disintegrating into a local patois. A revival was effected with the massive adult educational drive associated with Griffith Jones's circulating schools, a Methodist movement whose origins were independent of those in England. In effect, 'an *alternative society* was taking shape', and '*it was created in little more than one generation in the early nineteenth century*'.[85] The revival of the Madoc myth served the rhetorical purposes of Welsh nationalism at the time through its portrayal of a heroic and decisive nation involved in the discovery of America.[86]

Thus, Southey's *Madoc* rendered a contemporary nationalist myth into poetry. The revival of the Madoc myth in the 1790s coincided with the appearance of the first section of William Owen's Welsh–English dictionary in 1793, which was completed and issued in two volumes, with a grammar prefixed to the first, in 1803. The appearance of this dictionary was part of what Prys Morgan has called the 'Welsh Renaissance', which was a revival of interest in the history, antiquities, language, and literature of Wales in the eighteenth century. Owen's dictionary contained over 100,000 words, 40,000 more than in Johnson's English dictionary, and con-

83 Ibid. 136. 84 Ibid. 140. 85 Ibid. 149.

86 Prys Morgan, *A New History of Wales: The Eighteenth Century Renaissance* (Llandybie: Christopher Davies, 1981), 23.

ferred an enhanced status on the Welsh language. Southey was acquainted with William Owen and his work. Owen was 'full of Welsh information', but Southey felt he had never met a 'muddier minded man', and that there was 'abundant proof in his Dictionary how loose and inaccurate his knowledge of his own language is'.[87] Owen also showed Southey his translation of the *Mabinogion*, on which he worked towards the end of his life, but which never appeared. Southey praised Owen for translating these tales 'in so Welsh a syntax and idiom, that they would convey the full manner of the original'.[88] Southey also felt qualified to pronounce Owen's edition and translation of *The Heroic Elegies and other poems of Llywarch Hen* (1792) as inaccurate, although he admitted 'his version is better than none, and eminently useful to all who want information either in old history or in old manners'.[89] It is not clear how qualified Southey was to make these remarks, but they do indicate a deep interest in the Welsh Renaissance. He had met Iolo Morganwg, one of the key figures in the Welsh Renaissance, and described him vividly.[90] He described Edward Jones's *Musical and Poetical Relicks of the Welsh Bards* (1784), a work which was part of the attempt to record what was seen as a declining musical tradition, as containing 'much curious matter mixed with some ignorance and clumsily put together', and he favourably reviewed Edward Davies's *Celtic Researches*.[91]

Southey's deep interest in the Welsh Renaissance is also evident from his letters to his lifelong friend Charles W. W. Wynn, who was the great grandson of Sir William Williams. Williams had been interested in the history and literature of Wales, and purchased the valuable collection of manuscripts belonging to William Maurice, an industrious collector and transcriber of Welsh manuscripts. A small portion of these came into the possession of Charles Wynn in the early nineteenth century. Southey often addressed questions about Welsh culture to his friend, whom he considered a patron of Welsh scholarship. Even before Southey had established his reputation, he had approached Wynn for information on Welsh scholarship. In 1797 he wrote to him, 'I would your countrymen encouraged researches into their antiquities somewhat more' because 'I want

87 Southey, 'To C. W. W. Wynn', Jan. 1823, in *Selections*, iii. 373.
88 Southey, 'To C. W. W. Wynn', 16 June 1804, in *Selections*, i. 278.
89 Southey, 'To C. W. W. Wynn', 29 Aug. 1801, in *Selections*, i. 116.
90 Southey, 'To Henry Taylor', 24 Jan. 1827, in *Life*, v. 285.
91 Southey, 'To Joseph Cottle', 25 Aug. 1805, in *New Letters*, i. 395.

more Welsh poetry than is got-atable',[92] and he later asked him to point out 'what manners or superstition of the Welsh would look well in blank verse'.[93] He often expressed the desire to learn Welsh: 'I want badly to see your country, and, if it were a study that promised any success, to understand your language that I might get at the hidden treasures.'[94] Knowledge of Welsh was 'necessary to render *Madoc* as I intend to'.[95] He also considered moving to Wales because of 'the facility afforded of acquiring the Welsh language',[96] and after a visit to Wales, he felt his experience of the Welsh scenery ('I can call up the whole succession of rocks and streams and lakes and mountains with life-vividness') was useful for composing *Madoc*.[97]

Like *Thalaba* and *Kehama*, *Madoc* is a fantastical poem. In many ways, the poem is not just about the discovery of the Americas by Madoc; it is also about the regeneration of Welsh culture in America, and the establishment of Christianity there. One of Southey's friends, John Rickman, complained about this fictionalized history in *Madoc*. The establishment of Christianity in America by Madoc was too 'notoriously false'. Although poets had licence 'to vary circumstances and to invent incidents', some sort of deference had to be paid to historical facts.[98] Southey argued that Rickman was wrong to criticize his fictional history, since he never asserted that *Madoc* was 'historically true'.[99] To a certain extent, Southey was following Jones, who had considered the possibility of forming a mythology by separating myth from history.

The poetical fables of the old *Persians*, however curious or amusing, ought not to be mixed, like glittering drops, with the pure ore of true History: but, if some student of Eastern literature would amuse himself with collecting these fables, and reducing them to *a system of Persian mythology*, he would greatly assist every learner of the *Asiatick* languages.[100]

92 Southey, 'To C. W. W. Wynn', 12 Sept. 1797, in *New Letters*, i. 147.
93 Southey, 'To C. W. W. Wynn', 21 Feb. 1801, in *Life*, ii. 133–4.
94 Southey, 'To C. W. W. Wynn', 24 Sept. 1799, in *Selections*, i. 85.
95 Southey, 'To John James Morgan', 16 Mar. 1797, in *New Letters*, i. 122.
96 Southey, 'To William Taylor', 28 Nov. 1802, in *Life*, ii. 193.
97 Southey, 'To C. W. W. Wynn', 19 Apr. 1803, in *New Letters*, i. 312. By the late 18th century Welsh scenery had taken on a new significance; this change to a picturesque Wales owed a great deal to the increase of tourism in this period, and also to Richard Wilson's paintings of the Welsh landscape from the 1750s onwards (Prys Morgan, *A New History of Wales*, 103–4).
98 John Rickman, 'To Robert Southey', 27 June 1805, in *Life*, ii. 338.
99 Southey, 'To John Rickman', July 1805, in *Life*, ii. 339.
100 Jones, *Works*, v. 553.

But as a fictional history *Madoc* also accurately reflects the nature of the Welsh renaissance. There was a considerable element of forgery in the Welsh renaissance. Iolo Morganwg, who after 1815 was a national figure in Wales, was a prime example of how a process of cultural recovery was closely related to mimicry, forgery, and invention.[101] The recovery of the past was too slow for Morganwg, and what was recovered did not match his grand vision of the past. His earliest forgeries were poems in the fourteenth-century style of Dafydd ap Gwilym in 1789. He also included many forgeries in the three volumes of the *Myvyrian Archaiology of Wales* (1801–7), which was envisaged as an encyclopaedia of Welsh classics and was to be described by Matthew Arnold as 'the great repertory' of the 'treasures' of Welsh 'national literature'.[102] It took Welsh scholars about a hundred years to unravel his forgeries; a reliable canon of Dafydd ap Gwilym's poems did not appear until as late as 1952.[103]

Madoc is thus indicative of the ambiguities embodied in Morganwg's inability to distinguish between his role as a visionary and mythologist, and as a researcher and scholar. These ambiguities were brought to the fore in this age of national literary inventions and forgeries, ranging from James Macpherson's *Ossian* to Elias Lonnrot's *Kalevala* (1835; second edition 1849), the Finnish national epic composed from different types of folk poetry, lyrical fragments, and epic poems, some of them ancient, but shaped into an epic which was a nineteenth-century product.[104] However, this playful creativity in which fact and fiction merged to form a new kind of history raised important questions about the nature of historiography and the role of evidence in the narration of history. It also challenged the concept of forgery in any simple sense. The notion of mythological history had partly been given a new impetus by Sir William Jones's work in the *Asiatick Researches*, and particularly by his contention that Indian legendary and mythological material was itself a source of historiography. Also, as we have seen, Jones was not always able to maintain the distinction between history and 'poetical fables'.[105] However, the most profound alteration in the understanding of myth took place as a result of

[101] Morgan, *A New History of Wales*, 112.

[102] Matthew Arnold, *On the Study of Celtic Literature*, iii. 304.

[103] Morgan, *A New History of Wales*, 118.

[104] Kai Laitinen, *Literature of Finland: An Outline* (Helsinki: Otava, 1985), 59–64.

[105] See ch. 1.

certain trends in biblical, and especially German biblical, criticism in the late eighteenth and early nineteenth centuries.[106] The treatment of the Old Testament as oriental literature by Robert Lowth in *Lectures on the Sacred Poetry of the Hebrews*, in which he examined how the sacred poetry in the Old Testament was 'peculiarly appropriate to subjects the most solemn and sublime',[107] had already partly led to the relinquishing of claims of historical factuality in the Bible. Indeed, Alexander Geddes in his *Prospectus of a New Translation of the Holy Bible* (1786) prefigured the conclusions drawn by German biblical critics about the nature of faith, when he argued that it had been 'invincibly established' that large portions of the Scriptures were corrupt, and that the very notion of an agreement between the 'most recent and remote copies' of them is non-sensical. There can be 'no such thing in the world as any ancient authentic deed'; if there were, this would be a 'continual miracle'.[108] However, this does not in any way undermine their authority or the faith of the believer, which must be based on grounds other than those of the textual purity of the Scriptures.[109] Towards the end of the eighteenth century, Lessing's and Herder's insistence on the Hellenistic philosophy in the Gospels gave grounds for suspecting that they could not have been written in apostolic times, or even in a Judaic milieu. This placed an emphasis on the visionary element in historical experience.[110] But doubts about the historical accuracy of the Gospels, and indeed of the trustworthiness of all historical evidence and human testimony, became the basis for a redefinition and regeneration of religious faith. Faith was no longer justified on the basis of the authority of the Church or the biblical text.[111] In myth, fact and fiction merged to form a new kind of truth[112] and a new conception of history was defined which bridged the gap between fact and 'sacred story'.[113]

This notion of mythological history, in which the boundaries between the playful and the serious were indistinct, and those

[106] E. S. Shaffer, *'Kubla Khan' and the Fall of Jerusalem: The Mythological School in Biblical Criticism and Secular Literature 1770–1880* (Cambridge: Cambridge University Press, 1975), 105.

[107] Robert Lowth, *Lectures on the Sacred Poetry of the Hebrews . . . To Which are Added, the Principal Notes of Professor Michaelis* (London: J. Johnson, 1787), 42.

[108] Alexander Geddes, *Prospectus of a New Translation of the Holy Bible* (Glasgow, 1786), 16.

[109] Ibid. 16.

[110] Shaffer, *The Mythological School in Biblical Criticism*, 82.

[111] Ibid. 85.

[112] Ibid. 105.

[113] Ibid. 53.

between fact and fiction challenged, was fundamental to the way in which communities were perceived imaginatively to recreate themselves and their histories. Paradoxically, this imaginative playfulness was underpinned by a rhetoric of accuracy to originals which were either presumed to be unproblematically available, or were themselves reconstructed imaginatively. Mill's conception of the historian's task in terms of the judiciary, in which the weighing of evidence is crucial, was in part a reaction against this kind of mythological history. One of Mill's purposes in the *History* was to separate this merging of fact and fiction by redefining the criterion of accuracy in such a way as to drive a wedge between the imaginative creativity of mythological history and its paradoxical claims to accuracy.

Nationality as a Trick to catch the Vulgar

Thus, Southey's writings reflect a new-found awareness of cultures as artefacts, underpinned both by a form of history in which fact and fiction merged and a playful ability to move from one cultural perspective to another. But this sense of cultures as artefacts also informed his project to define a national culture for what was increasingly coming to be perceived as the fragmented and divided polity of contemporary England.[114] In 1793 Southey had written of epic poems: 'Some critic (is it not Addison?) observes that an Epic poem ought to be national—with all due deference the nationality is of much the same use as a tolling bell or a storm of thunder and lightning upon the stage—a trick to catch the vulgar.'[115] This notion of nationality as a stage trick 'to catch the vulgar' was not abandoned by Southey when he started to write for the *Quarterly Review* from 1810 onwards. It was in fact an important part of his conservative views developed in his essays for the *Quarterly Review* and in *Sir Thomas More: Or, Colloquies on the Progress and Prospects of Society* (1829). The concern to reunify fragmented polities is also evident in the imagery of reanimating bodies in *Thalaba* and *Kehama*, which reflected the larger concern of the

[114] For an account of these perceptions and their importance in defining the cultural ideal embodied in the notion of a gentleman, see J. Barrell, *English Literature in History 1730–80: An Equal, Wide Survey* (London: Hutchinson, 1983), 13–50.

[115] Southey, 'To G. C. Bedford', 14 July 1793, in *New Letters*, i. 28.

oriental renaissance in British India to gather and collect material on the basis of which indigenous polities could be reconstituted for the purposes of legal administration.

Southey's conservative views constituted a defence of the system of beliefs and established institutions from three challenges in the late eighteenth and early nineteenth centuries, namely the demands for the repeal of the Test and Corporation Act, the repeal of legislation against Roman Catholics, and parliamentary reform. Of these, the threat of Catholic emancipation was perceived as the most serious, and by the 1820s it was the most pressing issue.[116] It was the Catholic emancipation which opened the floodgates to the rhetoric of radical reform aimed at established institutions.[117] Southey frequently argued against Catholic Emancipation, on the grounds that Catholicism was 'inherently and necessarily intolerant' of other faiths, and so could not exist in a broad framework with other forms of Christian belief.[118] It was in this sense that the Anglican ascendancy justified itself on the principle of the toleration of other forms of Christian worship, but drew the distinction between this and the admission of non-Anglicans to political power.[119] But whilst commentators have stressed Southey's opposition to Catholic emancipation,[120] they have ignored his criticism of the consequences of the Reformation. It was in fact in response to what Southey perceived to be the consequences of the Reformation that he developed his notion of a national culture. In a letter of 1808, Southey exclaimed: 'The papists are, beyond all doubts Idolaters, in the strictest sense of the word; but in flying from idolatry, what a fearful chasm have we left between man and God! What a void have we made in the Universe!'[121] He realized that the 'outward and visible forms of Catholicism', the 'superstitious observances, the scaffoldings and trappings, the tools and trinkets of Popery',

[116] G. I. T. Machin, *The Catholic Question in English Politics 1820–1830* (Oxford: Clarendon Press, 1964), 1.

[117] J. C. D. Clark, *English Society 1688–1832: Ideology, Social Structure and Political Practice during the Ancien Regime* (Cambridge: Cambridge University Press, 1985), 408–14.

[118] Southey, 'To Bernard Barton', 19 Dec. 1814, in *Life*, iv. 92. Also 'To G. C. Bedford', 5 May 1807, ibid. iii. 87.

[119] Clark, *English Society 1688–1832*, 352.

[120] See e.g. Geoffrey Carnall, *Robert Southey and His Age: The Development of a Conservative Mind* (Oxford: Clarendon Press, 1960), 201, and Kenneth Curry, *Southey* (London: Routledge & Kegan Paul, 1975), 127–8.

[121] Southey, 'To James Graham', Apr. 1808, in *New Letters*, i. 474.

had kept religious faith alive in the populace.[122] In the *Colloquies*, Montesinos argues that the Reformation was beneficial in destroying devotion to 'stocks and stones, relics, beads, girdles, and scapularies, polytheism and idolatry', but More counters with the observation that 'You have taken all this from persons whose religion goes no farther, and you have substituted nothing in its place'.[123] Montesinos finally agrees with More that 'these puppet-shows of Popery have their use'.[124] In his *Journal of a Tour in Scotland*, the ruins of the Cathedral of Elgin made Southey 'groan over the brutal spirit of mob-reformation'.[125] There is a hint here of an association with the French Revolution, which Southey made explicit in his essay 'On the State of the Poor' (1812)[126] and later in the *Colloquies*, when More compares 'the great operating causes in the age of Reformation' with those 'in this age of revolutions'.[127] This comparison between the Reformation and the French Revolution had been made by Burke, and was to be developed by Tocqueville in his *Old Regime and the French Revolution*.[128] Like Burke, Southey considered religious indifference to be the real threat to the established institutions of the country,[129] but Southey saw this threat emanating not just from the French Revolution, which Burke had analysed largely in terms of the breakdown of religious, and not aristocratic, sanctions and norms,[130] but from the 'fearful chasm' and 'void' produced by the Reformation itself.[131] Thus, Southey's view of nationality as a trick to catch the vulgar was

[122] 'On the Means of Improving the People', (1818) in *Essays, Moral and Political*, 2 vols. (London: John Murray, 1832), ii. 126–7. This essay first appeared in the *Quarterly Review*, 19 (Apr. 1818), 79–118.

[123] *Colloquies* (London: John Murray, 1832), i. 155.

[124] *Sir Thomas More; or, Colloquies on the Progress and Prospects of Society*, 2 vols. (London: John Murray, 1832), ii. 98.

[125] *Journal of a Tour in Scotland*, 90.

[126] *Essays*, i. 80. This essay first appeared in the *Quarterly Review*, 8 (Dec. 1812), 319–56.

[127] *Colloquies*, i. 19.

[128] Robert Nisbet, *Conservatism: Dream and Reality* (Milton Keynes: Open University Press, 1986), 6.

[129] See Edmund Burke, *Reflections on the Revolution in France* (1790); ed. C. C. O'Brien (London: Penguin, 1984), 187, 201, 269.

[130] Clark, *English Society 1688–1832*, 97.

[131] In some ways, Southey anticipated part of Max Weber's argument in *The Protestant Ethic and the Spirit of Capitalism*, who asserted that with Protestantism a 'great historic process in the development of religions' came to its conclusion, and 'all [such] magical means to salvation as superstition and sin' were repudiated (Max Weber, *The Protestant Ethic and the Spirit of Capitalism*, trans. Talcott Parsons (London: Allen & Unwin, 1930), 105.

formed partly in response to what he perceived to be the consequences of the Reformation, consequences which made it difficult to ensure the loyalty of the populace to the established institutions of the country, since it had destroyed those 'puppet-shows' which were so effective in keeping such loyalties alive.

In private Southey stressed some unorthodox beliefs for a Christian,[132] but publicly he wrote as a semi-Erastian Protestant high churchman of the generation before the Oxford Movement.[133] G. F. A. Best has argued that the real defence of the established church rested on 'utilitarian' arguments about the expediency of its hegemony, and not questions about the truth of its doctrine.[134] The discrepancy between Southey's private and public views lends some force to this argument. It was Southey's *Book of the Church* (1824) which sealed his reputation as the ideologue for the Protestant polity. As early as 1810 Southey had considered ways of restoring waning loyalty to the Church of England. He proposed a project for a history of the heroes of the Church to vie with 'the extravagant fables of a romance of saintship' in Roman Catholicism, through which the population 'would learn to prize the faith which was purchased for them thus heroically, in proportion to the price which was paid for it'.[135] This project was completed with the publication of his *Book of the Church.* Thomas Moore singled it out as fighting the 'good old cause of bigotry' on behalf of Protestantism.[136] It generated a polemical battle, and heightened sectarian ecclesiology.[137] In his review of the *Book of the Church*, James Mill sneered at Southey as the 'story teller of the Church' whose publication was a 'poor imitation of a stale trick of the Roman church'.[138] His attacks on dissenters and Roman Catholics 'to set

[132] See e.g. Southey, 'To C. W. W. Wynn', 3 Dec. 1807, in *Selections*, ii. 31; 'To James Grahame', Apr. 1808, in *New Letters*, i. 472–4; 'To Thomas Southey', 23 Jan. 1811, in *New Letters*, ii. 6; 'To J. Neville White', 9 Jan. 1819, in *Selections*, iii. 112.

[133] S. Gilley, 'Nationality and Liberty, Protestant and Catholic: Southey's *Book of the Church*', in S. Mews (ed.), *Religion and National Identity* (Oxford: Basil Blackwell, 1982), 419.

[134] G. F. A. Best, 'The Protestant Constitution and its Supporters, 1800–1829', *Transactions of the Royal Historical Society*, 5th Series 8 (1958), 105.

[135] 'On the Evangelical Sects', *Quarterly Review*, 4 (May 1810), 513–14.

[136] Thomas Moore, *Memoirs of Captain Rock, the Celebrated Irish Chieftain, with some Account of His Ancestors, Written by Himself* (London: Longman, Hurst, Rees, Orme, Brown, Green, 1824), 49 n.

[137] Gilley, 'Southey's *Book of the Church*', 421–2, 432.

[138] James Mill, 'Southey's *Book of the Church*', *Westminster Review*, 3 (Jan. 1825), 190, 168. The younger Mill described this article as the 'most important' of

up the Church of England', made him a 'very zealous, at least, if not a very formidable, adversary' to religious liberty.[139] Southey also contemplated writing a companion work to his church history, in the manner of Warburton's *The Alliance between Church and State* (1736), called 'the Book of the Constitution', which would 'show the gradual but uniform amelioration of society'. The object of both works would be to defend the alliance of Church and state, and 'to make the rising generation feel and understand the blessings of their inheritance'.[140]

Southey's view of nationality as a stage trick was not just implicit in publications such as the *Book of the Church*; on a more significant level, it informed his notion of the role of a man of letters in formulating a national culture. Southey saw his role as a poet of the national order and as a man of letters as only partly consisting of recording and transmitting tradition.[141] More importantly he saw the transmission of tradition as involving its re-creation and re-formulation for the purposes of protecting established institutions against the polemic of radical rhetoric. In his analysis of the factors leading to the French Revolution, Edmund Burke had identified a new monied interest associated with 'the political Men of Letters', who, because they are 'fond of distinguishing themselves, are rarely averse to innovation'. It was this 'literary cabal' which had a 'regular plan for the destruction of the Christian religion', and which founded the two academies and 'the vast undertaking of the Encyclopaedia'.[142] This cabal achieved its purposes by manipulating public opinion.[143] Southey shared this fear of a cabal of radical intellectuals.[144] He referred to the effect Junius had on the nature of the popular press, describing him as 'the founder of that school of writers, who setting truth at defiance, compose the most auda-

his father's contributions to the *Westminster Review*, after the attacks on the *Edinburgh* and *Quarterly Review*; see J. S. Mill, *Autobiography and Literary Essays*, in *Collected Works of John Stuart Mill*, ed. John M. Robson and Jack Stillinger (Toronto: University of Toronto Press, 1981), i. 99.

139 Mill, 'Southey's *Book of the Church*', 177, 180.

140 Southey, 'To the Rev. Herbert Hill', 31 Dec. 1811, in *Life*, iii. 321.

141 For an explicit statement of this view of the man of letters as an heir and transmitter of a steadily accumulating body of knowledge, see Southey's review of vol. 8 of the *Asiatick Researches* in the *Annual Review* for 1807, 6 (1808), 643–54.

142 Burke, *Reflections*, 211, 213.

143 Ibid. 213.

144 'On the Rise and Progress of Popular Disaffection', in *Essays*, ii. 87. This essay first appeared in the *Quarterly Review*, 16 (Jan. 1817), 511–22.

cious misrepresentations upon a credulous public'.[145] It was because of Southey's fear of a radical literary cabal, and his awareness of the power of public opinion, that in 1831 he advised the then Lord Chancellor to establish 'as a political measure' some sort of academy 'with salaries for its members (in the nature of literary or lay benefices)', in order to ensure the loyalty of a 'certain number of influential men of letters', who otherwise would be enlisted 'in hostility to the established order of things'.[146] In his review of the *Colloquies*, Macaulay draws a comparison between Burke and Southey in terms of their overt political views,[147] but there is a deeper similarity in their self-conscious roles as intellectuals who defended the status quo against radical literary cabals.

Thus, Southey's role as a poet or spokesman of different nationalities, for example, in *Madoc* and the *History of Brazil*, was continuous with his conception of the man of letters as re-forming traditions in response to radical attacks on the status quo. Like Coleridge in the *Biographia Literaria* (1817) and in *On the Constitution of the Church and State* (1830) his defence of established institutions rested on a conception of the importance of defining a national culture for what was feared to be an increasingly disparate and fragmented polity.[148] Education was an important instrument in the formation of this culture; another major defect of the Reformation in England was that the 'platform of general instruction was not laid (as it ought to have been) when we passed from Popery to Protestantism'.[149] One of the best ways to ensure the loyalty of the populace to the state was to have a national system of education; since a government is secure 'in proportion as the great body of the subjects are attached to the institutions of their country, it necessarily follows that national

145 'Rise and Progress of Popular Disaffection', ii. 82–3. It had been the Junius letters of 1768–71 which highlighted the growing importance of public opinion as a factor in political society (D. E. Musselwhite, 'The Trial of Warren Hastings', in Francis Barker *et al.* (eds.), *1789: Reading Writing Revolution* (Colchester: University of Essex Press, 1982), 229).

146 Southey, 'To Lord Chancellor Broughman and Vaux', 1 Feb. 1831, in *Life*, vi. 133–5.

147 T. B. Macaulay, 'Southey's *Colloquies*', *Edinburgh Review*, 50 (Jan. 1830), 528.

148 William Stafford, 'Religion and the Doctrine of Nationalism in England at the Time of the French Revolution and Napoleonic Wars', in Mews (ed.), *Religion and National Identity*, 393.

149 'On the Means of Improving the People', ii. 138, 126; this essay first appeared in the *Quarterly Review*, 19 (Apr. 1818), 79–118.

education ought to be conducted in conformity to those institutions'.[150] Any system of national education must be 'the outwork and bulwark of the national church'.[151] National education is 'the base upon which everything must rest'.[152] It was not until 1833 that the Whig government decided to make an annual grant to elementary education, channelling its distribution through two national voluntary societies, the National Society for the Promotion of the Education of the Poor according to the Principles of the Established Church, and the dissenter-supported British and Foreign School Society. Southey's proposal for a coherent system of national education was therefore far-reaching in an age when the only state-aided schools were elementary schools, which provided rudimentary training for the labouring poor. A system of national education would be the best means of overcoming class and political conflict, by diffusing a cohesive ideology throughout the polity. It was also important as an instrument of 'moral culture' which had to 'keep pace with the increases of . . . material powers' unleashed by industrialization.[153] This would ensure that wealth would not be taken as 'the sole measure of . . . prosperity',[154] and that the predominant ideology of industrialization, by which 'one might suppose, that the great fabric of British prosperity rested upon cotton', and according to which the 'proper definition of man is a manufacturing animal',[155] would be undermined. As a unifying force, a system of national education would render 'civilization complete by extending it to those classes who are brutalized by the institutions of society'.[156]

For James Mill education was also to be the means by which the polity would be remodelled, but it was a polity based on very different principles from the one Southey advocated, and by means of an education which proceeded on very different assumptions. There was little emphasis on hierarchical subordination in Southey's views on education; indeed, there is a hint of egalitarian rhetoric in his argument for a national system of education, although the egalitarianism is limited more to the notion of a 'moral culture' in

[150] 'Of the Poor, and the Means Pursued by Society for Bettering Their Condition', in *Essays*, i. 230; this essay first appeared in the *Quarterly Review*, 15 (Apr. 1816), 187–235.

[151] 'On the State of the Poor', in *Essays*, i. 146.

[152] 'On the Means of Improving the People', ii. 138.

[153] *Colloquies*, i. 206.

[154] Ibid. i. 100.

[155] 'On Emigration', in *Essays*, ii. 267–8; this essay first appeared in the *Quarterly Review*, 37 (Mar. 1828), 539–78.

[156] *Colloquies*, i. 132.

which all can participate, and is not specifically related to economic benefits. This marks a break with eighteenth-century views on popular education; both its opponents and its champions believed that hierarchical subordination would not be dissolved by the spread of popular education.[157] Although Matthew Arnold was to advocate a state-supported system of education, his view of education was decisively class-structured. Nowhere does Southey suggest that the 'education of each class in society has, or ought to have, its ideal, determined by the wants of that class, and by its destination'. Southey's attitude to national education can be summed up by Arnold's description of the educational philosophy opposed to his own, 'Society may be imagined so uniform that one education shall be suitable for all its members.'[158] To a certain extent, this reflects the fact that 'class' was more a consequence than a cause of the establishment's collapse; in this period class denoted culturally defined groups rather than economically defined ones.[159] But populist rhetoric was in any case hardly the monopoly of political radicals. Indeed, James Mill's 'Essay on Government' which was seen by some as the political manifesto of the philosophic radicals,[160] in spite of Bentham's substantial disagreements with it,[161] was conspicuous for its lack of such rhetoric. Hazlitt argued that Southey's character as poet laureate and a courtier was superficial, and that 'Everything of him and about him is from the people'; he is 'decidedly *revolutionary*'.[162] But in fact there was no discrepancy between the office of poet laureate and populism, especially in an age of the increasing manipulation of popular ceremonies to enhance the image of the monarchy.

In other ways, though, Southey's views anticipated those of Matthew Arnold's. Arnold had a similar conception of the man of letters as binding together different classes in common respect for a national heritage. He also saw education as a civilizing agent, and

[157] Clark, *English Society 1688–1832*, 86.

[158] Matthew Arnold, *A French Eton or Middle Class Education and the State*, in *Matthew Arnold on Education*, ed. Gillian Sutherland (London: Penguin, 1973), 137.

[159] Clark, *English Society 1688–1832*, 71.

[160] See e.g. T. B. Macaulay, 'Utilitarian Logic and Politics', *Edinburgh Review*, 49 (Mar. 1829), 160.

[161] Bentham MS, University College London, 23 Apr. 1824, Box 34, fos. 302–3.

[162] William Hazlitt, *The Spirit of the Age; or, Contemporary Portraits* (1825), in *The Complete Works of William Hazlitt*, ed. P. P. Howe (London: J. M. Dent, 1932), xi. 80–1.

felt the need for a cultural agency, perhaps in the form of a literary academy, to supplement the unifying action of the state. Arnold's description of the state religion as representing *'all its citizens, without the fanaticism of any of them'*, almost defines Southey's views on religion as a social force.[163] Southey also hinted at 'the humanizing effects of literature, which has now first begun to act upon all ranks'.[164] The diffusion of literature 'carries with it a beneficial influence to the lower classes', even though it tends to diminish the number of scholars, and 'increases the multitude of sciolists'.[165] For Southey, however, the most valuable current literature was not imaginative literature, but travel literature, 'rich in material for the poet and the historian',[166] and what would now be termed anthropological literature, 'relating to the manners of other nations, and the condition of men in states and stages of society different to our own'.[167] Remedies for the problems of British society may be found in the 'laws, usages, and experience of other nations'.[168] In some ways, then, Southey prefigured Arnold's views, and also shared his general outlook; he did not have a philosophical system, and brought a flexible mode of thinking to bear on contemporary issues. But again there were also some significant differences. Although Southey's notion of a 'moral culture' is close to Arnold's conception of culture as seeking 'to do away with classes' by making the 'best that has been thought and known in the world current everywhere',[169] the term 'culture' does not have the same weight and complexity in Southey's vocabulary as in Arnold's. Arnold discussed the desirability of an academy in Britain in *The Literary Influence of Academies*; he stopped short of advocating the establishment of such an institution on the lines of the French Academy. Southey's interest in such an academy was explicitly political; an academy was needed to ensure the existence of a strong body of men of letters who would be loyal to the state, and defend the status quo against radical attacks. He had very little notion of criticism as a *'disinterested endeavour'*.[170]

The imagery of the shattering and reuniting of bodies in *Thalaba* and *Kehama* reflects Southey's concern to reunify and thereby

163 *Culture and Anarchy*, in *Prose Works*, v. 193. 164 *Colloquies*, ii. 418.
165 Ibid. ii. 420. 166 Ibid. ii. 382. 167 Ibid. ii. 365.
168 Ibid. ii. 383. 169 Arnold, *Culture and Anarchy*, v. 113.
170 Arnold, *The Function of Criticism at the Present Time*, in *Prose Works*, iii. 283.

reanimate fragmented polities. When Arvalan is smashed into pieces by Ereenia, Lorrinite comes to the rescue and 'the scatter'd members of the slain, | Obedient to her mighty voice, assumed | their vital form againt'.[171] Similarly, Arvalan's 'thin and essential spirit, rent and riven | With wounds, united soon and heal'd again'.[172] In both epics, figures come to life. Khawla tries to rekindle Hodeirah's corpse into life with her incantations; soon 'the still eye-balls roll'd, | The muscles with convulsive motions shook, | The white lips quiver'd'.[173] The 'Guardian of the garden' in which Laila is a prisoner suddenly comes to life. In *Kehama*, Kailyal lies 'silent and motionless' after she is rescued from the river by Ladurlad, who massages her back to life.[174] The pliable material of the human body is also moulded into shape. When Arvalan is dashed to the ground by Ereenia, he lies 'quivering there in gore', but his 'scatter'd members' are fashioned together.[175] Lorrinite's 'globe of liquid crystal' is made of the material of human eyes:

> A thousand eyes were quench'd in endless night
> To form that magic globe; for Lorrinite
> Had, from their sockets, drawn the liquid sight.
> And kneaded it, with re-creating skills,
> Into this organ of her mighty will.[176]

The imagery of figures coming to life foreshadows one of the themes of Mary Shelley's *Frankenstein* (1818), which like *Thalaba* and *Kehama*, is about giving 'form to dark shapeless substances', and bestowing 'animation upon lifeless matter'.[177] J. Drew has traced the influence of *Kehama* on *Prometheus Unbound*.[178] There are some other similarities between *Thalaba* and *Kehama*, and *Frankenstein*. *Kehama* was one of the first poems Shelley read to Mary when she came to live with him. In both *Thalaba* and *Frankenstein* regions of snow and ice figure largely.[179] Southey had been stirred by Mary Wollstonecraft's *Letters During a Residence in Sweden, Norway, and Denmark* (1796); in a letter of 1797, he

[171] *Kehama*, 119. [172] Ibid. 86. [173] *Thalaba*, 55.
[174] *Kehama*, 20. [175] Ibid. 119. [176] Ibid. 91.
[177] Mary Shelley, *Frankenstein* (1818: Harmondsworth: Penguin, 1968), 262, 312.
[178] J. Drew, *India and the Romantic Imagination* (Delhi: Oxford University Press, 1987), 235–40.
[179] See e.g. *Thalaba*, 393, 398, 400–1; also *Kehama*, 96; *Frankenstein*, 270, 276, 279, 362, 477–8.

wrote that she 'has made me in love with a cold climate, and frost and snow, with a northern moonlight'.[180] There is also a similarity between Eblis and Frankenstein's monster. Eblis is described as a 'Living Image, by the art | Of magic hands, of flesh and bones composed, | And human blood, through veins and arteries | That flow'd with vital action'.[181] The monster also compares himself to Satan at least twice.[182] Furthermore, the contrasting attitudes of Clerval and Frankenstein to oriental languages reflect the changing nature of oriental studies in the early nineteenth century. Clerval came to his university 'with the design of making himself complete master of the Oriental languages'; he had turned 'his eyes towards the East as affording scope for his spirit of enterprise'.[183] It was in the early nineteenth century that oriental studies became a specialized university discipline. The first European chair in Sanskrit was established at the Collège de France in Paris in 1815; on the initiative of Wilhelm von Humboldt, Germany followed suit in 1818. Clerval's and Frankenstein's contrasting attitudes reflect this transition from the dilettantism of gentlemanly pursuits to the formation of specialized university disciplines. But this hint of interest in the oriental renaissance in *Frankenstein* is not just peripheral; the monster learns human language by observing an Arabic speaker being tutored in French. It is not just the family of humans from which the monster is excluded, but also the Indo-European family of languages, in which each language can be translated into another.

The similarities between Southey's oriental epics and *Frankenstein* point to some deeper affinities between the two. In the latter, Felix instructs Safie by using Volney's *Ruins of Empires*, whose 'declamatory style was framed in imitation of the Eastern authors'.[184] Volney's *Les Ruines ou méditations sur les révolutions des empires* (1791) was an influential text for radical artisans, dissenters, and republicans in England in the 1790s; its fifteenth chapter on the

[180] Southey, 'To Thomas Southey', in *Life*, i. 311.

[181] *Thalaba*, 435. Frankenstein's monster has yellow skin which 'scarcely covered the work of muscles and arteries beneath' (*Frankenstein*, 270).

[182] *Frankenstein*, 364, 396.

[183] *Frankenstein*, 330. He intends to visit India in 'the belief that he had in his knowledge of its various languages, and in the view he had taken of its society, the means of materially assisting the progress of European colonization and trade' (ibid. 427–8). Frankenstein, on the other hand, learns Persian, Arabic, and Sanskrit, not to 'attempt a critical knowledge of their dialects', but only as a 'temporary amusement' (271).

[184] Ibid. 385.

vision of a new age was often circulated as a tract.[185] It surveyed the demise of cultures which had flourished in the past, and compared mythologies to argue that Christianity was a form of solar worship.[186] Its search for an explanation of the decay of cultures and a strategy for renewing them as part of a single world culture is analogous to the search for the 'principle of life' in *Frankenstein*.[187] Both radical and reactionary creeds attempted to shape idioms with which to reunify and reanimate cultures. The infusion of lifeless matter in *Frankenstein* has a further contemporary relevance as well, in an age when old legitimacies were being restored and renewed after the defeat of the French revolution. *Thalaba* and *Kehama*, and later *Frankenstein*, can be partly elucidated in the context of this concern on the part of the conservatism of the counter-revolution, and in the oriental renaissance, to reanimate and reunify cultures.

Dissecting the Dead: History as Progress

Sheridan Gilley has suggested that there is a continuity between the youthful radicalism of the Lake Poets, and their religious nationalism later, in which religion set the terms for patriotism.[188] The continuity in Southey's views is evident not only in his sense of cultures as artefacts, but also in his adherence to a philosophy of progress throughout his life, a philosophy which was defined within the complex context of the oriental renaissance.

In 'A Letter To William Smith, Esq., M.P.' (1817), referring to *Wat Tyler* (which was written during the summer of 1794 but published in 1817) he contended that if he were 'now to dramatize the same story there would be much to add, but little to alter', and he believed that he would have expressed the same sentiments, but would have opposed to them 'more enlarged views of the nature of man and the progress of society'.[189] He claimed that the 'pole-star of my course' had always been 'the removal of those obstacles by which the improvement of man-kind is impeded'. The 'whole

[185] Brian Rigby, 'Volney's Rationalist Apocalypse', in Barker *et al.* (eds.), *1789: Reading Writing Revolution*, 23–4.

[186] C. de Volney, *The Ruins; or, A Survey of the Revolutions of Empires, to Which is Added, the Law of Nature, by the Same Author* (4th edn., London: H. D. Symonds, 1801), 24, 229–31.

[187] *Frankenstein*, 311.

[188] Gilley, 'Southey's *Book of the Church*', 416–17.

[189] *Essays*, ii. 14–15.

tenour' of his writings bears witness to this.[190] It was Southey's belief in history as progress which determined his generally positive attitude to industrialization. In his essay 'On Emigration' (1828), he is unequivocal in describing industrialization as 'a necessary consequence of advancing science, and of that increased activity and spirit of enterprise which accompany the progress of civilization'.[191] Elsewhere he stressed that there would be accompanying problems to this progress; 'Some price is paid for every improvement in society, and every stage in our progress brings with it concomitant evils.'[192] He stresses that 'In the political, as in the natural body, it seems as if those important transactions in the system, which are necessary to its development, could not be performed without some degree of suffering or of danger.'[193] In the *Colloquies*, More's criticisms of the brutalizing effects of the industrial society on a section of the population, are not so much a condemnation of industrialization *per se*, than an exhortation 'to render civilization complete by extending it to those classes which are brutalised by the institutions of society'.[194] Although there has been progress, it has not been general. While 'some parts of the globe are progressive in civilization, others have been retrograde'; and even where 'improvement appears the greatest, it is partial'.[195] The *Colloquies* ends on an optimistic note, which is a paraphrase of Kant's description of history as 'eudaemonistic'; mankind exists in 'perpetual progression toward improvement'.[196] Southey refers to Kant's 'Universal History on a Cosmo-Political plan', and summarizes the latter's conviction of history as 'a steady and continuous, though slow development of certain great predispositions in human nature'.[197]

Sheridan Gilley has also argued that the English idea of liberty was not just the achievement of Macaulay's progressives, but was defined in the clash between reactionaries and radicals, who both

[190] *Essays*, ii. 21.

[191] 'On Emigration', *Essays*, ii. 217. This essay first appeared in the *Quarterly Review*, 37 (Mar. 1828), 539–78.

[192] 'On the Means of Improving the People', ii. 114.

[193] 'On the State of the Poor', i. 95.

[194] *Colloquies*, i. 132.

[195] Ibid. i. 44.

[196] L. W. Beck (ed.), *On History: Immanuel Kant* (Indianapolis: The Library of Liberal Arts, 1963), 139.

[197] *Colloquies*, ii. 408–9, 411. A translation of the 'Idea of a Universal History on a Cosmopolitan Plan' appeared in the *London Magazine*, 10 (Oct. 1824), 385–93.

contributed towards it.[198] Certainly Macaulay's review of the *Colloquies*, whose philosophy he rebutted with a strong avowal of the philosophy of progress,[199] ignored the equally strong avowal of history as progress by Southey, not just in the *Colloquies*, but also in his earlier essays. But Southey's view of history as progress was based less on what Gilley has called 'providentialist' interpretations of English history, and more on a reading of Kant's writings on human history as a whole. At any rate, Robert Nisbet's contention that conservatism in this period defined itself against the notion of history as progress as the 'very centre-piece of modernity',[200] stands in need of some revision. In some ways, the integration of the philosophy of progress by Southey into the body of his conservative thinking was less problematic than the espousal of the same notion of history by radicals such as Mill, who outrightly rejected Kantian epistemology.[201]

The predominance of liquid imagery in Southey's epics is important in the context of his search for a design in history. The 'brook's perpetual flow', and the 'unvaried murmuring' since the 'birth-day of the world', suggests the remorseless flow of time.[202] Near the ruins of Babylon, 'Alone unchanged, a free and bridgeless tide, | Euphrates rolls along.'[203] The 'Ancient Temples' of the submarine city are now empty and silent, 'Hearing no voice save of the Ocean flood'.[204] Sometimes this sensation of the flow of time is described as a perpetual present: 'Time is not here, nor days, nor months, nor years, | An everlasting Now of solitude!'[205] This changelessness suggests Kant's 'abderitism', in which the human race exists 'in eternal stagnation in its present stage of moral worth among creatures'.[206] The suggestion of the pure flow of time raises doubts as to the purpose of history. These doubts are wrestled with in *The Poet's Pilgrimage to Waterloo*, where the Satanic adversary tries to persuade the poet to 'Regard not what has been, nor what may be, | O Child of Earth, this Now is all that toucheth thee.'[207] He insists that the past teaches only one lesson: 'Look where thou wilt, the history of man | Is but a thorny maze without a plan!'[208] However,

198 Gilley, 'Southey's *Book of the Church*', 410.
199 'Southey's Colloquies', 563.
200 Nisbet, *Conservatism*, 92.
201 See ch. 5.
202 *Madoc*, 19; *Thalaba*, 395–6.
203 *Thalaba*, 184.
204 *Kehama*, 127.
205 *Thalaba*, 16.
206 Beck (ed.), *On History: Immanuel Kant*, 139.
207 *Works*, x. 61.
208 Ibid. x. 73.

like the *Colloquies* later, *The Poet's Pilgrimage* ends on an optimistic note.[209]

It is not just the fluvial imagery in *Thalaba* and *Kehama* which points to Southey's grappling with the problem of design in history. The imagery of figures coming to life in these epics is paralleled by that of living figures becoming statues or lifeless images. When Kailyal is confronted by Arvalan's spectre, she is rooted to the spot like a statue.[210] When she accompanies Juggernaut on his chariot as his bride, she seems like a 'bridal statue'.[211] Kailyal keeps watch on the shore for her father, 'statue-like'.[212] The dissection of bodies and the imagery of lifeless figures coming to life, or living figures being deprived of it, again points to Southey's belief in history as progress. In 1796, Southey wrote 'mangle the dead as you please', but the living must not be dissected.[213] In his review of a biography of Nelson in 1810, he again shows disrespect to the dead; 'not infrequently the dead have been embalmed, when for the instruction of posterity they ought to have been dissected.'[214] In *Madoc* the Hoamen's council-hall is decorated with the embalmed bodies of chiefs, and in *Kehama* there is a 'hall of Death' with the embalmed figures of old Kings, 'statues of actual flesh', in the submarine city.[215] Although Southey is fascinated with these embalmings, their lifelessness is also stressed. This indicates Southey's ambivalence towards the past and tradition, which consisted of a fascination and fear of being imprisoned with the dead. In his epics, there are frequent images of lifeless weights. When Ereenia stumbles to free himself from the rock he is chained to, he falls 'prostrate on his prison-bed of stone, | Body and chain alike with lifeless weight'.[216] After a six-day battle, Ladurlad finally kills the monster, which lay 'lifeless, underneath his grasp'.[217] This monster, 'hugest of the Ocean brood, | Weltering and lifeless, drifts toward the shore'.[218] According to Nisbet, conservatives view past tradition as a sacred deposit.[219] The lifeless weights in Southey's epics suggest that for him these sacred deposits were encumbrances, and not inheritances to cherish uncritically. They indicate an attempt to articulate a

[209] Ibid. x. 91. [210] *Kehama*, 35. [211] Ibid. 114.
[212] Ibid. 146.
[213] Southey, 'To G. C. Bedford', 29 Aug. 1796, in *Life*, i. 290.
[214] 'Lives of Nelson', *Quarterly Review*, 3 (Feb. 1810), 219.
[215] *Madoc*, 233; *Kehama*, 137–8. [216] *Kehama*, 140.
[217] Ibid. 142. [218] Ibid. 147–8. [219] Nisbet, *Conservatism*, 26.

notion of history as progress, which was to prefigure his later views. Above all, this attempt was made in the context of defining the 'Orient'. The comparison and contrast of cultures in the oriental renaissance also made possible the defining of a scheme of history for which the notion of progress was the organizing principle. This scheme of history was emerging in Mill's *History* with its reflections upon the 'rude' state of society among the Hindus, although, as shall be discussed below, he failed to articulate this scheme clearly because of the contradictions in his thought. But it was clearly defined in Hegel's characterization of the first stage in the development of *Geist* in world history in which 'the natural spirit is still immersed in nature and is not yet self-sufficient' in the 'oriental' world.[220] It was Jones's discovery of the affinity between Sanskrit and Greek and Latin which made this new world history possible, and one in which, as Romila Thapar has put it, the ancient Indian past was seen almost as 'a lost wing' of early European culture.[221] Thus, not only must the characterization of conservatism in terms of its opposition to history as progress be qualified; the attempt to integrate a notion of progress in the thinking of an author like Southey has to be seen in conjunction with the complex nature of the images he formed in his creation of an Orient in the epics considered here.

Guilty Renunciation or Guilty Government

It has been argued that Southey's epics reflect the importance of Jones's role in shaping some of the central concerns of the Oriental Renaissance. However, the epics also bear the imprint of the growing importance of another body of literature, which was on the whole opposed to the generally favourable views of Jones and his colleagues to non-European cultures, and to their emphasis on their integrity and viability. This growing body of work was missionary and evangelical literature. That this latter body of work was not always opposed to the work of orientalists is evident in Mill's *History*, which drew upon both bodies of literature in its attempt to transform thinking about British India;[222] but in the case of

[220] G. W. F. Hegel, Introduction to *Lectures on the Philosophy of World History*, trans. Duncan Forbes (Cambridge: Cambridge University Press, 1975), 130.

[221] Romila Thapar, 'Interpretations of Ancient Indian History', *History and Theory*, 7 (1968), 319.

[222] See ch. 5.

Southey, these two bodies of literature came to be represented as conflicting strands in his work, rather than as ways of thinking whose assumptions and prescriptions could reinforce each other at a deeper level.

It was Charles Grant's 'A Proposal for Establishing a Protestant Mission in Bengal and Behar' of 1787 which led to an awakening of interest in the evangelization of India. The intention of the 'Proposal' was to win the patronage of the government for missionary work in India. Grant sent a copy to both William Wilberforce and Charles Simeon; the latter was to become Grant's collaborator in the appointment and instalment of evangelicals as East India Company chaplains.[223] Grant's ideas were developed in his highly influential *Observations on the State of Society among Asiatic Subjects of Great Britain* (1792), which by 1820 was regarded in evangelical circles as an authoritative work on prescribing the form the relationship between Britain and India should take. This defined what it saw as the dilemma at the heart of the relationship between Britain and India: 'we cannot now renounce them [Indians] without guilt, though we may also contract great guilt in the government of them'.[224] The ultimate aim of British rule should be the 'moral improvement' of its subjects;[225] it was by conferring benefits of this nature that British rule in India could be justified.[226] This end could not be achieved through the administration of law or legal reforms;[227] it was through the propagation of Christianity that the real root of the problem in India could be tackled, namely the 'internal principles of depravity' in Indian cultures themselves.[228] The conservative policy of British rule was misplaced; it was 'proper and even necessary' to abandon this apparent non-interference policy 'when the state of society among the Hindoos calls for any new provision'.[229] To fulfil the imperatives of British rule as Grant defined them, it would be necessary to undermine the 'attachment of that people to their own modes and customs'.[230] Only the propagation of Christianity would enable this to take place. It would also

[223] A. T. Embree, *Charles Grant and British Rule in India* (London: Allen & Unwin, 1962), 118–20.

[224] Charles Grant, 'Observations on the State of Society among Asiatic Subjects of Great Britain, Particularly with Respect to Morals; and on the Means of Improving it: Written Chiefly in the Year 1792', in *Parliamentary Papers*, 10 (1812–13), paper 282, p. 23.

[225] Ibid. 91. [226] Ibid. 25. [227] Ibid. 27.

[228] Ibid. 27. [229] Ibid. 24. [230] Ibid. 80.

put British rule in India on a more secure footing by 'assimilating our subjects to our modes of thinking', and by establishing an 'identity of sentiments and principles'.[231] The introduction of Christianity as a unifying bond between rulers and ruled would inevitably augment agriculture and commerce in India.[232] Grant's *Observations* influenced William Wilberforce's attempt to have the so-called 'pious clause' introduced into the renewal of the East India Company's Charter in 1793, which failed because of the opposition to it by the Court of Directors, who were averse to allowing missionaries to operate in British India. None the less, the attempt marked the beginning of the Clapham Sect's association with social reform in India.[233] In April 1804 Grant became Deputy Chairman of the East India Company, and he was Chairman for the periods 1804–6, 1807–10, and 1815–16.[234] This position enabled him to ensure that the 'pious clause' was included in the 1813 Charter Act, albeit in a modified form. It no longer stipulated that direct government support be given to missionary activities in India but it legalized the entry of missionaries into India, and provided for the appointment of a bishop.[235] It also defined the 'duty' of British rule to be the promotion of 'the interests and happiness of native inhabitants', and the 'introduction among them of useful knowledge, and of religious and moral improvements'.[236]

The appearance of Grant's *Observations* coincided with the establishment of a number of missionary societies in this period, such as the Baptist Missionary Society in 1792, the London Missionary Society in 1795, and the Church Missionary Society in 1799.[237] In 1793 a number of denominations established *The Evangelical Magazine*, which tried to publicize the cause of proselytizing abroad, and in 1804 the British and Foreign Bible Society was established on a non-sectarian basis to encourage the international circulation of the Bible.[238] It was from 1794 onwards that the 'Periodical Accounts' of the Baptist Missionary Society were published. These included extracts from the letters and journal of

231 Ibid. 24, 104. 232 Ibid. 82. 233 Embree, *Charles Grant*, 152.

234 Ibid. 201, 205. 235 Ibid. 271.

236 Cited by M. A. Laird, *Missionaries and Education in Bengal 1793–1837* (Oxford: Clarendon Press, 1972), 67.

237 K. Ingham, *Reformers in India 1793–1833: An Account of the Work of Christian Missionaries on Behalf of Social Reform* (Cambridge: Cambridge University Press, 1956), 3.

238 K. P. S. Gupta, *The Christian Missionaries in Bengal 1793–1833* (Calcutta: Firma K. L. Mukhopadhyay, 1971), 8, 14.

William Carey, who had arrived in Bengal in November 1793; he later joined William Ward and Joshua Marshman at the Danish settlement of Serampore in 1800. This marked the beginning of the work of the Serampore trio. Carey was appointed a teacher at Fort William College in 1801;[239] the co-operation between Fort William College and the Serampore mission resulted in a systematic study of popular Bengali culture; it also provided the mission with useful weapons for mass evangelization.[240]

In *Kehama*, Southey quotes at length from the first volume of the Baptist translation of the *Ramayana*, which the 'excellent and learned Baptist missionaries at Serampore are at this time employed in printing and translating'.[241] Southey's favourable attitude to missionaries, particularly to the Baptist mission at Serampore in Bengal, is evident also in his prose works. In the *Annual Review* of 1803 he criticized the Church of England for neglecting its duty in spreading the gospel in the East, and argued that the Baptist missionaries should be seen as pioneers in the task the Church should take over.[242] Similarly, in the *Annual Review for 1803*, taking a stance similar to that of Charles Grant in his *Observations*, he asked: 'When will the East India Company be convinced that it is in their ultimate interest, as well as their immediate duty, to convert their subjects?'[243] In the *Quarterly Review* of February and May 1809, Southey recommended the Church to use dissenting missions as 'useful auxiliaries' and pioneers facilitating 'the success of the regular force'.[244] Southey also commends the success of the Roman Catholic Church in proselytizing in his review of Reginald Forbes's *Oriental Memoirs* (1814, 4 volumes) and laments that if 'we had served our God with half the zeal . . . the tree of life would long ere this have stuck deep roots in Hindostan'.[245]

This body of missionary writing on India, however, had a deeper and more profound influence on Southey than his explicit remarks suggest. It has been argued that the concern to tap new sources of creativity made available by the oriental renaissance is reflected in

239 Ibid. 35.

240 David Kopf, *British Orientalism and the Bengal Renaissance: The Dynamics of Indian Modernization 1773–1835* (Berkeley, Calif.: University of California Press, 1969), 71.

241 *Kehama*, 264.

242 'Baptist Missionary Society', *Annual Review for 1802*, 1 (1803), 218.

243 *'Asiatick Researches' Annual Review for 1803*, 2 (1804), 907.

244 'Baptist Missionary Society', *Quarterly Review*, 1 (Feb. and May 1809), 226.

245 'Forbes' *Oriental Memoirs*', *Quarterly Review*, 12 (Oct. 1814), 190.

the preoccupation with the plumbing and probing of depths in Southey's epics. The imagery of liquidity so predominant in these epics reinforces this sense of the tapping of new springs of creativity. However, the sense of chiaroscuro and refraction evoked in these images of depths also indicates the perilous nature of this tapping of new sources of creativity, as does the evocation of the overwhelming sense of flooding in the epics. Sometimes the latter is suggested through the emphasis on the 'everlasting roar' of springs and the surrounding oceans.[246] At the scene of the submerged city, 'the Ocean flood . . . roars forever on the restless shores'.[247] Sometimes the resounding waters fill everything: 'All living sounds had ceased, | Only the flow of waters was heard.'[248] The 'Simorg's vale' is described in terms of the unvaried sound of flowing water:

> No sound intruded on his solitude,
> Only the rivulet was heard,
> Whose everlasting flow,
> From the birth-day of the World, had made
> The same unvaried murmuring.[249]

When Thalaba rests on the shore in preparation for his final battle, 'The roar and raving of the restless sea, | The boundless waves that rose and roll'd and rock'd: | The everlasting sound | Opprest him.'[250] The sense of being swallowed up is also evident in *Kehama*, when the 'deaf Ocean o'er Ladurlad closed',[251] and in *Thalaba*, which ends with the flooding of the 'ocean-vault'. Southey also saw the *bellum servile* which haunted his imagination in terms of a deluge. In the *Colloquies*, More describes how 'the dikes and boundaries of social order began to give away' during his lifetime.[252] There is also a horrifically vivid picture of a *bellum servile*:

> Imagine the infatuated and infuriated wretches, whom not Spitalfields, St. Giles's, and Pimlico alone, but all the lanes and cellars of the metropolis would pour out: . . . a frightful population, whose multitudes, when gathered together, might almost exceed belief! The streets of London would appear to teem with them, like the land of Egypt with its plague of frogs: and the lava floods from a volcano would be less destructive than the hordes whom your great cities and manufacturing districts would vomit forth![253]

[246] *Thalaba*, 188; *Kehama*, 99.
[247] *Thalaba*, 127.
[248] Ibid. 221.
[249] Ibid. 395–6.
[250] Ibid. 442.
[251] *Kehama*, 128.
[252] *Colloquies*, i. 236.
[253] Ibid. i. 114–16.

The ambivalent nature of the imagery of liquidity in Southey's epics and his prose works points to the threat which the oriental renaissance also represented; namely, the possibility that the cultures uncovered by the renaissance would threaten the apparent superiority and uniqueness of the Graeco-Roman heritage which was so central to the definition of European notions of cultural superiority.[254] The imagery of flooding is indicative of the threatening nature of this prolificity; but it is also indicative of the danger of the imaginative expansion enabled by the renaissance undermining and subverting the task of legal codification, which was so central to the rejuvenation of established polities and the reinforcement of social stratification. It was the possible radical uses to which the oriental renaissance could be put in the work of comparativists such as Volney, Dupuis, Sir William Drummond, Erasmus Darwin, and Richard Payne Knight, which James Mill was also to react against.[255] Southey's own brand of conservatism was careful in its attempt to harness the rejuvenating effects of the renaissance to the project of conferring a new lease of life on the established regime and its tasks of legal codification.

Raymond Schwab has argued that 'To poets with a Latin education India brought the temptation, as against the routine of fragments, to write rivers of poems.'[256] Southey's oriental epics succumb to this temptation to write 'rivers of poems' in order to rival those of the oriental renaissance and neutralize the cultural threat which it posed by employing missionary and evangelical rhetoric which was so critical of non-European cultures in this period. It is this which explains what Jeffrey described as the 'very strange and unaccountable sucess' of Southey's epics.[257] Thus, Southey often expressed a low opinion of Indian or Middle Eastern literature in his epics. In a note in *Thalaba* he writes: 'A waste of ornament and labour characterises all the works of the Orientalists . . . The little of their literature that has reached us is equally worthless.'[258] He uses the excerpts from the translation of the

[254] For an analysis of this heritage and the role it played in shaping European notions of cultural superiority, see Martin Bernal, 'Black Athena Denied: The Tyranny of Germany over Greece and the Rejection of the Afroasiatic Roots of Europe: 1780–1980', *Comparative Criticism*, 8 (1986), 3–69. See also Schwab, *Oriental Renaissance*, 18, 268.

[255] See ch. 5.

[256] Schwab, *Oriental Renaissance*, 355. For a fascinating argument about the nature of 'Kubla Khan' as an 'epic' fragment, see Shaffer, *The Mythological School in Biblical Criticism*, chs. 1–2.

[257] *Edinburgh Review*, 17 (Feb. 1811), 431.

[258] *Thalaba*, 29–30.

Ramayana to protect his epic from the charge of extravagance by comparing it to 'this genuine specimen of Hindoo fable'.[259] He justifies the extravagance of his epics on the grounds of their resemblance to the extravagance of texts translated by European scholars, and so absolves himself of the responsibility for what Jeffrey called their 'wilful deformities' and the 'perversity of his manifold affectations'.[260] However, Southey is careful to profess adherence to the European aesthetic standards by which *Thalaba* and *Kehama* are condemned. In the preface to *Kehama*, he argues: 'The spirit of the poem was Indian, but there was nothing Oriental in the style. I had learnt the language of poetry from our own great masters and the great poets of antiquity.'[261] Southey betrays European aesthetic standards while professing an adherence to them, and the 'monstrosity' of his epics is legitimized by their fidelity to non-European standards. It is this double allegiance and betrayal which characterizes his epics, and which also enables his audience to enjoy the renaissance without being threatened by it. Southey often described *Thalaba* and *Kehama* as fantastic. He felt that the public would not take to *Kehama* because 'It is too strange, too much beyond all human sympathies';[262] 'sympathy is clearly out of reach and out of sight'.[263] *Kehama* is intended to 'take us out of ourselves, to carry us into the world of unrealities, to busy us with something flesh and blood, . . . and to make us perceive our imaginative power'.[264] Macaulay's comment on *Thalaba* and *Kehama* as 'gorgeous visions' with 'invention, grandeur, and brilliancy', but 'grotesque and extravagant', violating 'even that conventional plausibility which is essential to the works of art', was therefore an accurate estimate of Southey's conception.[265] The fantastic nature of Southey's epics allowed the imagination of Southey and his readers to revel irresponsibly in the Orient of his creation, while remaining faithful to the standards by which such revelry was condemned.

Thomas Moore's *Lalla Rookh* was both to provoke and mimic this reaction. It was able to do this because of the ambiguous relationship Moore had as an Irish patriot of Catholic background

259 *Works*, viii. 265.
260 *Edinburgh Review*, 17 (Feb. 1811), 429.
261 *Kehama*, p. xvii.
262 Southey, 'To Walter Scott', 6 Nov. 1810, in *Life*, iii. 180.
263 Southey, 'To C. W. W. Wynn', 29 Oct. 1808, in *New Letters*, i. 486.
264 Southey, 'To Thomas Southey', 5 Dec. 1812, in *Selections*, ii. 307.
265 Macaulay, 'Southey's *Colloquies*', 530.

with the fashionable London milieu he inhabited. The success of *Lalla Rookh* lay not in its pandering to the taste for the exotic, but in its intimate but parodic relationship with the popular imperial sensibility which it manipulated so well. *Lalla Rookh* touched on the nerves of an imperial sensibility, both confirming and caricaturing its expectations. Furthermore, two of the tales of *Lalla Rookh*, 'The Veiled Prophet of Khorassan' and 'The Fire Worshippers', are implicit denunciations of the Protestant ascendancy in Ireland, so that part of *Lalla Rookh* was an allegory of an imperialist politics closer to home. In this way, the character of *Lalla Rookh* as a slight work and the serious attention it received in its time, can be read in terms of the 'politics of the exotic', conducted from the perspective of a writer whose negotiation between a colonizing and a colonized culture was both humorous and full of pathos.

CHAPTER 3

THOMAS MOORE AND ORIENTALISM

Rebels in Cork are Patriots in Madrid

Moore's formulation of a sophisticated brand of orientalism stemmed from his ambivalent position as an Irish patriot of Catholic background who was also the 'god of drawing-room idolatry' in London society.[1] This reputation was partly based on his recital of Irish songs at social gatherings. In one of his letters home soon after his arrival in England in March 1799, he wrote to his mother, 'My songs have taken such a rage! even surpassing what they did in Dublin.'[2] He was to publish ten volumes of *Irish Melodies* between April 1808 and January 1834, and declared that they were the 'main bulwark of my reputation'.[3] He also felt that they would outlive *Lalla Rookh*.[4] His self-conscious role as an Irish songster (he sometimes depicted himself as a 'Minstrel of Erin'[5]) and his publication of the *Irish Melodies* reflected his serious standing as an Irish patriot. In a letter to Sir John Stevenson of February 1807, from which extracts were cited as part of the 'advertisement' to the first volume of *Irish Melodies* (1808), Moore felt 'very anxious that a Work of this kind should be undertaken', because 'our National Music has never been properly collected'. He looks forward to 'a better period both of politics and music' in Ireland, hinting that a rehabilitation of Irish culture, of which his *Irish Melodies* were a part, would rejuvenate Ireland politically as

[1] *Westminster Review*, 1 (Jan.–Apr. 1824), 20.

[2] Thomas Moore, 'To His Mother', 1 Mar. 1801, letter 38 of *The Letters of Thomas Moore*, ed. Wilfred S. Dowden, 2 vols. (Oxford: Clarendon Press, 1964), i. 304.

[3] Moore, 'To James Power', Feb. 1814, letter 367 of *Letters*, i. 304.

[4] Moore, 'To Thomas Longman', 23 Nov. 1837, letter 1,123 of *Letters*, ii. 821.

[5] *The Poetical Works of Thomas Moore*, ed. Thomas Moore, 10 vols. (London: Longman, Orme, Brown, Green, and Longmans, 1840–1), iv. 48.

well.[6] In *Memoirs of Myself*, Moore confessed that some of the prominent members of the United Irishmen were among the 'most intimate friends' of his family.[7] While a student at Trinity College, Dublin, Moore wrote two articles in 1797 and 1798 for *The Press*, the United Irishmen's newspaper. His close friend Robert Emmet, who died in the 1803 rebellion, persuaded him to desist from any other similar articles, since this would damage their cause.[8] Moore and his family were also friends of Edward Hudson, who was exiled from Ireland for his part in the May 1798 rebellion.[9] Moore persisted in this strain for some time. His *Memoirs of Captain Rock, The Celebrated Irish Chieftain* (1824) was seen by some reviews as publicizing the wrongs done to Ireland.[10] In his *Journal*, Moore mentioned a speech made by Edward George Stanley in the House of Commons on 6 May 1824, in which several passages from *Captain Rock* were read to illustrate Irish feelings towards the established Church.[11] Moore was seen as a spokesman for the Irish; it was in this role that Southey condemned him for supporting terrorism. He deplored what he saw as Moore's callous reference to the '*fun-stirring*' Captain Rock, and felt Moore 'may do well to reflect . . . before he composes any more songs, or biographies, which have a tendency to *make the fun stir*'.[12] The biography Southey referred to is Moore's *The Life and Death of Lord Edward Fitzgerald* (1831), in which Moore depicted Fitzgerald and the United Irishmen uprising of May 1798 in heroic terms. Moore felt that this biography reflected his persistent 'zeal for Ireland & her liberties',[13] and declared that he would continue to dedicate himself to 'that cause which has always been uppermost in my heart, which was my first inspiration and shall be my last, the

[6] Moore, 'To Sir John Stevenson', Feb. 1807, letter 144 of *Letters*, i. 116.

[7] *Memoirs of Myself, Begun many Years since, but Never, I Fear, to be Completed* (1833), in *Memoirs, Journal, and Correspondence of Thomas Moore*, ed. Lord John Russell, 8 vols. (London: Longman, Brown, Green, and Longmans, 1853), i. 18.

[8] Ibid. i. 57.

[9] Ibid. i. 48.

[10] *Westminster Review*, 1 (Jan.–Apr. 1824), 494, 503.

[11] *The Journal of Thomas Moore*, ed. Wilfred S. Dowden, 3 vols. (Newark: University of Delaware Press, 1983–6), entry for 10 May 1824, ii. 729.

[12] 'Moore's *The Life and Death of Lord Edward Fitzgerald*', *Quarterly Review*, 46 (Nov. 1831), 243, 253. Southey was referring to Moore's couplet in the Memoirs of Captain Rock: 'Through Leinster, Ulster, Connaught, Munster | ROCK'S the boy to make the fun stir!' (*Memoirs of Captain Rock, the Celebrated Irish Chieftain, with Some Account of His Ancestors: Written by Himself* (London: Longman, Hurst, Rees, Orme, Brown, 1824), 8.

[13] Moore, 'To E. R. Moran', 19 July 1832, letter 1,008 of *Letters*, ii. 751.

cause of Irish freedom'.[14] He refuted Daniel O'Connell's accusations of 'lukewarmness in the cause of Ireland, since the grant of Emancipation' (that is, the Catholic Emancipation of 1829) by pointing to 'the praises which he himself, under his own hand, bestowed upon me for the "courage" of my "Life of Lord Edward."'[15]

Moore also supported the Irish parliament, whose separate existence had been brought to an end by the Act of Union which came into force on 1 January 1801. He believed that it had kept alive 'an active political feeling' which had saved Ireland 'from decay and degradation'. Without the Irish Parliament, 'there never would have been enough of public spirit generated to produce the grand spectacle which Ireland exhibited in '82'.[16] This 'grand spectacle', which Moore elsewhere calls the '*Irish Revolution of 1782*',[17] was the virtual declaration of independence by Henry Grattan in 1782, based on a series of resolutions drawn up by Grattan, Henry Flood, and Charlemont in February 1782, the most important of which were those asserting the sole right of the Irish Parliament to legislate for Ireland, and declaring the powers exercised by the privy councils of the two kingdoms under Poynings' Law 'unconstitutional and a grievance'.[18] Moore eulogized Charlemont and Grattan.[19] He also contemplated a biography of Grattan; the latter's son seemed 'half inclined to transfer' the task to Moore, who declared, 'There is no task I should feel greater pride in.'[20] One of Moore's melodies was 'a remembrance' of him, in which 1782 is depicted as '*one* lucid interval, snatch'd from the gloom', when 'A nation o'erleap'd the dark bounds of her doom, | And for *one* sacred instant, touch'd Liberty's goal.'[21] It was because Moore supported Grattan's declaration of independence, that he described the Union as an 'ill-assorted marriage' between England and Ireland,[22] and later said, in no uncertain terms, 'The union I always detested the very thought of.'[23]

[14] Moore, 'To the Limerick Union', 8 Nov. 1832, letter 1,020 of *Letters*, ii. 759.

[15] Moore, 'To Cornelius Lyne', 26 Sept. 1834, letter 1,059 of *Letters*, ii. 786.

[16] *Journal*, entry for 14 Apr. 1823, ii. 627.

[17] *Captain Rock*, 234.

[18] J. C. Beckett, *A Short History of Ireland* (1952; 4th edn. London: Hutchinson University Library, 1971), 118.

[19] *Captain Rock*, 236.

[20] *Journal*, entry for 12 June 1823, ii. 644. The biography was completed by Henry Grattan and published in five volumes between 1839 and 1846.

[21] 'Shall the Harp, then, be Silent', in *Works*, iv. 49.

[22] Moore, 'To the Marquess of Lansdowne', *c.*1820, letter 594 of *Letters*, ii. 489.

[23] Moore, 'To the Marquess of Lansdowne', 7 Dec. 1830, letter 945 of *Letters*, ii. 707.

Moore's publications on Irish politics, and his desire to write a biography of Grattan, can almost be seen as a hagiography of the Irish nationalist heroes who struggled for Ireland's independence. But it was not just Moore's position as an Irish patriot in London society which was redolent with ambiguities; his standing as an Irish patriot was of a different order from O'Connell's, who linked the cause of Irish nationalism and the Roman Catholic Church.[24] This is not to say that Moore did not welcome the Emancipation of 1829; he himself had suffered from the disabilities of being a Catholic while he was in Ireland. He described the penal laws as 'demoralising', and added that it was not surprising if 'the recollection of such laws, and of their bigoted, though, in some cases, conscientious, supporters, should live bitterly in the minds and hearts of all who have, at any time, been made their victims'.[25] But Moore took Lord John Russell's advice that 'one could best serve the Catholics by keeping out of their ranks & joining their cause, *not* themselves,'[26] and so he did not join the Catholic Association, established in 1823 by Daniel O'Connell as an instrument of agitation for Catholic emancipation. Moore sometimes suggests that although Catholic emancipation was an important victory, the real goal should be the repeal of the Act of Union.[27] Also, Moore was ambivalent towards the faith into which he was born. He sometimes wrote as if he were not a Catholic at all. In 1815 he referred to Catholicism, 'though it be the religion of my fathers', as 'that wretched faith, which is again polluting Europe with Jesuitism and inquisitions, and which of the humbugs that have stultified mankind is the most dangerous and mischievous'.[28] He described Irish priests as 'low, miracle-working, whisky drinking'.[29] He occasionally argued that Catholic recalcitrance was also to blame for Ireland's troubles; 'They have done much towards the ruin of Ireland, and have been so well assisted by the Protestants throughout, that, between them, Ireland is at this instant as *ruined* as it need be.'[30] It is Catholic recalcitrance which he attacked in his

[24] Beckett, *Short History of Ireland*, 136.

[25] *Memoirs of Myself*, i. 29, 50.

[26] *Journal*, entry for 18 Aug. 1828, iii. 1153.

[27] Moore, 'To the Marquess of Lansdowne', 7 Dec. 1830, letter 945 of *Letters*, ii. 705–7.

[28] Moore, 'To Lady Donegal', 10 Apr. 1815, letter 429 of *Letters*, i. 359.

[29] Moore, 'To the Marquess of Lansdowne', *c.*1820, letter 594 of *Letters*, ii. 488.

[30] Moore, 'To His Mother', 1807, letter 158 of *Letters*, i. 126.

Letter to the Roman Catholics of Dublin (1810). In this pamphlet, Moore forcefully argued for the Roman Catholics to support independence from the papal authority in the appointment of bishops, since this would mollify Tory anxieties about Catholic emancipation, especially if the king were given the power to veto such papal appointments. Moore took pains to explain why the 'members of a persecuted religion, should turn for support, for counsel and consolation, to the visible head of that faith, for which they were suffering'. He also explained the need to 'seek, in a spiritual alliance abroad, some shelter from the storm of a temporal tyranny at home',[31] but he made it clear that, in order to qualify for a full participation in the British constitution, Irish Catholics must be prepared, as their fellow Catholics in England were, 'to exchange the rescripts and bulls of Rome, for the blessings of a free Constitution'. Freedom was 'too delicate a treasure, to be exposed unnecessarily' to the Pope's influence.[32] Moore went so far as to argue along lines that even Southey would have approved of, when he declared that 'as long as you cling close to the Court of Rome, you [cannot be] embraced by the British constitution'.[33] He was also anxious to justify the Protestant fear of entrusting the constitution to Irish Catholics as 'natural, just and well-founded', and described the Catholic fears of repudiating the Pope's influence as 'unmeaning, groundless and ungenerous'.[34] He ended by expressing a preference for the bigots 'who have the Constitution on their side', rather than the bigots who represented Catholic opinion.[35] It was of prime importance that the Irish Catholics join the people of England in their demands for political reforms, which cannot be ignored for long, and so join the ranks of the 'regenerators of that system, which statesmen of your own faith first gloriously founded'.[36] Moore's argument in the *Letter to the Roman Catholics of Dublin* seems to conflict with his view of the 1782 Declaration of Independence and the Union, but for Moore 'the dawn of independence' in 1782[37] was a lost opportunity; it was now important for Irish Catholics to win whatever they could within the framework of the Union. The *Letter to the Roman*

[31] *Letter to the Roman Catholics of Dublin* (London: J. Carpenter, 1810), 17. For an account of the veto controversy, see G. I. T. Machin, *The Catholic Question in English Politics 1820 to 1830* (Oxford: Clarendon Press, 1964), 13–15.

[32] *Letter to the Roman Catholics of Dublin*, 15.

[33] Ibid. 18–19.

[34] Ibid. 35.

[35] Ibid. 36.

[36] Ibid. 33.

[37] *Journal*, entry for 14 Apr. 1823, ii. 628.

Catholics of Dublin also indicated Moore's commitment to a secular politics, and a pluralist society in which different faiths could coexist peacefully; 'the mixture of religion, with this world's politics is as dangerous as electrical experiments upon lightning.'[38] This commitment is even more clear in the *Memoirs of Captain Rock*, where Moore argues that any church establishment is 'imminently calculated to serve the cause of discord, in whatever form it exists'. This is especially so in Ireland, where the creed of the majority of the populace is not the religion of the state.[39]

It is these ambiguities in Moore's position as an Irish patriot in London society which account for the ironic mode of writing in *Lalla Rookh* (1817) and *The Epicurean* (1827), in which different perspectives are played off against each other before the superiority of any single all-encompassing perspective emerges. The poem 'The Sceptic' (1809) expressed this ironic perspective and denied the possibility of arriving at any knowledge immune from doubt in 'the circle of human pursuits'.[40] This is partly because of cultural differences:

> you'll find the self-same man
> A sage in France, a madman in Japan;
> And *here* some head beneath a mitre swells,
> Which *there* had tingled to a cap and bells.[41]

But it is not just cultural differences which undermine the pretensions of any single perspective:

> Just as the mind the erring sense believes,
> The erring mind, in turn, the sense deceives . . .
> Self is the medium through which Judgement's ray
> Can seldom pass without being turn'd astray.[42]

Not only are individual minds deluded; 'Whole nations, too, the same delusion blinds,' and sometimes 'Rebels in Cork are patriots in Madrid.'[43] Moore's scepticism extended to histories; he touches on the close relationship between fiction and historiography, commented upon by Jones:

> . . . how oft we sigh,
> When histories charm, to think that histories lie!
> That all are grave romances, at the best . . .[44]

[38] *Letter to the Roman Catholics of Dublin*, 23.
[39] *Captain Rock*, 254.
[40] 'The Sceptic', in *Works*, iii. 67.
[41] Ibid. iii. 71.
[42] Ibid. iii. 73–4.
[43] Ibid. iii. 75.
[44] Ibid. iii. 76.

The works examined here reflect different ramifications of the sort of scepticism described in this poem, a scepticism which undermines any attempt, such as that made by Bentham and Mill, to establish universal principles of epistemology. Moore's sensitivity to the possibility of alternative perspectives, which is the basis of his ironic mode of writing, enabled him to treat issues of imperialism in *Lalla Rookh* from an angle unexplored by others, and in particular, to grasp the nature of the imperial sensibility of his readers in order to manipulate it for his own purposes. His brand of scepticism subverted this imperial sensibility by suggesting alternative narratives to its dominant one.

The Melodies of Ireland at Home in the East: Lalla Rookh *(1817)*

Moore first mentioned *Lalla Rookh* in 1811; he felt confident it would place him 'above the vulgar herd both of worldlings and of critics'.[45] After it was published in 1817, he was sure that it would 'set me higher in reputation than ever'.[46] It was *Lalla Rookh* which made him a public figure. *Lalla Rookh* purported to be an imitation of an oriental framework tale in which four stories are loosely held together. The framework tale is the journey of the Emperor Aurengzebe's daughter, Lalla Rookh, from Delhi to Bucharia to marry the son of the King of Bucharia. During the journey, she and her entourage are entertained by a Persian 'minstrel', Feramorz. Fadladeen, who is Aurengzebe's prime minister, is a Polonius-like figure who makes various criticisms of Feramorz's art. Lalla Rookh falls in love with Feramorz, but on arrival at her destination, he reveals himself as her husband to be. Of the four tales the first, 'The Veiled Prophet of Khorassan', and the third, 'The Fire-Worshippers', will be concentrated on here, since they are more interesting for our purposes. The contemporary reviews of *Lalla Rookh* are also significant. Whether favourable or not, they show a deep interest in the orientalism which it played upon, and accord *Lalla Rookh* an attention apparently out of all proportion to its merit. There are various reasons for this, which this chapter will consider. *Lalla Rookh* was widely read; Longman paid £3,000 for it, and still thought of it twenty years later as the 'cream of the

[45] Moore, 'To Mary Godfrey', 11 Sept. 1811, letter 195 of *Letters*, i. 160.
[46] Moore, 'To His Mother', 30 May 1817, letter 499 of *Letters*, i. 417.

copyrights'. By 1841, *Lalla Rookh* had gone through twenty editions, of which six had appeared in the first year of publication. Although critical opinion today would probably agree that *Lalla Rookh* is a slight work, its popularity and the serious critical attention given to it at the time have to be accounted for. The 'slightness' of *Lalla Rookh* is much more complex than it appears at first.

'The Fire-Worshippers' supplanted Southey's planned Persian epic;[47] and it also reflected the interest aroused in Zoroastrianism by Anquétil-Duperron's *Zend-Avesta*, which Gibbon had described as the 'Bible of the Ghebers'.[48] The subject matter of 'The Fire-Worshippers' is imperialism and its beleaguered cultures. In particular, it is a maudlin tale of the last resistance of the Iranians to the Arab conquerors. It dramatizes the belief which overcame the retreating Persians after the battle of al-Qadisiyah in AD 635 that, in Gibbon's words, 'the last day of their religion and empire was at hand'.[49]

The occasion for the story of 'The Fire-Worshippers' arises when the royal entourage rests in a grove in the vicinity of 'the ruins of a strange and awful-looking tower, which seemed old enough to have been the temple of some religion no longer known'.[50] The Princess conjectures that the 'tower might be a relic of some of those dark superstitions which had prevailed in that country before the light of Islam dawned upon it'.[51] Feramorz explains that the tower is the remains of a fire-temple, built by the ancient Persians, or 'Ghebers' as the Muslims called them, and he suggests an alternative narrative to that of 'the light of Islam':

> it was impossible . . . not to feel interested in the many glorious but unsuccessful struggles, which had been made by these original natives of Persia to cast off the yoke of their bigoted conquerors . . . and, as a native of Cashmere, of that Fair and Holy Valley, which had in the same manner become the prey of strangers, and seen her ancient shrines and native princes swept away before the march of her intolerant invaders, he felt a sympathy, he owned, with the sufferings of the persecuted Ghebers, which

[47] See ch. 2.

[48] Edward Gibbon, *The History of the Decline and Fall of the Roman Empire*, ed. William Smith, 8 vols. (London: John Murray, 1862), vi. 367.

[49] Ibid. vi. 294.

[50] *Lalla Rookh: An Oriental Romance* (London: Longman, Hurst, Rees, Orme, Brown, 1817), 170.

[51] Ibid. 171.

every monument like this before them but tended more to powerful awaken.[52]

Moore makes clear that the story of 'The Fire-Worshippers' has a 'doubleness of application'.[53] Feramorz relates the narrative from the perspective of the Ghebers. The fiends and demons of the Muslims are the gods and heroes of the Ghebers. To the Emir and his daughter Hinda, Hafed is simply a 'rebel fiend',[54] but there is a comic confounding of stereotypes when Hinda discovers Hafed is actually her secret lover.[55] There is an obvious suggestion here of an alternative Irish narrative to that of the Protestant ascendancy. Moore's stress on the 'bigotry' of the Arab conquerors was in contrast to Gibbon's depiction of Muslim rule in Iran; Gibbon claimed that the Muslims had guaranteed the civil and religious liberties of the Ghebers, and that the 'greatest part of the temples of Persia were ruined by the insensible and general desertion of their votaries'.[56] But Moore had a special interest in reinforcing the common view of the intolerance of Islam. Bernard Lewis argues that Catholic authors tried to discredit Protestant doctrine by likening it to Islam, depicting Muhammad as an early-day Protestant. Protestant theologians responded to the charge in one of several ways; by refuting it, by emphasizing their own hostility to Islam, by turning Catholic accusations against dissenters such as Unitarians (Gibbon had described Muhammad and his followers as Unitarians[57]), or by accepting the accusation and turning it to their own advantage.[58] The parallel between Muslim rule in Iran and British rule in Ireland is driven home with the suggested similarity between the intolerance of Islam and what Moore later called the 'pestilent bigotry' of Protestantism.[59]

This parallel between Islam and Protestantism was already hinted at in the first tale of *Lalla Rookh*, 'The Veiled Prophet of Khorassan'. Moore's conception of Al Mokanna as an impostor was probably influenced by the characterizations of Muhammad by Sale and Gibbon. Moore sometimes quotes from Sale's edition of the Koran.[60] In his preliminary discourse, although Sale assumes

[52] Ibid. 172.
[53] Ibid. 173 n.
[54] Ibid. 219.
[55] Ibid. 238, 250.
[56] *Decline and Fall of the Roman Empire*, vi. 368–9.
[57] Ibid. vi. 224, 240.
[58] Bernard Lewis, 'Gibbon on Muhammad', in G. W. Bowersock *et al.* (eds.), *Edward Gibbon and the Decline and Fall of the Roman Empire* (Cambridge, Mass.: Harvard University Press, 1977), 62.
[59] *Captain Rock*, 47.
[60] *Lalla Rookh*, 66.

Muhammad was an impostor, he argued that Muhammad's original purpose was to destroy idolatry and weed out the corruptions which Jews and Christians had introduced into monotheism, and thereby restore it to its original purity. He hints at a view which Gibbon was later to adopt, namely that Muhammad began in 'enthusiasm' and went on to imposture.[61] Gibbon described Muhammad's creed as 'free from suspicion or ambiguity'; the truths of Islam are sublime, perhaps 'too sublime . . . for our present faculties'.[62] Uniting an adjective and noun seldom joined in the eighteenth century, he applauds Muhammad's 'rational enthusiasm', and seems to admire Islam's 'independent spirit of fanaticism'.[63] But although Muhammad's original motives may have been those of 'pure and genuine benevolence', it is unfortunately the case that from 'enthusiasm to imposture the step is perilous and slippery'.[64] He used fraud and cruelty to propagate his faith, and so his character must have been 'gradually stained'.[65] Thus 'Of his last years ambition was the ruling passion; and a politician will suspect that he secretly smiled (the victorious impostor!) at the enthusiasm of his youth, and the credulity of his proselytes.'[66] In *Lalla Rookh* Al Mokanna is like the later Muhammad, who manipulates his millenial message and the enthusiasm it arouses in his followers for his own purposes, and is contemptuous of 'the credulity of his proselytes'. The concern with imposture in 'The Veiled Prophet of Khorassan' is with all forms of religious imposture, not just the imposture of Islam. There is certainly a hint of a parallel between the depiction of Islam as a reforming movement and its slide into bigotry and imposture, and Protestantism.

There is another serious purpose behind 'The Fire-Worshippers', which Moore was at pains to make clear. In his preface to the 20th edition of *Lalla Rookh*, Moore makes special mention of 'The Fire-Worshippers'. He claimed that he was at a loss with *Lalla Rookh* until he conceived of this tale, and then 'a new and deep interest in my whole task took possession of me. The cause of tolerance was again my inspiring theme; and the spirit that had spoken in the melodies of Ireland soon found itself at home in the East'.[67] In 'Paradise and the Peri', the story Feramorz relates before 'The

[61] Byron Porter Smith, *Islam in English Literature* (Beirut: American Press, 1939), 65–6.
[62] *Decline and Fall of the Roman Empire*, vi. 233–4.
[63] Ibid. vi. 232.
[64] Ibid. vi. 263.
[65] Ibid. vi. 263–4.
[66] Ibid. vi. 264.
[67] *Works*, vi, p. xvi.

Fire-Worshippers', the Peri catches the last drop of blood of a warrior who resisted Mahmud of Ghazni. In a long note, in which he refers to 'The Fire-Worshippers', Moore defended this depiction of a struggle for liberty:

> Objections may be made to my use of the word Liberty, in this and more especially in the story that follows it, as totally inapplicable to any state of things that has ever existed in the East; but though I cannot, of course, mean to employ it in that enlarged and noble sense which is so well understood at the present day, and, I grieve to say, so little acted upon, yet it is no disparagement to the word to apply it to that national independence, that freedom from the interference and dictation of foreigners, without which, indeed, no liberty of any kind can exist, and for which both Hindoos and Persians fought against their Mussulman invaders with, in many cases, a bravery that deserved much better success.[68]

Moore conferred a respectability on the struggles of colonized cultures, by describing them as national independence struggles. He also assumed that national identities existed on the basis of which struggles to resist 'the interference and dictation of foreigners' take place. This view was in marked contrast to that of James Mill, who argued that 'the aversion to a government, because in the hands of foreigners; that is, men who are called by one rather than some other name, with out regard to the qualities of government, whether better or worse, is a prejudice which reason disclaims.'[69]

Moore was to expand these suggestions of parallels between Ireland and the East in his *History of Ireland* (1838), in which he concurred with Jones's designation of Iran as the original centre of population.[70] He also suggested that there might be some connection between the 'pillar-temples, or Round Towers, which form so remarkable a part of Ireland's antiquities', and the Zoroastrian fire-temples of Iran.[71] Moore's argument for the oriental roots of Irish culture had already been publicized by General Vallancey, the most prominent Irish antiquarian of the time, in works such as the *Ancient History of Ireland Proved from the Sanskrit Books* and *Prospectus of a Dictionary of the Language of the Aire Coti, or Ancient Irish* (1802). Moore also emphasized the Phoenician influence on Ireland.[72] The Irish were a mixture of Celts and Phoenicians;

[68] *Lalla Rookh*, 378–9.

[69] James Mill, *The History of British India*, ed. H. H. Wilson, 10 vols. (London: James Madden, Piper, Stephenson, and Spence, 1858), ii. 342.

[70] *The History of Ireland*, 3 vols. (1838–46), i. 31.

[71] Ibid. i. 26–30.

[72] Ibid. i. 16.

as a seafaring race, 'every where upon the waters', it is likely that the Phoenicians established a colony in Ireland, since it was their 'system' to make 'colonisation the basis of their power'.[73] There is an implicit contrast between the Phoenicians and the English as colonialists. Part of the reason Ireland was a country of 'a variety of modes of devotion and doctrine' was because the Phoenicians characteristically 'set no limits to the varieties of creed and ritual, with which, in their career over the globe, they furnished their colonies'.[74] The 'early and long-continued intercourse which Ireland appears to have maintained, through the Phoenicians, with the East' would explain 'the varieties of worship imported to her shores', which were either 'incorporated with her original creed, or formed new and distinct rallying points of belief'.[75] Thus, the Phoenicians represent an earlier, oriental form of colonization, which is beneficial in its effects, in stark contrast to the intolerance of the later English colonialists.

Moore's stress on the oriental roots of Irish culture was part of the scholarly tradition established by the French scholar Samuel Bochart in the mid-seventeenth century, who suggested that Phoenician was the mother tongue of all the non-Romance languages of Western Europe, especially Gaulish and Breton.[76] The mainstream school about the westward progression of civilization was the Nordic/Teutonic school, which considered various Teutonic languages as a continuation of Scythian ones, and Celtic languages as a branch of the Nordic/Teutonic/Viking group. The Phoenician school was supported by those Irish, Welsh, and Scottish scholars who sought to vindicate Celtic antiquity against the Anglo-Saxon orientation of the 'Nordic' Scytho-Celtists.[77] In Moore's time, General Vallancey, who was among the founding members of the Royal Irish Academy, was the leading proponent of Phoenician Scytho-Celtism in Britain. Vallancey was a friend of Jones, who was well acquainted with his work. Jones felt Vallancey's work was unreliable; he even called it 'very stupid'. He felt his stress on the Persian influence on the Irish was inaccurate, and was sure his etymology was erroneous.[78] None the less he was also sure that the

[73] Ibid. i. 4, 10. [74] Ibid. i. 19–20. [75] Ibid. i. 32.

[76] Joseph Th. Leersen, 'On the Edge of Europe: Ireland in Search of Oriental Roots, 1650–1850', *Comparative Criticism*, 8 (1986), 95. [77] Ibid. 95–6.

[78] Sir William Jones, 'To the Second Earl Spencer', 1–11 Sept. 1787, letter 467 of *The Letters of Sir William Jones*, ed. Garland Cannon, 2 vols. (Oxford: Clarendon Press, 1970), ii. 768–9.

ancient language of Ireland did have some affinity with Sanskrit.[79] Sir William Betham (1779–1853), another prominent member of the Royal Irish Academy, was Vallancey's successor in this school of thought.[80] It was the Phoenicianist, rather than the Nordic, wing of Scytho-Celtism which best suited the sentiments of Irish patriotism. The Nordic school, which was dominant in England, held that the Celtic languages were a mere branch of tongues of Northern Europe, barbaric until the importation of civility from Rome and its heirs. Phoenicianism disagreed with the notion that civilization was by definition Graeco-Roman; and it impugned this Graeco-Roman tradition as intolerant and imperialist, linking its victims from Phoenicia to Ireland into a great tradition in its own right. The vanquished Celts were placed in this tradition of cultures whose cultivation was elevated over the military efficiency of the younger upstart cultures who suppressed this alternative tradition.[81] Moore's stress on the Phoenician and Persian influence on Irish culture was thus very much in agreement with this school of thought congenial to Irish patriotic sentiment.

Moore's depiction of Ireland as a country with a long tradition of absorbing different faiths and cultures was also part of another scholarly tradition, which sought to refute the barbaric image of Ireland current in Britain since the Norman conquest in the twelfth century. Irish antiquarians from Geoffrey Keating (*c.*1570–*c.*1644) to Charles O'Conor and Sylvestor O'Halloran in the eighteenth century invented a glorious pre-colonial past of cultural and political sophistication which was in sharp contrast to their present situation as colonial subjects. Macpherson's Ossian texts could not be used to validate this imagined past because the primitivism which the poems represented did not validate the depiction of the Irish pre-colonial past by these scholars.[82] Indeed, Macpherson's Ossian had actually reinforced the unfavourable views of early Irish society and its literature and history.[83] Moore's characterization of Ireland was not only part of a scholarly tradition which reacted against pejorative views of pre-colonial Ireland; it also

[79] Jones, 'To Joseph Cooper Walker', 11 Sept. 1787, letter 468 of *Letters*, ii. 770–1.

[80] Leersen, 'Ireland in Search of Oriental Roots', 99, 103.

[81] Ibid. 100–1.

[82] Clare O'Halloran, 'Irish Re-creations of the Gaelic Past: The Challenge of Macpherson's Ossian', *Past and Present*, 124 (Aug. 1989), 72.

[83] Ibid. 74–5.

heightened the contrast between contemporary Britain and pre-colonial Ireland.

Moore's stress on the oriental roots of Irish culture, and the suggested parallels between beleaguered oriental and Irish cultures, points to an analogy of a more pragmatic kind which was later explicitly drawn between Ireland and India, when Ireland became the first British colony in the nineteenth century to mount a nationalist challenge. In an article entitled 'Disintegration' (1883), Lord Salisbury saw Irish nationalism as the foremost threat to the British empire:

> The highest interests of the Empire, as well as the most sacred obligations of honour, forbid us to solve this question by conceding any species of independence to Ireland; or in other words, any licence to the majority in that country to govern the rest of Irishmen as they please.[84]

Salisbury looked upon India as a potential Ireland, and asked if Home Rule was granted to Ireland, 'how long can the final disintegration of the Empire be postponed?'[85] H. V. Brasted has shown that the Irish scenario offered glimpses of the treatment awaiting the Indian nationalist movement, and hints of the type of campaign that might be needed. Between 1870 and 1922, Ireland presented India with four different models of emancipation, embodied in Isaac Butt, Charles Stewart Parnell, Arthur Griffin, and Sinn Fein.[86] These models of parliamentary pressure, mass agitation, armed insurrection, and economic protectionism, provided Indian nationalist bodies and figures of varying shades of belief, from the Indian National Congress to Tilak, Aurobindo, and Motilal Ghose, with inspiration for differing strategies. This influence of Irish models on Indian nationalists continued until the Anglo-Irish treaty when Irish models then became less applicable.[87]

A Full Riot of Licentious Ideas

However, the popularity of *Lalla Rookh* cannot be explained by its denunciations (sometimes explicit and sometimes veiled) of the Protestant ascendancy in Ireland, and of British imperialism in

[84] Lord Salisbury, 'Disintegration', *Quarterly Review*, 156 (July–Oct. 1883), 594.
[85] Ibid. 594.
[86] H. V. Brasted, 'Irish Models and the Indian National Congress, 1870–1922', *Journal of South Asian Studies*, NS 8 (June–Dec. 1985), 25.
[87] Ibid. 36–7.

general. Its popularity can be accounted for by examining the peculiar character of its slightness as a literary work. Moore claimed that *Lalla Rookh* was translated into Persian.[88] In his *Journal*, Moore noted that a friend of his had been informed by the Persian ambassador's nephew that part of *Lalla Rookh* had been translated into Persian, 'nor can they believe there but that the whole work has been taken originally from some Persian manuscript'.[89] Moore was certainly at pains to stress the amount of research that went into his poem. It is clear that *Lalla Rookh* was in fact painstakingly researched, and these researches are displayed in copious annotations to the text, which refer to more than eighty separate works, including encyclopaedias, dictionaries, histories, English, French, and German travel books, translations from oriental literature, and scholarly essays by orientalists such as Jones. Moore claimed:

> I took the whole range of all such Oriental reading as was accessible to me; and became, for the time, indeed, far more conversant with all relating to that distant region, than I have ever been with the scenery, production, or modes of life of any of those countries lying most within my reach.[90]

He adds that 'whatever time and trouble this preparatory process may have cost me, the effects resulting from it, as far as the humble merit of truthfulness is concerned, have been such as to repay me more than sufficiently for my pains'.[91] Moore then cites authorities who had been in India, and whom he uses as sources, who testify to the detailed fidelity of *Lalla Rookh* to the oriental world. For example, he quotes Colonel Wilks, the author of *Historical Sketches of the South of India in an Attempt to Trace the History of Mysoor* (vol. i, 1810; vols. ii and iii, 1814) as saying in reference to *Lalla Rookh* that it proved 'reading over D'Herbelot is as good as riding on the back of a camel'.[92] Sir John Malcolm, who had a long career in India and was appointed governor of Bengal in 1827, and who was the author of, amongst other works, the *Political History of India* (1811), *History of Persia* (1815), *Sketches of Persia* (1827), and the *Government of India* (1833), attributed to Moore the 'truth of the historian'.[93]

88 *Works*, vi, p. xx.

89 *Journal*, entry for 6 Nov. 1820, i. 359.

90 *Works*, vi, p. xviii.

91 Ibid. vi, pp. xvii–xviii.

92 Ibid. vi, p. xviii. The reference is to Barthelemy d'Herbelot's *Bibliothèque orientale; ou Dictionnaire universel . . . des peuples de l'orient* (Paris, 1697).

93 *Works*, vi, p. xix.

Moore was therefore careful to make claims to authenticity and fidelity, just as Southey had done so in his oriental epics. But unlike Southey's epics, *Lalla Rookh* can be seen to play upon the anxieties of an imperial sensibility which Moore's ambiguous position in London society afforded him a shrewd grasp of. The peculiar character of the slightness of *Lalla Rookh* is also demonstrated by its reception by the journals of the day, of which Moore had obviously made a judicious estimate in *Lalla Rookh.* This is indicated by his use of Fadladeen as an 'anticipatory defence'.[94] Many of Fadladeen's criticisms are reiterated by the reviews. For example, he objects to 'the charms of paganism' portrayed in Feramorz's recitals, and comments:

> The profusion . . . of flowers and birds, which this poet had ready on all occasions . . . was a most oppressive kind of opulence to his hearers; and had the unlucky effect of giving to his style all the glitter of the flower-garden without its method, and all the flutter of the aviary without its song.[95]

The *Critical Review* agreed with this criticism of the 'eternal employment of images drawn from birds or flowers', and it claimed that before the end of *Lalla Rookh*, 'we are ready, without affectation, "to die of a rose in aromatic pain."'[96] Not surprisingly, it considered Fadladeen's remarks 'sagacious'.[97] The *British Review* remarked that 'we are constrained by the truth to confess, that we do adopt many of the strictures of the Great Chamberlain, as having sense and reason on their side',[98] and in the *Edinburgh Review*, Jeffrey argued that Fadladeen's remarks were generally 'smart, snappish, and acute'.[99]

The popularity of *Lalla Rookh*, and the serious attention it received, indicates that a popular imperial sensibility already existed in the early nineteenth century. Moore's accurate estimate of the reception of *Lalla Rookh* could not have been formed without an astute grasp of this imperial sensibility of the British public. Moore carefully plays upon this sensibility, and it is for this reason that *Lalla Rookh* elicited such serious attention. In the reviews of *Lalla Rookh* one can sense a therapeutic unloading of the anxieties of

[94] 'Moore's *Lalla Rookh*', *British Review*, 10 (1817), 36.

[95] *Lalla Rookh*, 336.

[96] 'Moore's *Lalla Rookh*', *Critical Review*, 5 (1817), 562.

[97] Ibid. 570.

[98] 'Moore's *Lalla Rookh*', *British Review*, 36.

[99] 'Moore's *Lalla Rookh*', *Edinburgh Review*, 18 (1817), 9.

this sensibility. *Lalla Rookh* touched on the nerves of this susceptibility, both confirming and caricaturing its expectations. The reviews in the *British Review*, the *Critical Review*, and the *Edinburgh Review*, were similar in tone: they combined censoriousness with an indulgent dwelling on the 'licentiousness' of *Lalla Rookh*. With *Lalla Rookh*, Moore's reputation as a 'licentious' writer was sealed.[100] All three reviews attributed to *Lalla Rookh* an unhealthy and exhausting surfeit, which distorts the perception of the 'real world'. The *British Review* criticized it for being 'cloyed' with too many 'stimulating sweets'; its 'sickliness' is such, that we grow tired 'of the deceptious glare, and long to see things as they are, however homely they may be'.[101] The *Critical Review* protested at the 'dazzling plumage of eastern ornithology', and at the 'profusion of affected and unnatural similes'.[102] Jeffrey dwelt longer on this quality of unhealthy and exhausting excess. The fault of the text lay in its 'excessive finery' and in 'the extravagance of excessive wealth'.[103] Its 'greatest fault' is 'the uniformity of its brilliancy' and 'the want of plainness, simplicity and repose'; its 'greatest defect' is that there is 'a cluster of beauties on every page'. Moore 'labours under a plethora of wit and imagination' and 'impairs his credit by the palpable exuberance of his possessions, and would be richer with half his wealth'.[104] Jeffrey objected to 'the excessive strength of the emotions that are sought to be raised', and 'the violence of their transitions, and the want of continuity in the train of feeling that is produced'.[105] Jeffrey also criticized Moore's eschewing of the real world: 'In order to avoid the debasement of ordinary or familiar life, the author has soared to a region beyond the comprehension of most of his readers.'[106] Successful narrative poetry is distinguished by 'the occasional familiarity, and even homeliness of their incidents, characters and sentiments'.[107] These criticisms are close to Mill's condemnation of the role of the imagination in literature, especially in Indian literature, in which 'the real occurrences of life are too familiar'.[108] The reviewers of *Lalla*

[100] Lord John Russell cited some verses which were circulating about *Lalla Rookh*: 'Lalla Rookh | Is a book | By Thomas Moore | Who has written four, | Each warmer | Than the former, | So that the most recent | Is the least decent' (*Journal*, entry for 10 July 1821, ii. 467).

[101] 'Moore's *Lalla Rookh*', *British Review*, 33.

[102] 'Moore's *Lalla Rookh*', *Critical Review*, 562, 581.

[103] 'Moore's *Lalla Rookh*', *Edinburgh Review*, 33.

[104] Ibid. 2–3.

[105] Ibid. 4–5.

[106] Ibid. 4.

[107] Ibid. 27.

[108] James Mill, *History of British India*, i. 115–16.

Rookh shared Mill's distrust of the imagination, especially in its revelry in the Orient of its creation, and his concern to tie language down to a world of measurable and concrete objects.

Much of the criticism of the unhealthy surfeit of *Lalla Rookh* is directed at the spectacle of the Perso-Islamic world which is paraded in it. It is also in the depiction of this spectacle that Moore provoked and mimicked the reactions of the reviewers which he anticipated so well. The longest description of this enamelled world is in 'The Veiled Prophet', when Azim wanders through an oriental version of a Spenserian Bower of Bliss.[109] Initially, Azim's reaction is one of puritanical distaste,[110] but he soon succumbs to this 'witching scene':

> So thought the youth; but, ev'n while he defied
> This witching scene, he felt its witchery glide
> Through every sense . . .
> All was too much for him, too full of bliss;
> The heart could nothing feel, that felt not this;
> Soften'd he sunk upon the couch, and gave
> His soul up to sweet thoughts, like wave on wave
> Succeeding in smooth seas, when storms are laid . . .[111]

Passages such as this mimicked and provoked the reaction of the critics to this type of oriental scene; namely, a mixture of puritanical distaste, and a desire to succumb irresponsibly to its soporific pleasures. In a sense, Moore 'staged' the imperial sensibility he had such a clear grasp of.

The exhaustion the reviewers testify to in *Lalla Rookh* is partly the result of this therapeutic unloading of the anxieties of the imperial sensibility, and was thus a measure of the success of *Lalla Rookh*. All three reviews were imbued with a language explicitly sexual in tone, and all three expressed the sort of unease James Mill had defined in relation to the threatening fecundity of Jones's Orient.[112] The *British Review* exclaimed 'we cannot help looking with profane scepticism upon this voluptuous detail'. It denounced Moore's 'sensual apparatus of stimulated desire' and his neglect of a subject matter of a 'manly and moral tendency'.[113] It also condemned Moore for diffusing 'over the mind a loose and rambling sense of pleasure'.[114] The review also saw the world in *Lalla Rookh*

[109] *Lalla Rookh*, 53–4. [110] Ibid. 57. [111] Ibid. 58–9.
[112] See ch. 5. [113] 'Moore's *Lalla Rookh*', *British Review*, 36.
[114] Ibid. 41.

as a conveniently distant locale for Moore's imagination to lend its 'faith to all the exaggerations of hyperbole in the description of Oriental voluptuousness'.[115] The *Critical Review* made a similar point: 'The author has purposely placed his scene on a continent where he could indulge all the gaudy splendour of art and nature.'[116] The *British Review* objected to the depiction of women in *Lalla Rookh*, which it links to the Orient as a convenient locale for Moore's imagination. If the scene were set in England, a 'full riot of licentious ideas' would not be possible, but this is not so if it is set in a harem, where a 'gilded corruption and voluptuous abandonment' are possible.[117] The *British Review* went further in expressing anxiety about British women reading *Lalla Rookh*. It reminded women readers that the stories of *Lalla Rookh* were from countries 'where women are merchandize, and men are their proprietors',[118] and it linked this to anxieties about the 'British Muse in her migration to the scenes of Oriental luxury'.[119] The review even goes so far as to suggest that the writing and reading of such works as *Lalla Rookh* was a threat to British masculinity:

> we must always raise our voices against all writings, in poetry or prose, in which we perceive a tendency to emasculate the British mind; to melt down its robust virtue, and to dissolve the chaste hardihood of its ancient character, by delusive exaggerations of vicious delights.[120]

In his study of the attitudes to race, sex, and class in nineteenth-century British India, K. Ballhatchet has examined the official attempts to control sexual relations between English men and Indian women, the criticisms these provoked, and the difficulties experienced by those individuals who transgressed the accepted conventions. These attitudes are also revealed in the jealousy to which British men in India, as males of the dominant élite, were prone, at the possibility of sexual relations between women of the élite and men of subordinate groups.[121] The reviews of *Lalla Rookh* clearly indicate the beginnings of these sexual and racial anxieties.

The *Edinburgh Review* and *British Review* also suggested that somehow Moore's *Lalla Rookh* was at the margins of language. Jeffrey saw Crabbe and Moore as 'the antipodes of our present

[115] Ibid. 31. [116] *Critical Review*, 5 (1817), 562.

[117] 'Moore's *Lalla Rookh*', *British Review*, 32. [118] Ibid. 35.

[119] Ibid. 32. [120] Ibid. 54.

[121] K. Ballhatchet, *Race, Sex and Class under the Raj: Imperial Attitudes and Policies and Their Critics, 1793–1905* (London: Weidenfeld & Nicolson, 1980), 5–6.

poetical sphere', who occupy 'the extreme points of refinement and homeliness'. He depicted them as occupying the perilous outposts of an empire: 'The outposts of all empires are posts of perils,—though we do not dispute that there is great honour in maintaining them with success.' He also complained that *Lalla Rookh* offers 'no points upon which our sympathies can readily attach'.[122] In the same passage as the *British Review* criticizes Moore for diffusing 'over the mind a loose and rambling sense of pleasure', it argues: 'To play upon the margin of meaning, where the colours of thought are blending into confusion, is a dangerous exercise of the poet's talent . . .'.[123] *Lalla Rookh* was seen to be at the margins of meaning, at a frontier where accustomed distinctions no longer hold, because it supposedly represented the perspective of an alien culture; but it was seen to be at the frontiers of British culture precisely because of its intimate and parodic relationship with the imperial sensibility it plays upon. Moore's play upon the margins of meaning is associated by the review with a 'loose and rambling' pleasure. Moore himself depicted the problem of erotic surfeit in *Lalla Rookh* in terms of a personal struggle against temptation:

> You are quite right about the conceits that disfigure my poetry; but you (and others) are quite as wrong in supposing that I *hunt* after them . . . my greatest difficulty is to *hunt them* away . . . In short, St. Antony's temptations were nothing to what an Irish fancy has to undergo from all its own brood of will-o'-the-wisps and hobgoblins.[124]

The allusion to St Antony points to Moore's other major orientalist work, *The Epicurean*, which is set in Egypt in the late third century, and is about the beginnings of Christian asceticism. Whereas *Lalla Rookh* both parodied and played upon the imperial sensibility of its readership, and defined an orientalism to elaborate an anti-imperialist stance, *The Epicurean* can be seen as the articulation of an orientalism involving the formulation of a truly catholic Christianity. This formulation included an attack on Epicureanism, which was interpreted by some contemporaries as an attack on the hedonistic ethic of utilitarianism. The role which the Orient played in Southey's and Moore's works not only points to the ways in which its creation constituted and reflected their contrasting

[122] 'Moore's *Lalla Rookh*', *Edinburgh Review*, 34, 5–6.

[123] 'Moore's *Lalla Rookh*', *British Review*, 41.

[124] Moore, 'To Leigh Hunt', 21 Jan. 1819, letter 570 of *Letters*, ii. 471.

political positions; it was also integral to the definition of a variety of positions in the discursive practices of the same author.

A Little Modesty in Belief and Unbelief

The Epicurean was originally conceived by Moore as a poetical narrative, and some fragments, which now bear the title of 'Alciphron', were written between September 1819 and November 1822, when Moore was travelling on the Continent to escape debt. *The Epicurean* was published as a novel in 1827, and by December of that year there was a fifth printing of it. It was soon translated into French, German, Italian (twice), and Dutch, and was reissued in 1839 with the original verse fragments forming an appendix. It is possible that Rider Haggard's *She* was influenced by *The Epicurean*; it is more than likely that it influenced Walter Pater's *Marius the Epicurean*.

In 1820 Moore noted down the plot of his verse narrative in his *Journal*.[125] This, with some minor differences, was also the plot of *The Epicurean*. The novel is set in the late third century AD. Alciphron, the 24-year-old leader of the Epicureans at Athens, is the first person narrator. The story opens with the celebrations of the anniversary of Epicurus' birth. The narrator makes clear that Epicureans were not 'refined voluptuaries', and that the 'purer part' of the Epicurean doctrine 'had long evaporated'.[126] Alciphron is visited by melancholy thoughts about the 'perishableness of myself and all around' while in the midst of these celebrations.[127] After the celebrations are over, Alciphron falls asleep and dreams of a 'pale and extinct landscape' in which 'An ancient and venerable man' approaches and advises him to seek eternal life at the shores of the Nile.[128] Alciphron thinks that the 'secrets of the antediluvian world' could be in Egypt,[129] and sets sail for Alexandria in the summer of AD 257. At Alexandria, he initially immerses himself in a round of banquets, until a grisly *memento mori* at a feast reminds him of his quest. He leaves Alexandria for Memphis, where he witnesses the festival of the moon.[130] He is especially

[125] *Journal*, 25 July 1820, i. 329–30.

[126] *The Epicurean*, in *Works*, x. 10.

[127] Ibid. x. 19.

[128] Ibid. x. 22.

[129] Ibid. x. 25.

[130] It was only in Hellenic times that Isis, whom the Greeks depicted as Selene, took a place alongside the more ancient moon deities. (Manfred Lurker, *The Gods and Symbols of Ancient Egypt: An Illustrated Dictionary* (London: Thames & Hudson, 1980), 82.)

struck by the beauty of one dancer, and by her 'innocent shame'.[131] After the ceremony, he goes to a necropolis nearby, where he sees two veiled figures disappear near a small pyramid. He finds the secret opening into it, and then an oratory on whose walls are painted symbols signifying the 'History of the Soul' according to 'the mystic wisdom of the Egyptians'.[132] In the middle of this 'chapel' is a lifeless female form 'enshrined within a case of crystal'; bending over this form is the 'young worshipper of Isis' he was so strongly attracted to.[133] Alciphron leaves the scene, and returns later to the chapel. He discovers another passage, which he follows. After various adventures, he finds before him a scene of the 'warmest pictures of Elysium'.[134] An aged man, who from his garb Alciphron takes to be a hierophant, welcomes him as an 'Aspirant of the Mysteries'.[135] Later the hierophant explains that Alciphron's adventures were an initiation through fire, water, and air, into the mysteries.[136] After a deep sleep, Alciphron awakes to be entertained again, and then is led to a 'small, solitary valley',[137] which is presided over by the statue of Osiris as god of the dead. Alciphron reveals his desire for the 'lovely maiden', and so the hierophant deems it necessary for him to be 'purified by saddening' in remaining amidst this solemn scenery.[138] The hierophant visits him later, and expounds his doctrines about the soul. As he describes the final resting place of the soul, Alciphron is again presented with a scene of 'those fields of radiance', which consists of 'young female spirits' in 'silent, but harmonious movement'. The hierophant then traces the 'melancholy History of the Soul', and yet again Alciphron is presented with a scene of this 'melancholy history'.[139] As the scene reaches its climax in the progress of the soul, Alciphron recognizes the actress to be 'the young Priestess of the Moon'.[140] He is now deemed fit for the 'last grand revelation of the Secret of Secrets' in the presence of the 'unveiled image of Isis'.[141] After a further exposition by the Priest, Alciphron is left in 'the Sanctuary of the Temple, alone and in utter darkness'.[142] He sees a female form emerge from the veils of Isis; it is the form of the woman with whom he is so infatuated. She leads him into the 'realms of day',[143] and they sail down a canal to the Nile, where she

[131] *Epicurean*, x. 53.
[132] Ibid. x. 63.
[133] Ibid. x. 63–4.
[134] Ibid. x. 90.
[135] Ibid. x. 91.
[136] Ibid. x. 104.
[137] Ibid. x. 100.
[138] Ibid. x. 104–5.
[139] Ibid. x. 112–14.
[140] Ibid. x. 118.
[141] Ibid. x. 121.
[142] Ibid. x. 125.
[143] Ibid. x. 137.

presents Alciphron with a 'small leaf of papyrus', on which is traced a map 'of a part of that mountainous ridge by which Upper Egypt is bounded to the east, together with the names, or rather emblems, of the chief towns in its immediate neighbourhood'.[144] This is the destination of her voyage. Eventually, he persuades her to relate her story to him. Her name is Alethe, and she is the daughter of Theora, who was one of the amanuenses of Origen at Alexandria. Although her parents were attached to 'Pagan worship',[145] Theora is deeply impressed by Origen's commentaries on the Scriptures, and is given a copy of one of the catechumen. After Origen leaves Alexandria, she leaves for Memphis with her husband, a Greek adventurer, who dies there, leaving Theora pregnant. She seeks employment in the service of the great temples 'by which so large a portion of the wealth and power of Egypt is absorbed',[146] and becomes a priestess of Isis. Theora starts reading her copy of the Scriptures, while still officiating in the temple. She begins to teach Alethe some general religious truths, but when it becomes clear that Alethe is to participate in the mysteries to ensnare converts, Theora tells her the whole truth. After Theora's death, Alethe plans an escape, and the 'solemn reception' of Alciphron gives her the opportunity to do so.[147]

Alciphron and Alethe then travel on the river to the destination on the map, and arrive at an 'awful chasm'.[148] They climb the steps and ladders to the summit of the rocks, where they meet Melanius, 'one of the first of those zealous Christians of Egypt', who followed the example of the hermit, Paul, to lead a life of contemplation in the desert. Alciphron's religious education begins here, as he listens to Melanius' discourses, and reads the Scriptures given to him. Initially, Alciphron pretends interest with a view to winning Alethe. Eventually they are married but it is a celibate 'marriage'. Meanwhile there are rumours of a change of policy by Emperor Valerian toward the Christians. The day after his 'marriage' Alciphron visits Antinoe where he witnesses the persecution of Christians. As he flees, he sees Alethe and Melanius on a barge with soldiers. He tries to rescue them and is wounded. The Tribune at Antinoe is one of Alciphron's old friends, and when Alciphron recovers, he tells him how bravely Melanius met his death, and how Alethe won the crowd's sympathy with her courageous stance, as a

[144] Ibid. x. 153–4.
[145] Ibid. x. 174.
[146] Ibid. x. 176.
[147] Ibid. x. 191.
[148] Ibid. x. 216.

result of which the Governor vetoed Orcus, the High Priest of Memphis, who proposed her immediate execution. The Tribune smuggles Alciphron into prison where Alethe is held, and he attempts to persuade her to revoke her faith. She refuses and dies from the poison in the crown of coral Orcus places on her head as a sign of Christian martyrdom.

Moore first conceived of *The Epicurean* after reading Thomas Maurice's *Observations on the Remains of Ancient Egyptian Grandeur and Superstition* (1818). It was Maurice's study which gave him the idea 'to write a Poem, the scene of which shall be laid in Antient Egypt—its monuments, its scenery, its religious symbols, all poetical . . .'.[149] Moore read extensively about Egypt between 1819 and 1821 but, more importantly, he had many conversations with the Baron Vivant Denon (1747–1825) during this period.[150] Denon was the author of the popular *Voyage dans la Basse et la Haute Égypte* (1802) and the vast *Description de l'Égypte* (1809). He had played a leading role in Napoleon's campaign in Egypt. After his return to France, he was appointed the Director-General of Museums in 1804. He was also responsible for numerous commemorative medals, several of which related to the Egyptian campaigns; the motifs of these medals combine references to Roman imperialism, ancient Egypt, the French campaign, and the European orientalist enterprise as he conceived it. So in some ways *The Epicurean* was catering for the Egyptomania at the time, as indicated by the exhibition of Giovanni Belzoni's finds, casts, and drawings in the Egyptian Hall of Piccadilly in May 1821.[151]

The subject of *The Epicurean* is the beginnings of Christian asceticism in the late third century in Egypt. In *The Epicurean* can be detected the beginning of a narrative to reconstitute Christianity as the repository of an original and unique revelation, which is partly why Moore called the novel a '*pious* story'.[152] There is also an ecumenical strand in the novel, and a marked tendency to what

[149] *Journal*, 16–17 Apr. 1819, i. 162.

[150] See the following entries in Moore's *Journal*; 22 Dec. 1819 (i. 269); 22–3 Aug. 1820 (i. 331); 14 Oct. 1820 (i. 351); and 5 July 1821 (ii. 465).

[151] P. A. Clayton, *The Rediscovery of Ancient Egypt: Artists and Travellers in the Nineteenth Century* (London: Thames & Hudson, 1982), 42. In his *Journal*, Moore mentions reading Belzoni's work on Egypt; see the entries for 4 Nov. 1820 (i. 358) and 4 June 1821 (ii. 456).

[152] Moore, 'To the Countess of Blessington', 8 Nov. 1829, letter 876 of *Letters*, ii. 162.

E. S. Shaffer has called mythological 'doubling', which involves a 'disconfirmation of unique revelation'. All gods become 'emanations' of other gods, and each mythological system becomes an 'internal' system to others.[153] In *The Epicurean* the capacity of each system to act as an internal system to others is used to constitute Christianity as perennially present in the mysteries it subsumed.

There is a marked interest in the Egyptian mysteries in the novel. Henry Chadwick has pointed out the parallels between the eastern mystery religions, with their professional priesthoods, and the evolution of Christianity. For example, there is an obvious parallel between Isis and Horus, and Mary and Jesus, while Mithraism had sacred meals not unlike the Christian Eucharist.[154] Christian asceticism did not develop from Judaism. The Manichaean Elect provided the model of ascetic practice which bore many affinities to Christian monasticism, and which for the most part antedated the latter in time. Manichaeism also possessed a firmer doctrinal basis for asceticism, and the specific similarities between the Manichaean and Christian styles of asceticism suggest the important influence of Mani on Christian asceticism, and in turn of the Indian prototypes on Mani.[155] The rites of the mysteries of Isis and their relation to Christianity, and the beginnings of Christian asceticism, closely connected with Manichaeism and the whole Gnostic world-view, are the subject matter of *The Epicurean*. Late Gnosticism was a distinctly literate and syncretistic tradition; it was 'an obvious product of Hellenistic syncreticism, i.e. of an atmosphere in which ideas from nearly any source were regarded as admissible'.[156] The atmosphere of Hellenistic syncreticism is carefully evoked in *The Epicurean*. Theora, Alethe's mother who is of Greek parentage, was one of Origen's amanuenses in Alexandria, when he was in the 'fullness of his fame both among Pagans and Christians';[157] Origen tried to reinterpret Christian concepts in a language familiar to the

[153] E. S. Shaffer, *'Kubla Khan' and the Fall of Jerusalem: The Mythological School in Biblical Criticism and Secular Literature 1770–1880* (Cambridge: Cambridge University Press, 1975), 184.

[154] Henry Chadwick, *The Early Church* (London: Pelican, 1967), 24–5.

[155] Jean W. Sedlar, *India and the Greek World: A Study in the Transmission of Culture* (Totowa, NJ: Rowman & Littlefield, 1980), 235, 250–1. Moore had some knowledge of Manichaeism through reading Isaac de Beausobre's *Histoire critique de Manichée et du Manichéisme* (1734–9) (*Journal*, 22 Jan. 1823, ii. 617).

[156] Sedlar, *India and the Greek World*, 138.

[157] *Epicurean*, x. 172.

Platonic tradition, mingling philosophical discussion with expositions of the Scriptures.[158] The first city Alciphron arrives at on his quest is Alexandria, 'the second Athens of the world'.[159] The narrator emphasizes the cosmopolitan character of the city; its population is 'the most motley miscellany of nations, religions, and sects, that had ever been brought together in one city'; there were Greek platonists, 'cabalistic Jews', Christian Churches, and fire-worshippers.[160] The evocation of the twilight and cosmopolitan world of late Gnosticism and Hellenistic syncreticism in *The Epicurean* is reinforced by the fact that towards the end of the third century there was a pagan revival and the university circle at Alexandria remained Neoplatonic in its outlook until the early sixth century.[161]

The evocation of this world is also evident in references to twilight in *The Epicurean*. In his first dream: 'The very sky . . . looked pale and extinct, giving the idea, not of darkness, but of light that had become dead, and had the whole region been the remains of some older world, left broken up and sunless, it could not have presented an aspect more quenched and desolate.'[162] When Alciphron meditates on the decline of Memphis from its former glory, he adds 'the mild moonlight . . . harmonised with her decline'.[163] When he retreats to the necropolis, he is in 'a mood of mind, as usual, half gloomy, half bright',[164] and when he is imprisoned in the 'rocky barrier', he observes 'the sunshine, like the water, exhausted in its descent, had now dwindled into a ghostly glimmer, far worse than darkness'.[165] These evocations of twilight reinforce the historical milieu of the twilight world of Hellenistic syncreticism. Also, most of the references to twilight are associated with exhaustion, and in the case of Alciphron's first dream, with the exhaustion of an old world awaiting the birth of a new one. The landscape of 'gardens, palaces, and spires' within the desert suggests a Christian landscape, perhaps the new Jerusalem. After the scene at Memphis, in the 'mild moonlight' resonant with decline, Alciphron describes the sunrise:

The sun had just risen, and, from the summit of the Arabian hills, was pouring down his beams into that vast valley of waters—as if proud of last

[158] Chadwick, *Early Church*, 34.
[159] *Epicurean*, x. 31.
[160] Ibid. x. 29.
[161] Chadwick, *Early Church*, 172.
[162] *Epicurean*, x. 22.
[163] Ibid. x. 23.
[164] Ibid. x. 56.
[165] Ibid. x. 109.

night's homage to his own divine Isis, now fading away in the superior splendour of her Lord.[166]

The fact that the Nile is at full flood when Alciphron visits Egypt again suggests the potential of growth and fertility. Jacob Bryant remarked that the deluge was 'looked upon as a great blessing: for from thence proceeded the plenty, with which the present world is blest';[167] here the postdiluvian world is also seen to possess possibilities of growth which the antediluvian world did not. The Nile is also at full flood when Alciphron sails from Memphis to Alexandria; since at Memphis begins the long chain of events which brings him to Melanius, the flood is associated with the rise of Christianity. The inundation of the Nile is set in the ambience of the Egyptian 'mixture of the melancholy and the voluptuous' and 'desolation and bloom', but when Alciphron and Alethe arrive at Melanius' hermitage, the verdant and arid landscape are clearly contrasted. There is a hint here that Christianity has broken out of the twilight world in which Alciphron has been moving. At the summit of the rocks which are Melanius' dwelling, there is a clear contrast between the 'fertility of the Nile on one side, and the lone, dismal barrenness of the desert on the other'.[168] This contrast is drawn again, between the 'rich plains, all teeming with cultivation to the water's edge, which seemed to offer up, as from verdant altars, their fruits to the sun', and the 'wide waste of sands, bleak and interminable, wearying out the sun with its sameness of desolation; bleak, burnt-up rocks, that stood as barriers, at which life stopped'. Surveying the scene from the summit of Melanius' hermitage, the narrator comments that the view 'embraced the two extremes of fertility and desolation; nor could the Epicurean and the Anchoret, who now stood gazing from that height, be at any loss to indulge their respective tastes, between the living luxuriance of the world on one side, and the dead, pulseless repose of the desert on the other'.[169] This reinforces the sense that Christianity has broken out of the twilight world of *The Epicurean*, and the panoramic view from the summit of the hermitage which embraces and transcends the two extremes indicates its success in doing so.

166 Ibid. x. 67–8.

167 Jacob Bryant, *A New System; or, An Analysis of Ancient Mythology: Wherein an Attempt is Made to Divest Tradition of Fable; and to Reduce the Truth to its Original Purity*, 3 vols. (1774; London: T. Payne, 1775), iii. 595.

168 *Epicurean*, x. 228.

169 Ibid. x. 237–8.

Most of Alciphron's adventures involving the Egyptian mysteries take place underground. When Alciphron slams shut the gates in this underworld, 'It seemed as if every echo through that vast, subterranean world, from the catacombs of Alexandria to Thebes's Valley of Kings, had caught up and repeated the thundering sound.'[170] He describes how the priest conducts him 'through the long range of illuminated galleries and shrines, that extend under the site upon which Memphis and the Pyramids stand, and form a counterpart underground to that mighty city of temples upon earth'.[171] This subterranean world is associated with a secretive, self-enclosed and self-referential religious experience, which Christianity is seen to break with. None the less, it is in this world that the first hints of Christianity appear. When Alciphron watches 'the young worshipper of Isis' ministering to the lifeless female form 'enshrined within a case of crystal',[172] he notices that she raises a silver cross from the shrine. In a footnote, Moore claims that the sign of the cross occurs in Egyptian hieroglyphics, where it symbolizes after-life. He adds that 'not only the custom of marking the forehead with the sign of the Cross, but Baptism and the consecration of the bread in the Eucharist, were imitated in the mysterious ceremonies of Mithra'.[173] The Egyptian cross Moore refers to is probably the Ankh, a hieroglyphic sign meaning 'life'; this sign, also called the *crux ansata*, became one of the symbols of the Coptic Church because of its cruciform shape.[174] Moore supposes that the sign of the cross and ceremonies similar to baptism and the Eucharist were imitated by Mithraic ceremonies, and did not precede the analogous ceremonies of the Church. When Theora dies, Alethe finds in the chapel a cross, 'which by a remarkable coincidence, is an emblem common to the Gentile and the Christian —being, to the former, a shadowy type of that immortality, of which to the latter, it is a substantial and assuring pledge'.[175] The cross of pre-Christian ceremonies presages the Christian cross, which represents the ultimate 'substantial and assuring pledge'; Christianity was always potentially present in the mysteries it subsumed. To a certain extent, this is represented by Alethe, who is described as a 'Christian . . . under the garb of a Memphian Priestess'.[176] When Alciphron escapes with Alethe to the outside world

170 Ibid. x. 78.
171 Ibid. x. 122.
172 Ibid. x. 63–4.
173 Ibid. x. 65–6.
174 Lurker, *Gods and Symbols of Ancient Egypt*, 27.
175 *Epicurean*, x. 189–90.
176 Ibid. x. 199.

the Christian narrative becomes stronger, suggesting that it has transcended this twilight world of primitive religious experience in which different myths merge with each other. Christianity becomes a truly catholic faith which contains elements of primitive religious experience, but transcends the subterranean, claustrophobic world of the mysteries. The ecumenical strand of the novel becomes harnessed to the Christian narrative. The narrator rarely uses the words 'Christianity' or 'Christ'. Theora talks of revealing to Alethe 'the divine truths';[177] and when Melanius relates Christ's life to Alciphron, Christ is not mentioned by name, but is referred to as the 'heavenly messenger', or the 'Mediator'.[178] The word Bible is also rarely used; more often than not, 'Hebrew scriptures', 'the Book of Life', or the 'sacred volume' are used.[179] In the historical milieu in which the action of the novel is set it was not clear what was orthodox or heretical in Christianity; Christianity had not yet evolved as a coherent set of doctrines nor was there an established canon of Scriptures. The hesitancy to use the terms 'Christianity' or 'Christ' is not just a matter of historical fidelity; this hesitancy hints at the transcendental nature of the truths of Christianity, which the text seeks to establish, truths which can only be suggested and not fully explicated, and which renew themselves continuously. In this way the apparent conflict between the ecumenical strand of the novel and the constitution of Christianity as the repository of an unique revelation is resolved; Christianity itself is seen to be ecumenical and truly catholic.

The narrator of Alethe's story explains that the main purpose of the 'education of the youth of the Temple', was to train them to 'give effect to the illusion of those shows and phantasms, in which the entire charm and secret of Initiation lay'.[180] The final scene of Elysium is formed 'to render it captivating alike to the sense of the man of pleasure, and the imagination of the spiritualist', and Alethe's beauty and grace 'rendered her a powerful auxiliary in such appeals to the imagination'.[181] Alethe's role in the mysteries is one which she also inadvertently plays for Christianity, since it is through her that Alciphron is led to Christianity.

The remark that the mysteries were designed to captivate 'the sense of the man of pleasure, and the imagination of the spiritualist' indicates that Moore was well aware of the re-evaluation of the

[177] Ibid. x. 188. [178] Ibid. x. 257. [179] Ibid. x. 260, 177.
[180] Ibid. x. 180. [181] Ibid. x. 181.

importance of sexual imagery in ancient classical religion, which was influenced by the growing knowledge of the sexual and fertility rites practised by pagan societies of the time.[182] Missionaries and ethnographers sought to comprehend phallic rites mentioned in ancient Hebrew and classical texts by comparing them with a particular Indian cult, and eighteenth-century scholars such as La Crequinère went to India in search of parallels between classical and Old Testament practices on the one hand, and Indian ones on the other, convinced that the variety of religions in the world sprang from one source.[183] Similarly, Mathurin Veyssière de la Croze's *History of Christianity in the Indies* (1724) described the linga worship as the worship of Osiris and Bacchus. As far back as the fifth century BC Herodotus had presented these two chthonic gods as identical. By the time of Plutarch, Osiris had been fully assimilated into the classical pantheon, and was the central figure in one of the popular mysteries in late antiquity, and also the main inspiration behind Plutarch's *De Iside et Osiride*. So La Croze revived a late antique syncretizing tradition, extending its scope to bring the Indian god Siva into relation with Osiris. He saw ancient Egypt as the centre of diffusion, and believed the Egyptians were responsible for originating and spreading phallic cults to other parts of the world. P. E. Jablonski's *Pantheon Aegyptiorum* (1750) also dealt with licentious rites practised in ancient Egypt, and drew the expected parallels between phallic cults from Egypt and India.[184] Moore uses Plutarch's *De Iside et Osiride* in *The Epicurean*;[185] he also refers to Charles Dupuis's seven-volume *Origine de tous les cultes ou la religion universelle* (1795), in which Dupuis sought to trace all religions to a common source, and argued that the origins of all human beliefs lay in the worship of the sun and stars on one hand, and the sexual organs on the other.[186] According to writers such as Dupuis, the iconography of ancient classical and Indian erotic art was based on the same fundamental ideas as expressed in their mythology, which articulated profound ideas in an allegorical or enigmatic form in order to conceal them from the populace and prevent their profanation.[187] In eighteenth-century writings on religion, allegorical writings were also intertwined with a more mystical conception of sexual imagery in ancient fertility and sexual

[182] Partha Mitter, *Much Maligned Monsters: The History of European Reactions to Indian Art* (Oxford: Clarendon Press, 1977), 73, 77.

[183] Ibid. 77–8.

[184] Ibid. 79–80.

[185] *Epicurean*, x. 41 n.

[186] Ibid. x. 54.

[187] *Much Maligned Monsters*, 86.

rites. Consistent efforts were made to relate mystical doctrines about sacred and profane love to androgynous divinities in ancient classical religions, and to search for corresponding ideas in Hinduism.[188] Richard Payne Knight made a thorough investigation of the relations between sexual love and religion in his *A Discourse on the Worship of Priapus*, the *Mystic Theology of the Ancients* (1786), and *An Enquiry into the Symbolic Language of Ancient Art and Mythology* (1818). He believed that sexual imagery in ancient religious art contained hidden meanings, and he proposed to turn to the corpus of Orphic texts in order to realize the true meaning of phallic rites. He also drew a contrast between the superstitious religion based on fear for the vulgar, and the secret and mystical religion which contained divine truths in allegories and symbols.[189] Jones's essay 'On the Mystical Poetry of the Persian and Hindus' in volume three of the *Asiatick Researches* (1792), summed up these different concerns about the relationship between erotic imagery and religious truths; his subject was

> a singular species of poetry, which consists almost wholly of a mystical religious allegory, though it seems on a transient view to contain only the sentiments of a wild and voluptuous libertinism: now, admitting the dangers of a poetical style, in which the limits between vice and enthusiasm are so minute as to be hardly distinguishable, we must beware of censuring it severely, and must allow it to be natural, though a warm imagination may carry it to a culpable excess . . .[190]

Thus, Moore was writing with a strong grasp of the context in which a reappraisal of the erotic was taking place, which was intimately connected with a re-examination of the sexual imagery in Hinduism and ancient mystery cults, and also an investigation into the relationship between sacred and profane love. The enactments of the mysteries as a mixture of the erotic and spiritual, and the conflict in Alciphron between the ascetic and the voluptuary, are related to the more general question of the nature of erotic imagery in religion. Although Alethe plays the same role for Christianity as she does for the mysteries, the emphasis on the celibacy of her 'marriage' to Alciphron suggests that Christianity has broken from the erotic imagery of its predecessors, and especially from the matriarchal systems associated with such cults.

188 Ibid. 97–8.

189 Ibid. 100–1.

190 Sir William Jones, 'On the Mystical Poetry of the Persians and Hindus', *Asiatick Researches*, 3 (1792), 165.

Given the attempt to show that Christianity has broken from matriarchal systems, there is an added significance in the description of the sunrise in Memphis, after the night of the celebrations of Isis. The sun poured his beams 'into that vast valley of waters—as if proud of last night's homage to his own divine Isis, now fading away in the superior splendour of her Lord'.[191] In some ways, too, the novel underlines the dangers of erotic imagery in religion. Alciphron's erotic attachment to Alethe remains confused with his religious yearnings; in the end a surfeit of the erotic remains unharnessed to the purposes of spiritual edification. This is made clear in a passage which typifies his confusion:

> though I acknowledged not a heaven, I worshipped her who was, to me, its type and substitute. . . . Even passion itself felt a holy fear in her presence—like the flame trembling in the breeze of the sanctuary—and Love, pure Love, stood in place of Religion.[192]

Perversely, although Alciphron sees her as a type of heaven, rather than leading him on to the supposedly spiritual truths she embodies, his erotic love itself becomes deified. Embarrassingly, Alciphron's attention returns to the erotic forms in which these truths are hidden.

The ecumenical strand in *The Epicurean* and its emphasis on 'those pure particles of truth which lie at the bottom of all religions'[193] are continuous with Moore's own brand of liberalism and his commitment to a pluralist society. In the *Memoirs of Captain Rock*, Moore argues that all sects are 'more or less founded' on a 'principle of exclusion'.[194] His attempt to constitute a truly catholic faith in *The Epicurean*, which even includes elements of the ancient mystery cults and their matriarchal aspects, is his answer to this sectarian 'principle of exclusion'. The closest Moore comes in expressing religious belief in his *Journal* is when he declares 'the worship of one, gracious, benevolent God . . . I trust is enough'.[195] Moore's modest faith is also expressed in a letter to Lord Byron in 1822:

> Boldness, and even licence, in politics, does good, actual present good; but, in religion, it profits neither here nor here after; and, for myself, such a horror have I of both extremes in this subject, that I know not *which* I hate most, the bold, damning bigot, or the bold, annihilating infidel. . . . much

[191] *Epicurean*, x. 67–8. [192] Ibid. x. 200. [193] Ibid. x. 183.
[194] *Captain Rock*, 252. [195] *Journal*, Oct. 1818, i. 58.

as we are in the dark, even the wisest of us, upon these matters, a little modesty, in unbelief as well as belief, best becomes us.[196]

It is possible that the portrayal of a catholic faith in *The Epicurean* was partly meant to be a criticism of utilitarianism and its hedonistic philosophy. Moore had satirized the 'Benthamite spinsters', as he called them in his *Journal*,[197] in a poem called 'Ode to the Sublime Porte' in *The Times* of 3 November 1826. The target of his attack was Bentham and the philosophic radicals as a whole, as well as their 'darling Review', the *Westminster*. In his *Journal* Moore described the Benthamites as 'quite different from other people',[198] and found their whole school 'quizzible'; their 'method of analysis might be transferred so easily to some ludicrous question, and travestied'.[199] He also felt that political economists made the perennial mistake of 'endeavouring to find something of *fixed* value, where as no such thing exists',[200] and he described Macaulay's critique of Mill's 'Essay on Government' as 'admirable'.[201] Part of the reason Moore was later to call the Benthamites 'deadly enemies of mine',[202] were the cutting reviews *The Epicurean* and the *Letters and Journal of Lord Byron*, and the earlier *Fables for the Holy Alliance*, received at the hands of the *Westminster Review*.[203]

In his *Autobiography*, John Stuart Mill was to describe his father as an Epicurean, although he almost immediately qualified this;[204] that some of Moore's contemporaries viewed utilitarianism as a modern-day, and degenerate, form of Epicureanism is evident in Peacock's review of *The Epicurean* in the *Westminster Review* of April–July 1827. Peacock accused Moore of a complete misrepresentation of the ancient Epicureans, which is the result of a 'profound ignorance of everything truly classical'. Since this

196 Moore, 'To Lord Byron', 9 Feb. 1822, letter 619 of *Letters*, ii. 503.

197 *Journal*, 31 Mar. 1830, iii. 1298.

198 Ibid. 30 Mar. 1824, ii. 724.

199 Ibid. 23 Nov. 1824, ii. 777.

200 Ibid. 15 Aug. 1825, ii. 822.

201 Ibid., 17 June 1829, iii. 1230. For an account of and the articles in the debate about Mill's 'Essay on Government', see Jack Lively and John Rees (eds.), *Utilitarian Logic and Politics: James Mill's 'Essay on Government', Macaulay's Critique and the Ensuing Debate* (Oxford: Clarendon Press, 1978).

202 *Journal*, 13 Dec. 1830, iii. 1336.

203 'Moore's *Fables for the Holy Alliance*', *Westminster Review*, 1 (Jan.–Apr. 1824), 18–26; 'Moore's *Letters and Journals of Lord Byron, with Notices of His Life*', *Westminster Review*, 12 (Jan.–Apr. 1830), 270–304.

204 John Stuart Mill, *Autobiography and Literary Essays*, in *Collected Works of John Stuart Mill*, ed. John M. Robson and Jack Stillinger (Toronto: University of Toronto Press, 1981), i. 50.

characterizes the 'vast majority of the reading public', the popularity of *The Epicurean* is of no surprise.[205] Moore's misrepresentation of Epicureanism accords with the 'vulgar notion' of this philosophy. In other words, Moore is like the poets Peacock is so scathing about in *The Four Ages of Poetry*, who 'address their minstrelsy' to that 'much larger portion of the reading public, whose minds are not awakened to the desire of valuable knowledge, and who are indifferent to anything beyond being charmed, moved, excited, affected, and exalted'.[206] Moore had not only misrepresented Epicureanism; his depiction of Christianity as a simple and sublime religion, superior to the intolerant faiths it supplanted, was also inaccurate. It was of prime importance that humanitarians liberate men from such a 'mass of misrepresentation'.[207] To this effect, Peacock stated the correct version of Epicurus' teachings, and defended utilitarianism:

> Epicurus taught that happiness is the end of life: that there is no happiness without pleasure: that all pleasure in itself is good, and that all pain is in itself evil; but that present pleasure is to be avoided in the prospect of future pain, and that present pain is to be endured for the sake of future pleasure: that the true and only permanent pleasure of man is peace of body and mind: that the state in which the body is without pain, and the mind without pertubation, is the perfect health of the whole man: that the peace of the body is to be obtained especially by two means—Temperance . . . and Fortitude . . . Thus Epicurus taught that general utility, or as Bentham expresses it, 'the greatest happiness of the greatest number,' is the legitimate end of philosophy; and it is curious to see the same class of person decrying the same doctrine as impracticably dry, when the word utility precedes the word pleasure, and as too practically voluptuous when the word pleasure precedes the word utility. So much are small minds the slaves of words.[208]

Thus, the various positions Moore articulated in his oriental works were in strong contrast to some aspects of utilitarianism. Whilst James Mill attempted to place liberal imperialism on an entirely new footing, Moore created an Orient in *Lalla Rookh* which was integral to an anti-imperialist stance. *The Epicurean*'s representation of Christianity as a truly catholic faith was in part perceived to be an implicit criticism of the secular idiom and hedonistic ethic of Utilitarianism. The novel used the mythological

[205] 'Moore's *The Epicurean*', *Westminster Review*, 8 (Apr.–July 1827), 355.

[206] *The Works of T. L. Peacock* (London: Richard Bentley and Sons, 1875), iii. 337.

[207] 'Moore's *The Epicurean*', 377.

[208] Ibid. 373–5.

parallels, which were used by what has been called infidel radicalism in its attempts to undermine the claims of Christianity to a unique revelation,[209] for the contrary purpose of depicting Christianity as actually subsuming its antecedents in what Pusey was to call its 'higher unity'.[210] In its project to formulate an idiom for a far-reaching critique of the conservatism of the time, *The History of British India* struggled to break not just with the patriarchalist idioms of the British *ancien régime*, but also with such traditions as infidel radicalism. Above all, the orientalism which Mill defined played a central role in the articulation of his radical rhetoric in the *History*. In particular, it attacked orientalism as the product of undisciplined imaginations, and indeed as an important underpinning of positive views of the imagination, views which were both epistemologically unsound and politically dangerous. In doing so, it was attacking the very grounds on which Southey's and Moore's orientalism had been based, as it tried to create a new way of thinking which severed the intimate relationship between imagination and desire which Mill argued had determined the nature of British thinking about India.

It has already been argued that conflicting influences can be detected in *Thalaba* and *Kehama*.[211] Part of these conflicts are also evident in a similarity of approach between Southey and Mill. In the *Edinburgh Review* of January 1810, Mill had refused to accept the argument of scholars like Jones and his colleagues that only those personally acquainted with India and its languages were qualified to write about it. Mill countered that the European who has never visited India knows the facts that such scholars have related; these facts are only of value in so far as inferences can be drawn from them. The 'untravelled European', if he makes these inferences, is superior to the orientalist scholar.[212] In some ways, *Thalaba* and *Kehama* were poetic renderings of these 'facts'; and the prefaces and notes are the conclusions drawn from them. Furthermore, Southey's epics represent themselves as accurate renderings of the cultural material they are supposedly based upon; knowledge of other cultures was not felt to be totally reliant on a

209 See ch. 5.

210 E. P. Pusey, *An Historical Enquiry into the Probable Causes of the Rationalist Character Lately Predominant in the Theology of Germany*, 2 vols. (London: C. and J. Rivington, 1828), i. 145.

211 See ch. 2.

212 'Voyage aux Indies Orientales', *Edinburgh Review*, 15 (Jan. 1810), 367.

personal acquaintance with them. Southey's epics are placed between what Mill saw to be the naïve creation of an Orient that was culturally and materially rich, and the disillusioned view of it as poverty-stricken. It was the conflicting nature of thinking about India and the Orient, evident in such works as Southey's, which Mill was to try to break away from so decisively in *The History of British India*. It was his aim not just to rectify the 'singularly defective' knowledge of India in the British community, but also to perform the 'labour of extracting and ordering the dispersed and confused materials of India, once and for all'.[213] It was in acknowledgement of this attempt to define a new idiom to deal with British India that the younger Mill described his father's *History* as the 'commencement of rational thinking on the subject of India'.[214]

[213] Mill, *History of British India*, i, pp. xix, xv.

[214] James Mill, *Analysis of the Phenomena of the Human Mind* (1828); 'With Notes Illustrative and Critical', by Alexander Bain, Andrew Findlater, and George Grote; ed. with Additional Notes by John Stuart Mill, 2 vols. (1869), p. xiii.

CHAPTER 4

JAMES MILL'S *THE HISTORY OF BRITISH INDIA*

Introduction

The History of British India's main fame rests on its transformation of utilitarianism into what one scholar has described as a 'militant faith'.[1] This chapter explores the role which British India played in James Mill's thinking, a role whose complexity has been neglected by scholars who view the *History* as simply an attempt to apply a version of utilitarianism to British India.

It is important to make clear from the outset that both Bentham's and Mill's opposition to colonization was not as relevant to British India as at first it might appear, except in so far as Mill was in agreement with East India Company policy of actively hindering the settlement of non-official Europeans in British India. In 'Emancipate Your Colonies!' and the 'Essay on Colonies' in the supplement to the fifth edition of the *Encyclopaedia Britannica*, Bentham and James Mill were referring to colonization as the settling of areas by a mother country with members of its own population. What they had in mind were colonies such as Canada and Australia in their time, and Greek and Roman colonies in times of antiquity. Their characterization of colonial government as inefficient, corrupt, and perpetuating the interests of the ruling few, and their opposition to monopolistic trading practices, had obvious relevance to the case of British India, and indeed Mill was to criticize British India on these very grounds in his *History*. But the main thrust of their opposition to colonization was not centred on India, for the simple reason that India was not a colony which had been settled by Europeans. The overwhelming mass of Europeans in India were employed by the East India Company, the armed forces,

[1] Duncan Forbes, 'James Mill and India', *Cambridge Journal*, 5 (Oct. 1951–Sept. 1952), 31.

or the Crown. It is doubtful that a community dominated by official employment, recruited in Britain and intent on returning there, can be said to constitute a 'colonial' society. Furthermore, the practical obstacles to the growth of non-official European settlement in British India were reinforced by a body of prohibitions. Until 1833 the Company had the right to control migration to India by licence. It is also clear that the Company viewed the arrival of private Europeans in India as politically dangerous.[2]

This distinction between British India and other colonies was implicit in Bentham's and Mill's articles on colonies. Thus, although Mill was at pains to point out that India never yielded a 'tribute', and especially not one which could pay for the expenses of governing India, this was part of a larger argument demonstrating the superiority of free trade over monopolistic practices which could never be profitable.[3] Indeed, the main purpose of Mill's article was to consider whether emigration and colonization were effective means of solving the problems resulting from overpopulation.[4] In particular, he criticized the deportation of delinquents to the colonies as inefficient and ineffective, and argued that the real solution to such problems lay in Bentham's *Panopticon*.[5] Mill's article has to be seen against the background of debates since the late eighteenth century on the relative merits of imprisonment and deportation for delinquents[6] and the advocation of schemes of emigration by Robert Horton and Edward Gibbon Wakefield in the 1820s and 1830s respectively.[7] It was not written with British India primarily in mind. In 'Emancipate Your Colonies!', which was written in 1793 and published in 1838, Bentham made a clear

[2] P. J. Marshall, 'The Whites of British India: A Failed Colonial Society?', paper delivered at the Institute of Commonwealth Studies, University of London, 12 Nov. 1988.

[3] 'The Article Colony', reprinted from the Supplement to the *Encyclopaedia Britannica* (London: J. Innes, *c*.1820), 17.

[4] Ibid. 13.

[5] Ibid. 14–15.

[6] This was also the background to Bentham's formulation of the Panopticon scheme. See L. J. Hume, 'Bentham's Panopticon: An Administrative History—1', *Historical Studies*, 15 (Oct. 1973), 704.

[7] Donald Winch, *Classical Political Economy and Colonies* (London: London School of Economics and Political Science, 1965), 52–5 and 73–84. Robert Southey's views on colonization as a social safety valve were close to those of Horton and Wakefield. See 'On the Rise and Progress of Popular Disaffection', *Quarterly Review*, 16 (Jan. 1817), 511–22, in *Essays: Moral and Political*, 2 vols. (London: John Murray, 1832), ii. 33–107 and esp. 'On Emigration', *Quarterly Review*, 37 (Mar. 1828), 539–78, in *Essays* ii. 207–75.

exception to his argument in the case of British India. In doing so, he made a distinction between the French West Indies, whose population was French and therefore 'ripe for self-government', and the British East Indies, whose population was not of European origin and for whom, therefore, another form of government was justifiable:

> Would the declaration of rights translate into *Sanscrit*? Would *Bramin*, *Chetree*, *Bice*, *Sooder*, and *Hallochore* meet on equal ground? If not, you may find some difficulty in giving them to themselves . . . If it is determined that they must have masters, you will then look out for the least bad ones that could take them: and after all that we have heard I question whether you would find any less bad than our English company.[8]

In some ways, this prefigures John Stuart Mill's reflections on the forms of government most appropriate for Britain's dependencies,[9] and the problems which both the younger Mill and his father grappled with when they defined forms of liberal imperialism which were different in character from its earlier instances.

As H. H. Wilson pointed out in his edition of the *History*, for James Mill India was a testing ground for some of Bentham's theories.[10] To a certain extent, *The History of British India* was an extension of Bentham's more moderate *Essay on the Influence of Time and Place in Matters of Legislation* (1793) in which, in order to arrive at a system of laws universally applicable, Bentham suggests transplanting English laws to Bengal, which formed as strong a contrast as possible to England: 'Till a lawgiver, who having been bred up with English notions, shall have learnt to accommodate his laws to the circumstances of Bengal, no other

[8] Jeremy Bentham, 'Emancipate Your Colonies! Jeremy Bentham to the National Convention of France, January 1793' (1838), 16. A similar distinction was to be made by John Stuart Mill, when in 1858 he stressed that the pressing question with regard to the proposed abolition of the East India Company was 'in what manner Great Britain can best provide for the government, not of three or four millions of English colonists, but of 150 millions of Asiatics, who cannot be trusted to govern themselves'. 'A President in Council the Best Government for India' (1858), *Writings on India*, ed. J. M. Robson, Martin Moir, and Zawahir Moir, in *Collected Works of John Stuart Mill* (Toronto: University of Toronto Press, 1990), xxx. 201.

[9] e.g. see *On Liberty* (1859), in *Collected Works*, xviii. 224, ch. 18 of *Considerations on Representative Government* (1861), in *Collected Works*, xix, and *Writings on India*, in *Collected Works*, xxx.

[10] James Mill, *The History of British India* (1817); ed. H. H. Wilson, 10 vols. (London: James Madden, Piper, Stephenson, and Spence, 1858), i, p. xi.

part of the globe can present a difficulty.'[11] But there were differences between Bentham and Mill, which became evident in the *History*. It was these differences which enabled Mill to transform utilitarianism into a militant faith. This chapter argues that Mill's aesthetic and linguistic beliefs were central to this transformation. The role of these beliefs in Mill's formulation of utilitarianism has been neglected by scholars, as has their part in Mill's criteria for the writing of history itself. These criteria were defined in opposition to the prevalence of mythological histories and their role in the definition of cultural identities in the late eighteenth and early nineteenth centuries.

Mill was the theorist of the new brand of radicalism which displaced the agrarian radicalism of the 1820s.[12] His fame also rests on his role as a teacher and guide to a generation of utilitarians, of whom Ricardo, Place, Grote, and of course John Stuart Mill were the most notable.[13] John Stuart Mill described his father as being for many years 'the soul of what is now called the advanced Liberal party',[14] and Alexander Bain described him as the spokesman of the middle classes when they were agitating for 'better government and better legislation to suit the extension of manufactures and commerce'.[15] In fact, Bain gives Mill a central place in the Reform Movement.[16] Mill's ideal society or polity appears to have been one in which an educated bourgeoisie, untainted by excessive wealth or poverty, predominated.[17] His 'Essay on Government', written for the supplement to the fifth edition of the *Encyclopaedia Britannica*, first appeared in 1820. This essay defined the ideology of philosophical radicalism, and the alliance of utilitarianism and political radicalism.[18] Although Mill argued for virtual universal male suffrage, his essay closed with a paean to the middle classes, whom he hoped would take the lead in reforming society, since it was their

[11] *The Works of Jeremy Bentham*, ed. John Bowring (Edinburgh: William Tait, 1843), i. 172.

[12] William Thomas, *The Philosophic Radicals: Nine Studies in Theory and Practice 1817–1841* (Oxford: Clarendon Press, 1979), 96.

[13] James Mill, *Selected Economic Writings*, ed. and introduced by Donald Winch (Edinburgh: Oliver and Boyd, 1966), 15.

[14] James Mill, *Analysis of the Phenomena of the Human Mind* (1828); ed. John Stuart Mill, 2 vols. (London: Longmans, Green, Reader, and Dyer, 1869), p. xv.

[15] Alexander Bain, *James Mill: A Biography* (London: Longmans, Green, and Co., 1882), 446.

[16] Ibid. 447.

[17] Mill, *Economic Writings*, 13.

[18] Jack Lively and John Rees (eds.), *Utilitarian Logic and Politics: James Mill's 'Essay on Government', Macaulay's Critique and the Ensuing Debate* (Oxford: Clarendon Press, 1978), 4.

interests which were identical with society as a whole. It was the 'middle rank' of society which was 'the most wise and the most virtuous part of the community'.[19] As Alan Ryan has pointed out, by this Mill meant that the middle classes had the qualities of economically rational agents, that is, industry, providence, and a sound knowledge of their interests.[20] Mill also believed that this class would set an example to the working classes.[21] In this Mill was followed by his son, who also looked forward to a general *embourgeoisement* of society, in which all enjoyed a decent competence, and leisure enough for self-cultivation.[22]

However, although Bentham and Mill played a role in the Reform movement, there were significant differences between the nature of their radicalism and that of others, such as Major John Cartwright's. As early as 1780, Bentham described himself as a 'system-maker' and a 'system-builder'.[23] It was this attempt in Bentham's and Mill's work to build systematic models in their critique of what in 1828 Bentham called 'priest-ridden, lawyer-ridden, lord-ridden, squire-ridden, soldier-ridden England',[24] which distinguished their political radicalism from other forms of radicalism in the early nineteenth century. This stress on an all-encompassing and systematic approach was also the characteristic feature of the *History*, a text which reinforced Mill's position as a spokesman for the philosophic radicals.[25] *The History of British India* shaped a theoretical basis for the liberal programme to emancipate India from its own culture. This was in accordance with James Mill's emphasis on the importance of theory to practice: 'The fact is, that good practice can, in no case, have any solid foundation but in sound theory.'[26] However, this chapter argues

[19] James Mill, *Essays on Government, Jurisprudence, Liberty of the Press, and Law of Nations: Written for the Supplement to the Encyclopaedia Britannica* (London: J. Innes, *c.*1825), 31–2.

[20] Alan Ryan, 'Two Concepts of Politics and Democracy: James and John Stuart Mill', in Martin Fleisher (ed.), *Machiavelli and the Nature of Political Thought* (1972; London: Croom Helm, 1973), 94.

[21] Mill, 'Government', 32.

[22] William Thomas, *Mill* (Oxford; Oxford University Press, 1985), 85.

[23] Bentham MS, University College London, projected letter to Edmund Burke, 1780, Box 169, fo. 74.

[24] Bentham to Daniel O'Connell, 15 July 1828, in *Works*, x. 595.

[25] *The History of British India by James Mill*, ed. William Thomas (Chicago: University of Chicago Press, 1975), p. xii.

[26] James Mill, 'Essay on Education' (written for the 5th edition of the *Supplement to the Encyclopaedia Britannica*, 1815–24), in *James Mill on Education*, ed. W. H. Burston (Cambridge: Cambridge University Press, 1969), 44.

that the distinctive feature of the systematic approach formulated in the *History* was its self-reflexivity. The *History* was not just a critique of Indian cultures and British rule; more importantly, in using British India as a testing ground for utilitarianism, it was fashioning a critique for British society itself. It is this self-reflexivity in Mill's thought, along with the role which linguistic and aesthetic beliefs played in it, which has been neglected by scholars eager to represent the *History* as simply an attempt to apply utilitarianism to British India.

It was precisely the systematic and all-encompassing aspect of Mill's political theorizing which Macaulay criticized in his review of Mill's 'Essay on Government'.[27] However, in a speech to Parliament in 1833 supporting the proposed Charter Act, which was to put an end to the East India Company as a trading body, Macaulay considered the question of whether India was now capable of self-government. He cited in support of his negative reply 'the author of a History of India, which, though certainly not free from faults, is, I think, on the whole, the greatest historical work which has appeared in our language since that of Gibbon'.[28] The prominence given to Mill's views in 1833 by Macaulay, in spite of his earlier attack on his 'Essay on Government' in 1829, demonstrates the importance of utilitarianism amid the new forces attempting to effect change in British India. The *History* became a standard work for East India Company officials, and eventually a textbook for candidates for the Indian civil service.[29] It was also the official textbook of the Company's college at Haileybury.[30] With its publication and James Mill's subsequent appointment at the East India Company as Assistant Examiner in 1819, and Chief Examiner in 1830, J. S. Mill claimed his father had 'effected a great amount of good, and laid the foundation of much more, to the many millions of Asiatics for whose bad or good government his country is responsible'.[31] In his *Autobiography*, J. S. Mill first mentions his father as the author of the *History*, and comments on its important influence on Indian administration.[32]

[27] T. B. Macaulay, 'Utilitarian Logic and Politics', *Edinburgh Review*, 49 (Mar. 1829), 185.

[28] T. B. Macaulay, 'Government of India', in *The Works of Lord Macaulay*, 12 vols. (London: The Albany Edition: 1898), xi. 555.

[29] Forbes, 'James Mill and India', 23.

[30] Mill, *History*, ed. Thomas, p. xii.

[31] Mill, *The Human Mind*, p. xiv.

[32] John Stuart Mill, *Autobiography and Literary Essays*, ed. John M. Robson and Jack Stillinger, in *Collected Works*, i. 29.

But as Eric Stokes has warned, undue attention must not be paid to formal statements of policy aims, since these are not a reliable indication of the working practice of British rule.[33] The limited effect of utilitarianism on British rule in India is reflected in H. H. Wilson's edition of Mill's *History*. Horace Hyman Wilson, who left India in 1833 to become the first Professor of Sanskrit at Oxford University, first edited Mill's *History* in 1840. His footnotes and additions are conceived in a very different spirit from Mill's. He attributed practical success of a different kind to the book, when he wrote, 'a harsh and illiberal spirit has of late years prevailed in the conduct and councils of the rising service in India, which owes its origin to impressions imbibed in early life from the History of Mr. Mill'.[34] It is often assumed that the *History* is a confident text, indicative of the growing power of the British in India, and the ascendency of utilitarianism as a progressive creed.[35] Both Bentham and Mill had a firm belief in the power of reason to change things for the better. But the *History* not only reflects the ambivalence to imperialism which characterized philosophical radicalism as a whole. Far from being a confident text, it reveals the contradictions in Mill's philosophy, which result in a loss of nerve in dealing with India. It is not the utilitarian Mill, but his editor Wilson, who clearly expresses a confidence in the role of the British in India. Wilson warns the reader early on that Mill has 'entered the lists' against Jones, because of the latter's 'exalted, and it may be granted, sometimes exaggerated descriptions of their [the Hindus'] advance in civilization'.[36] In his defence of Jones, Wilson was representing yet another strand of imperialism, which was later to be described by Kipling as the 'White Man's Burden'. Thus, Wilson's edition of *The History of British India* is composed of three strands, each defined by the other: Jones's 'orientalism' as defined and attacked by Mill's philosophic radicalism, which is in turn countered by Wilson, who defends Jones, and in the process elaborates the notion of the 'White Man's Burden'. Wilson's edition of Mill's *History* is therefore not simply a reflection of the limited effects of utilitarianism on British rule in India; it also

[33] Eric Stokes, 'The First Century of British Colonial Rule in India: Social Revolution or Social Stagnation?', in *The Peasant and the Raj: Studies in Agrarian Society and Peasant Rebellion in Colonial India* (Cambridge: Cambridge University Press, 1978), 30.

[34] Mill, *History*, ed. Wilson, i, p. xiii.

[35] e.g. see Eric Stokes, *The English Utilitarians and India* (1959; Oxford, Clarendon Press, 1963), 47–8.

[36] Mill, *History*, ed. Wilson, i, p. xii.

exemplifies the way in which intellectual traditions define both each other and the contexts in which they struggle to emerge.

The Art of Legislation for the Benefit of Empires

John Stuart Mill described the preface to *The History of British India* as 'among the most characteristic of my father's writings'. It conveyed 'a picture which may be entirely depended on, of the sentiments and expectations with which he wrote the *History*'.[37] These sentiments and expectations were influenced by Bentham's notion of the legislator's task. Bentham was adamant that the legislator should be concerned chiefly with what the law ought to be ('censorial jurisprudence'), using the utilitarian criterion of the greatest happiness of the greatest number as a guide, rather than with what the law is ('expository jurisprudence'). It is in the 'censorial line that there is the greatest room for disquisitions that apply to the circumstances of all nations alike'.[38] He defined his purpose as being to formulate 'a common standard, by which the several systems of law prevailing in every country may respectively be compared, and thereby their mutual agreements and disagreements represented, their comparative excellences and defects exhibited to view'.[39] It was for this reason that he described *Principles of Morals and Legislation* as a work of 'universal jurisprudence'.[40] In *Of Laws in General*, a continuation of *Principles of Morals and Legislation* completed in 1782 but never published by the author, Bentham envisaged the establishment of a school to teach 'the art of legislation for the benefit of empires', which would create a 'sort of universal *harmony of the laws*'.[41] These ideas were developed in his *Essay on the Influence of Time and Place in Matters of Legislation*, which celebrated 'legislators who, having freed themselves from the shackles of authority, have learnt to soar above the mists of prejudice, know as well how to make laws for one country as for another: all they need is to be possessed fully of the facts'. Once these are known, 'all places are alike'.[42] Thus, part of the legis-

[37] J. S. Mill, *Autobiography*, 29.

[38] Jeremy Bentham, *An Introduction to the Principles of Morals and Legislation* (1789), ed. J. H. Burns and H. L. A. Hart, in *The Collected Works of Jeremy Bentham* (London: The Athlone Press, 1970), 295.

[39] Ibid. 274.

[40] Ibid. 295.

[41] Bentham, *Of Laws in General*, ed. H. L. A. Hart, in *Collected Works*, 242–4.

[42] *Works*, i. 179–81.

lator's task consisted of comparing and contrasting legal traditions by using the general principle of utility, on the basis of which existing laws and institutions were criticized.

Similarly, in *A Fragment on Mackintosh* (1835) James Mill considered the two sets of circumstances worthy of attention in the framing of laws. These were those which 'all nations have in common', and those which 'each nation has peculiar to itself'.[43] The first set are the most important 'beyond comparison'. It is of prime importance that there should be men with knowledge of this set, since:

> the only men who can appreciate the circumstances which are accidental to this or that particular people, are the men who best understand that far more important part of the circumstances constituting their condition, which they have in common with the men of other communities. The operation of the minor circumstances can only be judged of by knowing the bearing upon them of the fundamental, and the predominant.[44]

The History of British India was an attempt to define these fundamental and predominant circumstances in order to arrive at 'general principles of law, detached from its accidental and national forms', principles which the authors of jurisprudential plans in British India had neglected.[45] Following Bentham's distinction between censorial and expository jurisprudence, in the *History* Mill stressed that the important question was 'not what *is* done in the courts of law, but what *ought* to be done'.[46] Furthermore, censorial jurisprudence would be a critique of not just Hindu and Muslim law as it had been defined under British rule, but English law as well. Bentham had made it clear in the *Essay on the Influence of Time and Place in Matters of Legislation* that the transplantation of English law to Bengal would reveal the weaknesses of the former, so that any legal reforms deemed necessary in Bengal would be apposite to the English legal system,[47] and in *Principles of Morals and Legislation* he had argued not only that the legislator will discover that 'every nation is liable to have its prejudices and its caprices', which it is his task 'to look out for, to study, and to cure', but also that in his attempt to forge a legal system for all cultures, the legislator is himself involved in a 'kind of perpetual lesson' which serves 'at once as a corrective to his

43 James Mill, *A Fragment on Mackintosh* (London: Baldwin and Cradock, 1835), 142.
44 Ibid. 143.
45 Mill, *History*, ed. Wilson, iii. 352.
46 Ibid. v. 87.
47 *Works*, i. 184–5.

prejudices, and as a check upon his passions'.[48] It was in keeping with this 'perpetual lesson' at the heart of the task of legislation that Mill used India to attack English legal institutions. Indeed, after he had finished the *History* he contemplated writing a critical history of English law, which would be 'capable of teaching law to all' and which would 'exhibit, in full, a system of jurisprudence to the world'.[49] Such a project would have been a logical development of *The History of British India*, in which Mill claimed that a 'faithful history of the laws of England would exhibit no less wonderful proofs, in the misery which it has brought, and still obstinately brings, upon the people of England'.[50] Mill made many Benthamite criticisms of English law in the *History*. He condemned the jurisprudential plan behind the Regulation Act of 1773 which established the Supreme Court in Bengal, because of the 'unfortunate inattention of its authors to the general principles of law',[51] and he criticized the language of English law for 'its studied intricacies and obscurities'.[52] Its procedures are 'loaded with minute formalities', and 'rendered unintelligible, tedious, and expensive, by technical devices'.[53] If any 'considerable progress towards improvement' is to be made in India, it is important that the British emancipate themselves from 'the deep-rooted prejudice, that English law is the standard of perfection to which everything should be fitted'.[54] For Mill, as for Bentham, India provided the opportunity to reveal the inadequacies of the English legal system and to arrive at a code of laws which could be universally applicable. In order to arrive at this code Mill also criticized Hindu and Muslim law as he knew it, although he did praise their judicial procedures for being free from delay, trouble, and expense.[55] Indeed, the compilation of laws by pandits in British India was such a 'disorderly compilation of loose, vague, stupid, or unintelligible quotations and maxims, selected arbitrarily from books of law, books of devotion, and books of poetry',[56] that Mill took it upon himself to classify Hindu law.[57] This classification followed Bentham's mode of analysis *Of Laws in General*.[58] However, in spite of his attack on certain aspects of

[48] Bentham, *Introduction to the Principles of Morals*, 184, 274.
[49] Macvey Napier papers, Add. MS 34612, fos. 212–13, Mill to Napier, 5 Aug. 1818.
[50] Mill, *History*, ed. Wilson, iv. 242.
[51] Ibid. iii. 352.
[52] Ibid. iv. 220.
[53] Ibid. v. 355.
[54] Ibid. v. 425.
[55] Ibid. ii. 359; see also 'Affairs of India', *Edinburgh Review*, 16 (Apr. 1810), 157.
[56] Mill, *History*, ed. Wilson, v. 426.
[57] Ibid. i. 159–200.
[58] Bentham, *Of Laws in General*, chs. 16–18.

Hindu law, for example on punishment,[59] it is important to reiterate that this attack was paralleled by just as severe an attack on English law itself. It is for this reason that it is difficult to understand R. Iyer's characterization of Mill's *History* as complacent and insensitive in its approach to other cultures.[60] It is also this self-reflexivity in Mill's *History*, which used British India to fashion a critique of British law in particular and British society in general, that has been ignored by analyses which characterize Mill's *History* as simply a 'hegemonic' text which had a dominating influence within what has been described as the 'Anglo-French imperial formation'.[61] Mill's criticism of Hindu, Muslim, and British law was in keeping with the Benthamite schema of comparing and contrasting legal systems in order to arrive at a comprehensive code of law based on the principle of utility which could be universally applicable. This was in keeping with the universalistic character of the greatest happiness principle itself.[62] It was only in this way that the confusion of codes and courts in British India could be overcome and replaced by a single and comprehensive code, and the legal system in England itself reformed.

However, there were some differences between Bentham and Mill which were reflected in their attitudes to the existing indigenous institutions in India. In the *Essay on the Influence of Time and Place in Matters of Legislation* Bentham had urged the legislator to have two tables, one consisting of particulars relating to the body of laws taken as the standard, and the other of circumstances influencing the sensibility and character of the people for whom alterations are to be made.[63] In his suggestion of the tables of data, Bentham was following his own method in *Principles of Morals and Legislation* where he lists the circumstances influencing sensibility.[64] The quantity of pain and pleasure produced in men is not dependent entirely on the exciting causes, nor is it uniformly in proportion to those causes. Rather, it is dependent on the 'primary influencing circumstances', such as health, strength, 'hardiness' and 'bodily imperfections', and the 'secondary influencing circumstances', such as Sex, Age, Rank, Education, Climate, and Religious

[59] Mill, *History*, ed. Wilson, i. 175–83.

[60] R. Iyer, 'Utilitarianism and All That', *South Asian Affairs*, 8 (1960), 31.

[61] Ronald Inden, *Imagining India* (Oxford: Basil Blackwell, 1990), 45.

[62] Frederick Rosen, *Jeremy Bentham and Representative Democracy: A Study of the Constitutional Code* (Oxford: Clarendon Press, 1983), 205–6.

[63] *Works*, i. 173.

[64] Bentham, *Introduction to the Principles of Morals*, 51–72.

Profession.[65] The legislator has to take into account these circumstances influencing sensibility when he undertakes his legislative task. This position was reflected in the *Essay on the Influence of Time and Place in Matters of Legislation*, in which Bentham urged caution in reforms, and the paying of a certain amount of regard to indigenous institutions. He advised using them as far as possible to effect reforms, rather than substituting them wholesale.[66] H. H. Wilson agreed with Bentham, arguing the necessity of patience, and not forcing 'on exotic reforms out of season', if they were 'to take root and live'.[67] Bentham's caution may also have been related to his awareness at an important stage of his career that a system of law must provide security for community expectations.[68]

In his *History* Mill made it clear that a 'full account of the character and circumstances' of the people of India was necessary 'for the understanding of the subsequent proceedings and events'.[69] His account of the character and circumstances of Indians was similar to Bentham's circumstances influencing sensibility, which had to be enumerated in order to calculate levels of felicity and predict the probable consequences of certain measures should they be put into effect. Mill sometimes advocated Bentham's cautious approach towards indigenous institutions. In an article on Indian affairs in the *Edinburgh Review* of April 1810, he recommended using Hindu institutions to effect law reforms: 'You might thus have a perfect code of laws, with such modifications as not to shock the prejudices and manners of the people, and with all the authority which the Brahmenical character, and the most sacred names could attach to it.'[70] Similarly, in the *History* he stressed that 'unless the administration of justice yield the *sense* of security [to the public], it fails of accomplishing one of the most important of its ends'.[71] But the general tenor of the *History* was opposed to this cautious approach. John Stuart Mill pointed out that his father made no distinction between theory and practice, and that he trusted 'too much to the intelligibleness of the abstract, when not embodied in the concrete'.[72] James Mill was less prepared than Bentham to compromise with the material of the world, and was

[65] Ibid. 52.

[66] Bentham, *Works*, i. 179.

[67] Mill, *History*, ed. Wilson, iii. 450.

[68] G. J. Postema, *Bentham and the Common Law Tradition* (1986; Oxford: Clarendon Press, 1989), 210.

[69] Mill, *History*, ed. Wilson, i. 106.

[70] Mill, 'Affairs of India', 157.

[71] Mill, *History*, ed. Wilson, v. 110.

[72] J. S. Mill, *Autobiography*, 35, 27.

committed to a vigorous reason shaping the matter of the world according to its own dictates. Referring to his father's views on religion, his son described how his 'intellect spurned the subtleties by which men attempt to blind themselves' to the 'open contradiction' between the notion of a benevolent creator and a world 'so full of evil'. However, the 'Manichaean theory of a Good and an Evil Principle, struggling against each other for the government of the universe, he would not have equally condemned; and I have heard him express surprise, that no one revived it in our time.'[73] Mill's belief in reason shaping the recalcitrant material of the world could be seen as a form of Manichaeism itself.

Mill also defined his conception of the role of the historian in the preface to his *History*. The preface defends Mill's credentials to write on India, without having visited the subcontinent, and without knowledge of any Indian languages. Mill's intention is to write 'A Critical History', which is 'a judging history'.[74] The critical historian is explicitly compared to a judge:

> He who, without having been a percipient witness in India, undertakes, in Europe, to digest the materials of Indian history, is placed, with regard to the numerous individuals who may have been in India, and of whom one has seen and reported one thing, another has seen and reported another thing, in a situation very analogous to that of the judge, in regard to the witnesses who give their evidence before him.[75]

Mill criticizes 'the fond credulity with which the state of society among the Hindus was for a time regarded' by such scholars as Jones.[76] This 'fond credulity' is partly attributable to 'the vague and indeterminate notions' he had of 'the signs of social improvement'. He attached 'no fixed and definite assemblage of ideas' to the term civilization.[77] Whatever the difficulty of describing 'the characteristics of the different stages of social progress', it is possible to formulate a scale of progress from a 'joint view of all the great circumstances' of nations. It is from 'an accurate comparison, grounded on these general views, that a scale of civilization can be formed, on which the relative positions of nations may be accurately marked'.[78] Mill made clear the standards he employed:

[73] Ibid. 43.
[74] Mill, *History*, ed. Wilson, i, p. xvliii.
[75] Ibid. i, p. xxv.
[76] Ibid. ii. 84.
[77] Ibid. ii. 109–10.
[78] Ibid. ii. 110.

In looking at the pursuits of any nation, with a view to draw from them indications of the state of civilization, no mark is so important, as the nature of the *End* to which they are directed . . . Exactly in proportion as *Utility* is the object of every pursuit, may we regard a nation as civilized. Exactly in proportion as its ingenuity is wasted on contemptible and mischievous objects, though it may be, in itself, an ingenuity of no ordinary kind, the nation may safely be denominated barbarous.[79]

It was this scale of civilizations which justified despotic rule over 'lower' societies until they were capable of self-government. The formulation of this scale was based on the Benthamite notion of the universal legislator, who from his superior position could take a more comprehensive view of cultures and their differences, and so achieve command of a set of laws which could be universally applicable.

Mill's argument in the preface is designed to illustrate 'the superiority of the comprehensive student over the partial observer'.[80] The observer in India suffers from a 'well-known and important law of human nature'; 'in a cursory survey . . . the mind, unable to attend to the whole of an infinite number of objects, attaches itself to a few; and overlooks the multitudes that remain.' The objects to which the mind is attracted are those 'which fall in with the current of his [*sic*] thoughts; those which accord with its former impressions; those which confirm its previous ideas'.[81] It is not the 'mental habits which are acquired in mere observing, and in the acquisition of language', but those involved in 'combination, discrimination, classification, judgement, comparison, weighing, inferring, inducting, philosophizing in short', which are 'the powers of most importance for extracting the precious ore from a great mine of rude historical materials'.[82] In *A Fragment on Mackintosh* Mill defined the purpose of philosophy as tracing 'particular phenomena to a general principle, and always from the less general to the more general',[83] and in his work on psychology he stressed that it was through generalization on the events of the past that we can make arrangements for the future. The 'great law of our nature' is the 'anticipation of the future from the past'; upon the correctness of our ideas of the past 'depends the faculty we possess of converting the powers of our nature into the instru-

[79] Ibid. ii. 105.
[80] Ibid. i, p. xxvi.
[81] Ibid. i, p. xxv.
[82] Ibid. i, p. xxiii.
[83] Mill, *Mackintosh*, 274.

ments of our will; and of bringing to pass the events we desire'.[84] In the *History* Mill argued that one of the characteristics of a 'rude and early state of society' was precisely the absence of this ability to generalize.[85] He even attributes Tipu Sultan's defeat to the lack of this ability to take 'a marshalling view of a great whole', as a result of which he was unable to anticipate accurately the 'distant consequences' of certain acts and events, including those he himself initiated.[86] In *A Fragment on Mackintosh* it was precisely this which Mill defined as irrational: 'To act, without regard to consequences, is the property of an irrational nature.'[87] For Mill civilized humans are calculators who try to choose the most efficient means to achieve clearly defined ends. This is only possible if evidence is standardized and evaluated systematically; since this is the case, this sort of 'instrumental rationality' gives rise to what Ernest Gellner has called 'world-levelling, unificatory epistemologies'.[88]

Given Bentham's insistence on the importance of circumstances influencing sensibility as data for the legislator, it would be wrong to attribute a 'world-levelling' epistemology to him. The term is perhaps more appropriate for the approach implicit in Mill's *History*, which on the whole paid little attention to cultural, linguistic, or religious differences. It was a unificatory epistemology which Bentham's and Mill's work defined when they grappled with the problem of legislating for empires and the hierarchy of mental activity upon which such legislation could take place. This unificatory epistemology is demonstrated by Bentham's argument in an 1817 manuscript that the 'interest of the community is the same, in its general description under all circumstances and at all periods subj. to be so governed as that the greatest happiness of the greatest number shall constantly be produced'.[89] It was in keeping with the general thrust of the argument in this manuscript that Bentham defined probity in *Parliamentary Reform* as the pursuit of that 'line of conduct' which is 'most conducive to the general good of the whole community', by which he meant 'the whole of the British empire'.[90] Mill's argument in the 'Essay on Colonies' in which he

[84] Mill, *The Human Mind*, i. 130–1.
[85] Mill, *History*, ed. Wilson, i. 133.
[86] Ibid. vi. 104.
[87] Mill, *Mackintosh*, 164.
[88] Ernest Gellner, *Relativism and the Social Sciences* (Cambridge: Cambridge University Press, 1985), 76.
[89] Bentham MS, University College London, Box 104, fo. 437, 'Tory and Whig Fallacies', 1 Dec. 1817 (in copyist's hand).
[90] Jeremy Bentham, *Plan of Parliamentary Reform, in the Form of a Catechism with Reasons for Each Article* . . . (London: R. Hunter, 1817), 2.

disagreed with Adam Smith's contention that a monopoly of colonial trade is always disadvantageous to the mother country is based on a similar assumption. Where colonial trade is in the hands of an exclusive company (the implicit reference is to the East India Company), the other country may obtain 'a given quantity of the goods of the colony for a less quantity of her own than otherwise she would do'.[91] He elaborates on this:

> The exclusive company, by limiting the quantity of the goods of the mother country which they choose to send to the colony, might compel the colonists to give for that limited quantity any quantity of the produce of their own land and labour, which their desire to obtain the goods of the mother country would admit.[92]

However, when the mother country gains, the colony loses, and on utilitarian grounds this means that 'the quantity of happiness [is] diminished upon the whole', because the colony is not a different country, but part of the same country. Such a policy is 'exactly the same sort of policy, as if Yorkshire were to be drained and oppressed for the benefit of Middlesex'.[93] In the *History*, Mill claimed on similar grounds that 'the aversion to a government, because in the hands of foreigners; that is, men who are called by one rather than some other name, without regard to the qualities of government, whether better or worse, is a prejudice which reason disclaims'.[94] Wilson disagreed with this; many of the problems of British rule arise from 'the evils inseparable from the sovereignty of strangers'.[95] It is important to stress that Mill was not in any way racist. He never expressed a belief in inherent racial differences as accounting for different forms of society. On the contrary, his argument in the 'Essay on Colonies' demonstrates his belief that the universalistic character of the principle of utility renders such considerations irrelevant.

Armed with this notion of the historian's task based on a unificatory epistemology, Mill dismissed objections which he anticipated, for example by Wilson, of the 'author's imperfect knowledge of the country, and unacquaintance with any of the languages spoken in it'.[96] Mill concluded:

[91] James Mill, 'Essay on Colonies', in *Papers on Colonial Policy* (1838), 20.
[92] Ibid. 20. [93] Ibid. 22. [94] Mill, *History*, ed. Wilson, ii. 342.
[95] Ibid. vii. 413. [96] Mill, *History*, ed. Wilson, i. p. viii.

As soon as everything of importance is expressed in writing, a man who is duly qualified may obtain more knowledge of India in one year in his closet in England, than he could obtain during the course of longest life, by the use of his eyes and ears in India.[97]

This was in direct opposition to what Jones had felt to be the necessary qualifications of a historian. Jones firmly believed that 'No man ever became a historian in his closet,'[98] and he vindicated the perspective of the local observer:

You judge rightly . . . that we are the best judges here of all that relates to ourselves. In Europe you see India through a glass darkly: here, we are in a strong light; and a thousand little *nuances* are perceptible to us, which are not visible through your best telescopes, and which could not be explained without writing volumes.[99]

Wilson agreed with Jones about the 'benefits derivable from personal observation', and the value of 'local knowledge'.[100] Jones, in a letter to Thomas Maurice, the author of *Indian Antiquities* (1793–1800) and the *History of Hindostan* (1795–8), stressed the importance of relying on primary sources in Persian and Sanskrit if Maurice wanted to compose a reliable history of India.[101] Jones's work itself demonstrates the importance he placed on acquiring a thorough knowledge of Indian languages. Mill on the other hand argued that cultures can actually be understood better in translation and from a distance. Too much sympathy with Indian cultures undermines the possibility of a thorough understanding of them. It is only by distancing oneself from Indian cultures that they can be seen in sharp relief and the targets of reform clearly formulated. Mill's argument bears some resemblance to a similar point of view put forward by Ernest Gellner. It is possible that sympathetic, positive interpretations of indigenous assertions are the result not of a sophisticated appreciation of their context, and the nuances of the culture generally, but rather of naïvety.[102] Excessive indulgence

97 Ibid. i, p. xxiii.

98 Sir William Jones, 'To Viscount Althorp', 18 Sept. 1780, letter 249 of *Letters of Sir William Jones*, ed. G. Cannon, 2 vols. (Oxford: Clarendon Press, 1970), i. 440.

99 Jones, 'To the Second Earl Spencer', 4–30 Aug. 1787, letter 764 of *Letters*, ii. 743.

100 Mill, *History*, ed. Wilson, i, p. viii.

101 Jones, 'To Thomas Maurice', 10 Oct. 1790, in 'Letters of Sir William Jones and His Correspondents', ed. G. Cannon, *Comparative Criticism*, 3 (1981), 184–5.

102 Ernest Gellner, 'Concepts and Society', in Bryan R. Wilson (ed.), *Rationality* (1970; Oxford: Basil Blackwell, 1985), 33.

in charity, especially in contextual charity, can blind us to what is the best and worst in the life of societies: 'in the social sciences at any rate, if we forgive too much we understand nothing'.[103] Mill's *History* was a criticism of the 'fond credulity' of those who formed erroneous views of Indian society; in many ways, it was an attack on the naïvety of sympathy which perpetrated such errors and on the epistemology upon which it was based. Scholars have been quick to note the unsympathetic and uncharitable tone of Mill's *History*,[104] but they have failed to give attention to the rigour and detail of the argument behind this lack of sympathy, and its relation to the rest of Mill's carefully articulated body of ideas. Furthermore, in his attack on the dominant ideology of British society, Mill was careful to maintain a similar lack of sympathy, and also a critical distance, which he was able to do by using India as an alien background against which the workings of this ideology were exposed.

Ironically, although Mill defined his position against Jones's, his position is reliant on the latter's in so far as he could not form any stance on Indian cultures without using the translations of Jones and his colleagues. Furthermore, to a certain extent Mill's position was implicit in Jones's. Jones saw the learning of languages as a means to an end, which implied that languages were transparent vehicles of knowledge.[105] It would seem that Mill shared this assumption. His very reliance on Jones's work suggests this; he was not disputing the possibility of translation so much as the authenticity of the texts, and the testimony regarding Hindu culture. Also, in the debate between the Anglicists, orientalists, and vernacularists in India, Mill took a vernacularist stance. The Anglicist position was represented by Macaulay's Minute on Education of 2 February 1835, in which he defined the aim of British educational policy in India to be the creation of 'a class of persons, Indian in blood and colour, but English in taste and intellect', which could only be achieved through using English as a medium of instruction.[106] The debate culminated in a triumph for the Anglicists, with Bentinck's

[103] Ibid. 42, 47.

[104] e.g. see R. Iyer, 'Utilitarianism and All That', 31; Thomas, *Mill*, 68; and O. P. Kejariwal, *The Asiatic Society of Bengal and the Discovery of India's Past, 1784–1838* (Delhi: Oxford University Press, 1988), 124.

[105] See ch. 1.

[106] Macaulay's Minute on Education, in Colonel W. F. B. Laurie (ed.), *Sketches of Some Distinguished Anglo-Indians*, 2 vols. (London: 1888), i. 183.

Resolution of 5 March 1835, in which he ruled that 'the great object of the British government ought to be the promotion of English literature and science through the medium of the English language'.[107] In his testimony before a Parliamentary Select Committee in 1832 on the renewal of the Company's Charter, Mill made it clear that he had doubts about English as a medium of instruction in India. In this he was probably influenced by the Serampore Baptist missionaries,[108] and was in direct opposition to Southey's views which were close to the Anglicist position.[109] Mill recommended vernacular translations as a medium of modernization, and did not approve of substituting English for Persian in the courts. He felt it appropriate to use the languages of the parties involved, that is, the vernaculars.[110] It has been argued that the real influence on Macaulay's Minute was evangelicalism, not utilitarianism.[111] Thus Mill felt that the Indian vernaculars were just as efficient as mediums of instruction for 'useful' learning as English, and so shared Jones's view of languages as transparent vehicles of knowledge, and as somehow equivalent to each other. To a certain extent Jones also believed that a culture could be understood efficiently in translations of its important texts. His digest of Indian laws was designed for British judges with little or no knowledge of Indian languages. It was presumed that the digest would give them a good working knowledge of the norms of Indian cultures. It was H. H. Wilson, though, who dominated policy making in education from 1820 until 1833.[112] His conservatism was evident not only in his opposition to such reforms as the abolition of suttee in 1829, but

[107] Percival Spear, *The Oxford History of Modern India 1740–1975* (Delhi: Oxford University Press, 1978), 206.

[108] M. A. Laird, *Missionaries and Education in Bengal 1793–1837* (Oxford: Clarendon Press, 1972), 230–1, 234.

[109] See e.g. his letters to John Rickman, 23 Dec. 1803, in *The Life and Correspondence of Robert Southey*, ed. C. C. Southey, 6 vols. (London: Longman, Brown, Green, and Longmans, 1849), ii. 243, and to C. W. W. Wynn, Apr. 1807, ibid. iii. 77; also 'On the State of the Poor', in *Essays*, i. 155. For a discussion of the emergence of English language and literature as a discipline, and the ideological underpinnings of this, see Chris Baldick, *The Social Mission of English Criticism* (Oxford: Clarendon Press, 1983), 70, and Gauri Viswanathan, *Masks of Conquest: Literary Study and British Rule in India* (London: Faber and Faber, 1990), ch. 1.

[110] J. F. Hilliker, 'English Utilitarians and Indian Education', *Journal of General Education*, 27 (Apr. 1975–Jan. 1976), 104.

[111] Elmer H. Cutts, 'The Background of Macaulay's Minutes', *American Historical Review*, 58 (Oct. 1952–July 1953), 826.

[112] G. and N. R. Sirkin, 'John Stuart Mill and Disutilitarianism in Indian Education', *Journal of General Education*, 24 (Apr. 1972–Jan. 1973), 232.

also in his educational policy, in which he influenced John Stuart Mill. Mill's draft dispatch of 1836, entitled 'Recent Changes in Native Education', condemned the new educational policy inspired by Macaulay and advocated a return to the previous policy in which funds and resources were directed to the teaching of Sanskrit, Arabic, and Persian. He drew a distinction based on Wilson, between the 'learned Indians', that is, the sacerdotal classes, who were dedicated to learning for its own sake, and other classes, who were interested in education for mainly economic motives. Sanskrit and Arabic learning were appropriate for the former, and should be patronized by the government; the other classes, interested in education for utilitarian reasons, should finance themselves.[113] It is possible that Mill's fears of a mass society, without the leadership of a cultural élite, influenced him in supporting Wilson's policy, which was based on concentrating on Sanskrit and Arabic at the expense of the vernaculars, and patronizing the learning of the sacerdotal classes.

The Relentless Tyranny of the Dead

Mill's stance on the relationship of the past to the definition of cultural identities was influenced by his conception of the role of the historian, and the world-levelling epistemology and the hierarchy of mental activity upon which it was based. Mill's enthusiasm to take on the world and mould it according to the universal dictates of the philosophic reason is nowhere more evident than in his philosophy of 'the science' of education, of which he claims 'the whole science of human nature is . . . but a branch'.[114] In his 'Essay on Education' he emphasized that 'all the differences which exist between classes or bodies of men is the effect of education . . . it is education wholly which constitutes the remarkable difference between the Turk and the Englishman'.[115] Of prime importance is the enquiry into how the mind 'with those properties which it possesses, can, through the operation of certain means, be rendered most conducive to a certain end'.[116] This end is defined as 'rendering the human mind to the greatest possible degree the cause of human happiness'.[117] Mill followed Locke in asserting that the

[113] Sirkin and Sirkin, 'Disutilitarianism', 246–7.
[114] Mill, 'Essay on Education', 45. [115] Ibid. 52. [116] Ibid. 45.
[117] Ibid. 41.

mind is a *tabula rasa*; the principle governing it is the association of ideas. The purpose of education is to 'work upon the mental successions' which constitute human thought since it is upon these successions that 'all the differences between the extreme of madness and of wickedness, and the greatest attainable heights of wisdom and virtue' are based.[118] Education has to find the means of making 'in the most perfect manner, those repetitions on which the beneficial sequences depend'.[119] Education has performed its 'most perfect work' when the individual becomes 'to the greatest degree, the source of utility to others, and of happiness to himself'; this is achieved when 'the grand sources of felicity are formed into the leading and governing ideas'.[120] Like Southey, Mill was aware of the political importance of education; he described political education as the 'keystone of the arch'.[121] But for Mill education was political in a much deeper sense; it was the basis on which society could be remodelled on entirely new principles. For Southey, education was a diffusion of the principles of the established Church to unify English culture and to win the allegiance of the populace in manufacturing districts which had grown up beyond the pale of the traditional Anglican parochial structure.[122] He had no conception of education as an instrument for remodelling human society *de novo*.

There appears to be a discrepancy in Mill's philosophy between the ability of reason to mould the materials of the world, and the description of the mind as passive upon which his science of education is based, but what is of importance here is his rejection of any inherent or hereditary traits in the human mind. This entailed a refusal to acknowledge for practical purposes any inherent or hereditary traits of Indian cultures and a rejection of Jones's contention that some sort of historical narrative could be recovered from Indian legendary and mythological material. He also ignored the development in such branches of historical research as numismatics and epigraphy.[123] Mill was sceptical about the picture conveyed by Jones and the Asiatic Society 'of an

[118] Ibid. 52. [119] Ibid. 58. [120] Mill, *The Human Mind*, ii. 378.

[121] Mill, 'Essay on Education', 117.

[122] On the significance of changes of population distribution for the authority of the Anglican Church, see J. C. D. Clark, *English Society 1688–1832: Ideology, Social Structure and Political Practice during the Ancien Regime* (Cambridge: Cambridge University Press, 1985), 372–3.

[123] Kejariwal, *The Asiatic Society of Bengal*, 43–4, 57.

antecedent period, when the sovereigns of Hindustan were masters of great power and great magnificence'. Instead he argued, far from being a culture of great antiquity, Hindu culture is immature and exhibits characteristics of 'the rudest and weakest states of society'.[124] It was almost universally accepted by scholars in the early nineteenth century that ancient Hindu texts and the Puranas contained exaggerated ideas about the antiquity of Indian civilization, and that their chronologies conveyed little factual information about ancient history.[125] Some of these questions were also clearly defined in such controversies as that between John Bentley and H. T. Colebrooke.[126] In addition, Colebrooke's paper on the inscriptions on the pillar known as the lat of Firuz Shah, had ascertained the date of one of them at AD 1164 and not 67 as Jones had thought.[127] But although Mill's scepticism may have been reinforced by some of these observations, and also by the famous case of Francis Wilford's essay 'On the Sacred Isles of the West', which became a byword for European credulity exploited by the forgeries of pandits,[128] it was based on a notion of education which believed society could be remodelled on rational principles. India was a *tabula rasa* where the British were to create the right environment to introduce and perpetuate 'those repetitions on which the beneficial sequences depend'. It is here that Mill's authoritarianism comes to the fore. As he was to explain later, the mind does not of its own accord initiate a beneficial sequence of ideas: 'We perform moral acts at first, from authority. Our parents tell us, that we ought to do this, we ought to do that.'[129] This is the source of the authoritarianism in Mill's version of liberal imperialism. John Stuart Mill developed these elements in his father's ideas to argue that despotism is justified when dealing with 'barbarians', until such time as they 'have become capable of being improved by free and equal discussion'.[130] The younger Mill described his father's *History* as a

> book which contributed largely to my education . . . the number of new ideas which I received from this remarkable book, and the impulse and

[124] Mill, *History*, ed. Wilson, ii. 114–15.

[125] Kejariwal, *The Asiatic Society of Bengal*, 87.

[126] Ibid. 88–9.

[127] Ibid. 92–3.

[128] For an account of this affair, see ibid. 101–2. Wilford's essay appeared in vol. 8 of the *Asiatick Researches*.

[129] Mill, *Mackintosh*, 259.

[130] J. S. Mill, 'On Liberty', in *Utilitarianism*, ed. Mary Warnock (London: Fontana Press, 1985), 136.

stimulus as well as guidance given to my thoughts by its criticisms and disquisitions on society and civilisation . . . made my early familiarity eminently useful to my subsequent progress.[131]

William Thomas attributes Mill's preoccupation with backward and progressive social states in his political writings to the influence of his father's *History*.[132] In a letter to Francis Place in 1814, the elder Mill mentions that 'John is now an adept in the first 6 books of India'.[133] James Mill's scheme of education for his son was based on associationist psychology, and the assumption that the mind is a *tabula rasa*. In many ways, his son's intellectual upbringing, itself so heavily influenced by the *History*, pointed to a possible parallel with the education of India from the childhood the British found it in, to the adulthood of self-government.

Mill's scepticism concerning the antiquity of Indian civilization was therefore partly based on the dictates of his associationist psychology. His views on Indian culture were determined not by their history, but by the criterion of utility which he elaborated as a scale by which to assess cultures. Furthermore, the view that the present state of Indian culture is a decline from a former state of 'high civilization' was 'a saving hypothesis',[134] because it was used as a sentimental defence against any attempts to recast the foundations of British rule in India and thereby to reform Indian cultures. For both Bentham and Mill the past was of little relevance when dealing with questions of the reform of institutions. Mill's rejection of inherent or hereditary traits in his associationist psychology was also important for his objections to the assumptions of common law theory and his ideas on legal traditions and the role they played in defining and characterizing communities. The central ideas of common law theory were expressed in Blackstone's *Commentaries on the Law of England* (1765–9). For Blackstone, common law was not made by the monarch, judiciary, or parliament; rather, it expressed a deeper reality merely discovered and declared by them. This deeper reality was, in Postema's phrase, 'historically evidenced national custom'.[135] The conviction of the authority of the law relies on the sense that its rules and practices are continuous with the life and history of the community shaped by it; law is immanent

[131] J. S. Mill, *Autobiography*, 28–9.
[132] Thomas, *Mill*, 2.
[133] Francis Place papers, Add. MS 35, 152, fo. 119b, 7 Dec. 1814.
[134] Mill, *History*, ed. Wilson, ii. 114.
[135] Postema, *Bentham and Common Law*, 4; see also 9 and 11.

in the historical process in which communities emerge.[136] Common law was not a structured system flowing from a set of first principles, nor could it be traced back to such a priori principles.[137] Both Bentham and Mill denied that arguments of precedence had any weight when considering the nature of institutions and their effect on human happiness. In a manuscript of 1794–5, Bentham argued that 'Of all tyrannies, the most relentless is that of the dead'. He described Burke's philosophy as 'absurd and mischievous' because it 'subjugates the well-informed to the ill-informed ages'.[138] Mill made a similar criticism in the *History*, when he wrote that 'In the case of public institutions, Mr. Burke had . . . worked himself into an artificial admiration of the bare fact of existence; especially ancient existence.'[139] This sort of criticism was in keeping with the general tendency in the *History* to belittle the ignorant past from the standpoint of the enlightened present.[140] More specifically, Bentham objected to the 'superstitious respect for antiquity' in common law theory; as a system based on precedent, the problem was that precedent became an avowed substitute for reason.[141] Furthermore, statute law had this great advantage over common law, which was that it was written and enacted, and so 'may be seen all the world over'.[142] It was embodied in a publicly accessible form which was open to scrutiny and revision. As *lex non scripta*, common law was a form of customary law, whose sources consisted of records, reports, and treatises; these treatises were the 'shadow of the shadow of a shade', and yet it was this shadow which was 'worshipped as the substance'.[143] Their 'Formularies of Precedents' meant that from a given set of data each person extracted whatever law he fancied he was able to.[144] There was no established rule to measure by, nor any standard to appeal to; 'all is uncertainty, darkness, and confusion'.[145] Mill made a similar point about the obscure and confused nature of common law in his chapter on the trial of Warren Hastings in the *History*. He described it as 'nothing but notes, taken by anybody, of what has been done, without any kind of law, in this and the other instance, in the several courts'. It was this which made the law not just 'voluminous and obscure', but

[136] Ibid. 6–8.

[137] Ibid. 13.

[138] University College London MS, 'Parliamentary Reform', 1794–5, Box 44, fo. 5.

[139] Mill, *History*, ed. Wilson, v. 201.

[140] e.g. see ibid. i. 29, 93.

[141] Postema, *Bentham and Common Law*, 279.

[142] Bentham, *Of Laws in General*, 185 n.

[143] Ibid. 188.

[144] Ibid. 189–92.

[145] Ibid. 184.

also 'dreadfully uncertain'.[146] The obscurity of customary law rested not just in the patchwork nature of its sources, but also on the fact that it depended 'in a great degree upon habits which are not perceptible out of the particular circles in which the practice of it is carried on'.[147] It was this obscurity, reflected, maintained, and perpetuated by fearful jargon and mysterious procedures, which lay at the basis of the monopoly of lawyers 'against the rest of the people', and a further monopoly 'of the illustrious in the profession itself against the obscure'.[148] It was these integral characteristics of common law which removed the possibility of intelligent citizenship; common law sought to undermine rational individual judgement and foster blind submission to authority, both in conduct and thought.[149] It was for this reason that Bentham wrote, 'Written law is the law for civilized nations' and customary law is for 'brutes'.[150] By replacing common law's myth of natural law with the rational principle of utility, Bentham hoped that a code of law could be arrived at which would define anew a social and political framework for interaction. Such a social order would not rest on habitual obedience, but on a submission which would not entail the surrender of judgement. It would be a rational form of obedience in which citizens would assent to the laws they were governed by, since these laws would have their source in a sovereign authority which they would recognize, and would be formulated in a clear, simple, and publicly accessible language.[151] It was only in this way that the '*seductive influence*' of sinister monarchical and aristocratic interests, which was exercised by the force of 'will on will', could be replaced by the felicitous influence of 'understanding on understanding'.[152]

The central importance of censorial and universal jurisprudence in Bentham's conception of the legislative task for the benefit of empires was in direct opposition to the notion of law and legislation which underlay the common law tradition. For Bentham and Mill law did not arise out of experience; on the contrary, it shaped and defined it. The primary function of law was not regulative but constitutive; law was a principle of order by which social reality

146 Mill, *History*, ed. Wilson, v. 205, 210.

147 Bentham, *Of Laws in General*, 185 n.

148 Ibid. 189.

149 Postema, *Bentham and Common Law*, 275.

150 Bentham, *Of Laws in General*, 153.

151 Postema, *Bentham and Common Law*, 277–8, 368. For Bentham's definition of law as a set of commands issuing from a sovereign, see *Of Laws in General*, 1.

152 Bentham, *Plan of Parliamentary Reform*, p. cxxxvi.

was constituted, and not simply an instrument through which power was wielded and behaviour regulated.[153] This conception of law was also in opposition to the assumptions upon which the legal administration in British India was based, assumptions which were close to the central ideas of the common law tradition.[154] Mill's criticism of the compilation of laws by pandits as loose, disorderly, vague, and arbitrary, and his criticism of their legal monopoly,[155] were in keeping with his and Bentham's attack on common law. But this attack was not just an assault on a legal tradition. Edmund Burke gave political expression to the central ideas of common law tradition.[156] These ideas were given a new lease of life by the revitalized conservatism of the late eighteenth and early nineteenth centuries,[157] which refurbished them as the terms in which to describe and defend the uniqueness of cultures and their integrities as they had evolved in history against what Burke called 'metaphysical and alchemistical legislators'.[158] Bentham's and Mill's attack on the common law tradition was thus also an attack on the ruling political ideology of the early nineteenth century. It is this aspect of Mill's *History* which has been overlooked by Ranajit Guha when he criticizes it for its disregard of the pre-British Indian past which created the necessary 'void' to be filled by the experiments of Western invention.[159] It was not just the disregard of an Indian past which was central to Mill's radical rhetoric, but the disregard of the British past and its invocations by the ruling political ideology of the time in the common law tradition. This formed the basis for his critique of the dominance of that ideology in British society. It was also on this assumption of being able to proceed *de novo* that Mill's 'science' of education was constructed, a science which was applicable not just to Indian cultures, but to British society as well.

Mill hoped that his *History* would 'form a kind of era in the writing of history & render it impossible to acquire reputation by such flimsy things as have hitherto passed for history'.[160] By basing

153 Postema, *Bentham and Common Law*, 175, 80.

154 See ch. 1.

155 Mill, *History*, ed. Wilson, i. 151–2.

156 Postema, *Bentham and Common Law*, 29, 81.

157 See ch. 1.

158 Edmund Burke, *Reflections on the Revolution in France*, ed. C. C. O'Brien (London: Penguin, 1984), 300.

159 Ranajit Guha, 'Dominance without Hegemony and its Historiography', *Subaltern Studies*, 6 (Delhi: Oxford University Press, 1989), 284–9.

160 Add. MS 35, 153, fo. 32, James Mill to Francis Place (in Place's hand), 6 Jan. 1818.

his notion of the historian on Bentham's conception of the legislative task, he was able to combine in the *History* two types of literature on the East India Company, which have been identified by Ranajit Guha as the literature of plans and the literature of polemic.[161] The *History* was both a polemical and a theoretical work. But the conception of the role of the historian and the writing of history was also formulated in opposition to the mythological histories of the late eighteenth and early nineteenth centuries, in which, as in Indian records, 'fable stands in the place of fact'.[162] It was also an attack on the common law tradition for which history was expressive of a community's sense of identity, and for which what was important was not the objective identity of the whole or part of the body of law over time, but the conviction of continuity upon which the believed identity of a people rested.[163] It is for this reason that Mill was so emphatic about basing his *History* on 'facts', and that he drew such a sharp distinction between facts and fictions. Unlike the New England historians, such as Prescott, who did not want to write like 'technical jurists', and whose histories used dramatic techniques to give the reader the illusion of participation in actions of heroic grandeur,[164] Mill did write like a technical jurist. When he wrote his account of the trial of Warren Hastings, Hastings and Francis were still alive. Mill did not bother to consult them; parliamentary reports and impeachment proceedings were his only sources.[165] He also uses the occasion to discuss the nature of legal evidence.[166] As William Thomas has pointed out, the *History* had large tracts of narrative punctuated by passages of theory.[167] The subject matter of the narrative was not heroic action in which the reader was invited to participate imaginatively; for Mill the story of British India was a sorry saga of stupidity and greed. Nor was there any sense of pathos in the depiction of the decline of cultures, as there was in the writings of the New England historians; for Mill the decay of such cultures was desirable.

[161] Ranajit Guha, *A Rule of Property for Bengal: An Essay on the Idea of Permanent Settlement* (New Delhi: Orient Longman, 1982), 20–1.

[162] Mill, *History*, ed. Wilson, i. 112. See ch. 2.

[163] Postema, *Bentham and Common Law*, 72, 22.

[164] David Levin, *History as Romantic Art: Bancroft, Prescott, Motley, and Parkman* (Stanford, Calif.: Stanford University Press, 1959), 9–11, 19.

[165] Mill, *History*, ed. Thomas, 17.

[166] Mill, *History*, ed. Wilson, v. 74 et seq.

[167] Thomas, *Philosophic Radicals*, 117.

It was not just the New England historians whose conception of history and whose practice of historical writing differed so much from that defined and exemplified in *The History of British India*. S. T. Coleridge's approach to assessing institutions in their historical contexts in *On the Constitution of the Church and State* (1830) also affords a strong contrast to Mill's methodology. It was not only addressed to the 'parliamentary leaders of the Liberalists and Utilitarians', whom he deemed responsible for the Catholic emancipation and the growing chorus for parliamentary reform;[168] it was also an explicit attack on the consequentialism of such doctrines as utilitarianism, or what Coleridge called the 'Guess-work of general consequences'.[169] Coleridge believed that every institution has an 'idea' which can be discovered and stated in terms of its original purpose and its 'ultimate aim'.[170] The method of distilling the essence or idea of an institution is to subject the present institution to historical study, stripping it of its temporal manifestations as one goes back through the historical stages of its development, until its original purpose and aim is laid bare. It is only by grasping the idea of the national Church in this way that its existing state can be judged. The central question is 'in what respects the existing institution still answers the original purpose, and continues to be a means to necessary or most important ends, for which no adequate substitute can be found'.[171] It was in this way that Coleridge hoped to salvage what authority the established institutions of the country had after the Catholic emancipation. In the process, he defined a method of assessing institutions which was in strong contrast to the utilitarian approach of ascertaining their influence on human happiness by using Bentham's felicific calculus, for which questions of historical precedent were of no great importance. But it was not just Mill's conception of history and the historian which was in sharp contrast to that expressed by such figures as Coleridge. *The History of British India* can also be seen as an attack on the influence of aesthetic and linguistic ideas on a brand of conservatism prevalent at the time. The *History* indicates how important aesthetic concepts were for political creeds in the early nineteenth century, and how they were related not just to ways of thinking about British India, but also to ways of defending societies and envisaging new political orders.

[168] S. T. Coleridge, *On the Constitution of the Church and State*, in *The Collected Works of Samuel Taylor Coleridge*, ed. John Colmer (Princeton, NJ: Princeton University Press, 1976), x. 68.

[169] Ibid. x. 68.

[170] Ibid. x. 12.

[171] Ibid. x. 56–7.

CHAPTER 5

SUSCEPTIBLE IMAGINATIONS

Oriental Rhetoric on the Riches of India

Between 1797 and 1818 petitions to Parliament favouring extended or universal male suffrage were rejected either because they were printed or because of the language in which they were written. Sir Francis Burdett submitted over 500 petitions allegedly containing almost a million signatures, which were rejected on these grounds. Burdett drily remarked that 'it was of the utmost importance to the country that they should come to some decision, in order that the people might know in what language the House would be inclined to lend their ears to grievances.'[1] Trials for sedition, discussions in Parliament, comments in newspapers, and responses to petitions relied on the notion of vulgarity to argue against the concept of extended or universal male suffrage.[2] To speak or write vulgar language demonstrated the vulgarity of one's class, and so one's moral and intellectual inability to participate in political culture. It was only refined language which was capable of expressing intellectual ideas and worthy sentiments. Vulgar language was limited to the expression of sensations and passions.[3] This notion of the vulgar and polite in language was the organizing principle of the first dictionary of the English Language. This was Samuel Johnson's *Dictionary with a Grammar and History of the English Language* (1755). In the Preface Johnson explained that he had excluded the language of the 'laborious and mercantile part of the people' because it was 'fugitive cant'.[4] His dictionary was based on the written, and not the spoken, word, and he hoped that the various dialects of English would die out. Like the unifying power of the British constitution, English was seen and used as a means of

[1] Olivia Smith, *The Politics of Language 1791–1819* (Oxford: Clarendon Press, 1984), 32–3.
[2] Ibid. 29.
[3] Ibid. 2.
[4] J. Barrell, *English Literature in History 1730–80: An Equal, Wide Survey* (London: Hutchinson, 1983), 158.

confirming the unity of the nation.[5] It was this conservative ideology, embodied in Johnson's dictionary, which political radicals attacked. Radicals had to justify the political capabilities of the disenfranchised by defending and proving the worth of their language, which was deemed 'vulgar' and so an indication of their inability to become responsible citizens.[6]

To a certain extent, Bentham's and Mill's ideas of language can be understood in this context of a preoccupation on the part of political radicals with the alliance between notions of linguistic and of political communities. Thomas Paine's *Rights of Man* (1791) was not just an attack on the political ideology of Burke's *Reflections*. Paine stressed how forms of address in courtly culture were part of the 'puppet show of state and aristocracy', and how these had contributed to the mystique of the Crown,[7] but the very style of *Rights of Man* was an attack on notions of linguistic propriety which were used to buttress conservative political ideology. It was written in a language which was alleged not to exist, namely an intellectual vernacular prose.[8] Its use of colloquial tone and rhetoric showed that important issues could be addressed in the language of common speech.[9] The clear and accessible language of the book reflected its emphasis on its simple political creed as consisting of universal truths which could be assented to by all.

Paine's book was influential in the reform movement of the 1790s, and its circulation was one of the reasons for the passage of repressive legislation.[10] As Cobbett's *A Grammar of the English Language* (1819) demonstrated, questions of language continued to be important with political radicals in the post-war period.[11] Although Paine belonged to a very different radical tradition from Bentham,[12] the latter shared the general preoccupation of radicals of different traditions with such issues. Central to Bentham's project to recast the legal and political framework of society was the formulation of a clear and publicly accessible language of political and legal morality, which would replace the studied intricacies and obscurities of the common law. It was only in this way that what Postema has aptly described as Bentham's 'jurisprudential protestantism' could succeed and his ideal for every man to be his

[5] Ibid. 111. [6] Smith, *Politics of Language*, pp. vii–viii.

[7] Thomas Paine, *Rights of Man* (1791; Harmondsworth: Penguin, 1984), introduction by Eric Foner, 59. [8] Smith, *Politics of Language*, 36.

[9] Ibid. 16. [10] Ibid. 60–6; [11] Ibid. 242.

[12] For Bentham's attack on the Rights of Man school, see below, 188–9.

own lawyer could be fulfilled.[13] But the work which had most influence on Bentham's and Mill's theories of language was Horne Tooke's *The Diversions of Purley* (vol. i, 1786; 1st edition of vol. ii, 1805, 2nd edition of vol. i, 1798). Tooke saw naming as the essence of language and showed that all words could be traced through etymology to the names of sensible objects. He sought to demonstrate the dependence of thought on language and to create a system of language which when applied to 'all the different systems of Metaphysical (i.e. verbal) Imposture' would do away with metaphysics, which in his view included 'all general reasoning, all Politics, Law, Morality and Divinity'.[14] Bentham found Tooke's ideas useful, especially when he grappled with what he had called 'the pestilential breath of fiction' in *A Fragment on Government* (1776). Bentham agreed with Tooke that all words were resolvable into references to real objects: 'In so far as any origin at all can be found for it, it is in a material import that the origin of every word possessing an immaterial import is to be found.'[15] He is adamant that 'All our psychological ideas are derived from physical ones—all mental from corporeal ones.'[16] Like Tooke, he was anxious to expose verbal imposture; for example, he defined 'paraphrasis' as 'transmuting into a proposition, having for its subject some real entity, a proposition which has not for its subject any other than a fictitious entity'.[17] But he was careful to distinguish between those fictions which were pernicious, such as 'fabulous' fictions whose separate existence 'is capable of becoming a subject of belief',[18] and those which were necessary for language and thought,[19] and which have 'a sort of *verbal* reality'.[20] He believed priests and lawyers often employed fictions to deceive and thereby govern,[21] but what he was particularly concerned to expose was the use of legal fictions by common law, which had been praised by Black-

[13] Gerald J. Postema, *Bentham and the Common Law Tradition* (Oxford: Clarendon Press, 1989), 425–7.

[14] Hans Aarsleff, *The Study of Language in England, 1780–1860* (1967; Minneapolis: University of Minnesota Press, 1983), 13.

[15] C. V. Ogden, *Bentham's Theory of Fictions* (London: Kegan Paul and Co., 1932), 63. [16] Ibid. 59. [17] Ibid. 86. [18] Ibid. p. xxxv.

[19] Ibid. 16.

[20] Ibid. 137. For the difficulty that this posed for Bentham's own reliance on fictions, and the relationship between this and the changing nature of his political philosophy, see L. J. Hume, 'The Political Function of Bentham's Theory of Fictions', *Bentham Newsletter*, 3 (Dec. 1979), 18–27.

[21] Ogden, *Bentham's Theory of Fictions*, 18.

stone as the life-blood of the law.[22] In fact, he went so far as to describe customary law as 'a fiction from beginning to end'.[23]

Mill claimed that Tooke had shed 'more light upon the subject of language than all the labours of all the grammarians and philosophers who have gone before him during two thousand years',[24] and as late as 1815 he described Tooke's work as the 'best introduction . . . to all logical studies'.[25] Tooke borrowed two assumptions about the nature of language from Locke, namely that it aimed to communicate our thoughts, and to do so quickly or 'with dispatch' in order to make speed of discourse approach the speed of thought. So Tooke makes abbreviation the cornerstone of his theory.[26] Mill agreed with Tooke on the importance of abbreviation in language.[27] He also believed Tooke's account of abstraction to be 'completely satisfactory'.[28] His indebtedness to Tooke is revealed by the epigraph placed at the head of the chapter on abstraction in the *Analysis of the Phenomena of the Human Mind*. Tooke's insistence that words could be traced through etymology to the names of sensible objects meant that language could be analysed in terms of Mill's psychology by reference to sensation and the association of ideas.[29] When discussing the concept of motives in *An Introduction to the Principles of Morals and Legislation*, Bentham wrote that in everyday language motives are seen as intrinsically good or bad; this is the result of a 'perverse association of ideas', and he intends to invent a new vocabulary involving 'the steady adherence to the one neutral expression, rejecting altogether the terms, of which the import is infected by adventitious and unsuitable ideas'.[30] Similarly, Mill's *History* attempted to invent a new vocabulary to deal with British India, purging the subject of the 'perverse association of ideas', an attempt which was influenced by Tooke's philosophy of language. Interestingly, the adoption of Horne Tooke's work by the utilitarians was a historical fact of the 'utmost importance' for

[22] Postema, *Bentham and Common Law*, 271.

[23] Bentham, *Corrigenda for Of Laws in General*, in *Collected Works of Jeremy Bentham*, ed. J. H. Burns and H. L. A. Hart (London: The Athlone Press, 1970), 193.

[24] James Mill, 'Horne Tooke's *Diversions of Purley*', *Literary Journal of Domestic and Foreign Literature*, 1 (1806), 13.

[25] Francis Place papers, Add. MS 35, 152, fo. 161, Mill to Place, 6 Sept. 1815.

[26] Aarsleff, *The Study of Language*, 46.

[27] Mill, 'Horne Tooke', 2.

[28] Ibid. 12.

[29] Aarsleff, *The Study of Language*, 94.

[30] Jeremy Bentham, *An Introduction to the Principles of Morals and Legislation* (1789), *Collected Works*, 102.

the study of language in England.[31] This was because language study remained philosophical rather than historical or philological much longer than on the Continent, where the new philology, founded by Jones, developed into a new and independent historical discipline. It was not until the 1830s that two Anglo-Saxon scholars, Benjamin Thorpe and John Mitchell Kembell, brought the new philology to England.[32] But for Mill there was a close relationship between linguistic and aesthetic notions; it was not just in opposition to Jones's notions of language that Mill adapted Tooke for his own purposes. He was also to rebut Jones's aesthetic creed, and in particular his version of a notion of the imagination, which was to be transformed in Mill's own time by such thinkers as Coleridge.

Whereas one of Bentham's favourite targets for attack was the legal fictions of common law, Mill's target in the *History* was the fiction of the economic and cultural riches of India. He frequently condemned European travellers in India and East India Company officials for exaggerating India's wealth. For example, he blames Clive for creating the myth that India 'overflowed with riches',[33] and he castigated English credulity for accepting 'the exaggerations of Oriental rhetoric on the riches of India', which made them believe that 'a country which they saw was one of the poorest, was nevertheless the most opulent upon the surface of the globe'.[34] It was this credulity, prompted by the inclination to believe 'what flatters their desires',[35] which created a vicious circle whereby disillusionment led to the sacrifice of a governor-general to appease disappointment, which then led to further fantasizing, with fancies pampered anew 'with endless hopes and delusions'.[36] Mill was describing a mock ritual of expectation, disillusionment, sacrifice, and then guilt-free expectation again. Furthermore, the hope of riches from India led to 'the rage of extorting more and more' from it,[37] which increased the poverty of India, which in turn led to more exploitation in the frantic search for this mythical oriental wealth. Mill was not alone in arguing that the wealth of Bengal had been greatly exaggerated. In his Minute of 18 June 1789 John Shore had

[31] Aarsleff, *The Study of Language*, 96. [32] Ibid. 161.

[33] James Mill, *The History of British India* (1817), ed. H. H. Wilson, 10 vols. (London: James Madden, Piper, Stephenson, and Spence, 1858), iii. 307.

[34] Ibid. iii. 213. [35] Ibid. iii. 213. [36] Ibid. iii. 307.

[37] Ibid. vi. 43.

pointed to the devastating effect of the 1770 famine on the economic condition of Bengal, and stressed that the zemindars 'are almost universally poor' and were not, as some observers claimed, 'wallowing in wealth and luxury'.[38] He also pointed to the fact that since the 1760s the English had shifted from importing silver into Bengal to shipping it out. This resulted in a diminishment of specie, a diminishment likely to intensify with the necessity of 'supplying China, Madras and Bombay, with money'.[39] In fact, as P. J. Marshall has pointed out, the Permanent Settlement of 1793 reflected pessimism about the extent to which wealth could be extracted from Bengal or improvement achieved; the British had voluntarily renounced any increase from taxation to be raised from the land.[40] Since the land revenue was fixed in this way, the Company tried to increase its revenue from other sources, such as duties on internal trade which had been abolished in the 1780s. These duties were restored in the early nineteenth century, but this did little for the financial solvency of the Company in India. It was the tea-trade with China which provided the whole profit of the East India Company, and into which the Company was directing all its commercial energies even before the abolition of its monopoly of Indian trade by Parliament in 1813.[41]

But Mill's attack on the fiction of Indian wealth was rooted in a definite economic doctrine. He takes a strict economic view of imperialism in India:

> If India affords a surplus revenue which can be sent to England, thus far is India beneficial to England. If the revenue of India is not equal to the expense of governing India, then is India a burden and drain to England. This is only an application of the principle, according to which the advantage or disadvantage of new territory, in general is to be estimated.[42]

As Wilson points out, according to this principle, 'this is to affirm that during the greater number of years in which we have been in possession of India it has been of no benefit at all'.[43] In *Commerce Defended* (1807), which launched his career as a propagandist for

[38] John Shore, 'Respecting the Permanent Settlement of the Lands in the Bengal Provinces', 18 June 1789, in *Parliamentary Papers*, 7 (1812), 182.

[39] Ibid. 183.

[40] P. J. Marshall, *Bengal: The British Bridgehead: Eastern India 1740–1828* (Cambridge: Cambridge University Press, 1987), 127, 46.

[41] Michael Greenberg, *British Trade and the Opening of China 1800–42* (1951; New York: Monthly Review Press, 1979), 3.

[42] Mill, *History*, ed. Wilson, vi. 471.

[43] Ibid. vi. 472.

the radical cause, Mill had moved away from Adam Smith's 'vent-for-surplus' view of the gains from trade. Mill argued that the 'production of commodities creates, and is the one and universal cause which creates a market for the commodities produced'. In other words, since 'a nation always has within itself a market equal to all the commodities of which it can possibly have to dispose', it can never be 'overstocked either with capital or with commodities; as the very operation of capital makes a vent for its produce'.[44] This means that foreign commerce does not 'furnish a vent for the produce of the country'. It is on the basis of this argument that he denies the importance of colonies as markets in *Elements of Political Economy*.[45]

In his 'Essay on Colonies', written for the supplement to the *Encyclopaedia Britannica* during 1817[46] Mill brought together Ricardian and Benthamite ideas on the question of the benefits and purpose of holding colonies. In the *Principles of Political Economy*, Ricardo believed Smith erred in suggesting that it would not be a profit to a nation to impose trade restrictions, because of the effect on the allocation of world resources. Ricardo felt there were some advantages of exclusive trading rights to the mother country in so far as the colonies were obliged to buy goods which they could have acquired more cheaply from other countries. In this way, an outlet was provided for goods which could not otherwise have been disposed of in world markets at the same prices.[47] Mill agreed with this but he showed that since this involved a loss to the colonies, it was undesirable on utilitarian grounds. Smith had argued that a monopoly of colonial trade raised the general level of profit. Mill used Ricardo to argue that this was not the case. The level of profits is determined by producing wage goods on marginal lands. Relative prices are determined by the relative quantities of labour embodied in commodities, and the general level of prices by the quantity of labour required to produce or acquire gold relative to other goods.[48] Mill cited Ricardo's authority for arguing nothing 'can raise the profits of stock, but that which lowers the wages of

44 James Mill, *Selected Economic Writings*, ed. Donald Winch (Edinburgh: Oliver and Boyd, 1966), 135. 45 Ibid. 319–20.

46 Macvey Napier papers, Add. MS 34, 612, fo. 140–1, Mill to Napier, 22 Aug. 1817.

47 Donald Winch, *Classical Political Economy And Colonies* (London: London School of Economics and Political Science, 1965), 40.

48 Winch, *Classical Political Economy*, 42.

labour'. Since there is nothing in the monopoly of colonial trade which does this, it is 'impossible that the monopoly of the colony trade can raise the profits of stock'.[49] Rent makes no difference to the argument, since it is the joint produce of labour and capital, and is the 'produce, exclusively, of a particular degree of fertility in particular lands, and is yielded over and above a return to the whole of labour and capital employed upon that land, over and above a return equal to the joint produce of an equal portion of labour and capital in any other employment'.[50]

So Mill demonstrated to his satisfaction that India is of no economic benefit to Britain, and it is a 'moral impossibility, that a colony should ever benefit the mother country, by yielding it a permanent tribute'.[51] In 'Emancipate Your Colonies!', written in 1792 but published in 1830, Bentham had also argued against the advantages of the monopoly of colonial trade, on the basis that 'it is *quantity of capital*, not extent of *market*, that determines the quantity of trade'.[52] But he also introduced a number of other points into the debate. He pointed out the inconveniences of government at a distance,[53] and also the corrupt patronage involved in governing colonies.[54] In his 'Essay on Colonies', Mill stressed the inefficiency of government from a distance. He believed that all governments will spend as much as they can find 'it possible or safe to extract from the people'. He also believed that the 'farther servants are removed from the eye of the master, the worse, generally speaking, their conduct will be'. If the home government is sure to overspend, the colonial government will be even worse.[55] Colonies provide a source of power and patronage for ruling élites, and they are 'a grand source of wars'. This, again, is to the advantage of governments, since 'the power of all governments is greater during war than during peace'.[56] He is left to conclude that the real purpose of colonies is '*to produce or prolong bad government*', and to perpetuate the power of the ruling few.[57] Empires sustain the power of the aristocracy, for whom the myth of the economic riches of India is a justification of Britain's role as an imperial nation.

[49] James Mill, 'The Article Colony', reprinted from the Supplement to the *Encyclopaedia Britannica* (London: J. Innes, c.1820), 25.

[50] Ibid. 26. [51] Ibid. 18.

[52] Jeremy Bentham, 'Emancipate Your Colonies!' Jeremy Bentham to the National Convention of France, January 1793', 7. [53] Ibid. 2–3.

[54] Ibid. 16. [55] Mill, 'The Article Colony', 18. [56] Ibid. 32.

[57] Ibid. 31.

For Mill, the sinister influence of the aristocracy in the affairs of the British empire was demonstrated in the 'aristocratical prejudices' of the Permanent Settlement,[58] which tried to establish 'an aristocracy upon the European model'.[59] In opposition to this land revenue system, Mill supported the ryotwari system. This was based on a direct settlement with each peasant for his individual holdings, eschewing all intermediaries. The Collector was given magisterial powers, which gave him control of the district police and the power of summary punishment. It was also based on the conviction that in Southern India, as opposed to Bengal, this had been the original land tenure system, which together with the institution of the village, had substantially survived.[60] The ryotwari system could be seen to be in some agreement with utilitarianism as far as simplification of law to a compact code which respected Indian tradition, and an accurate survey and record of landed rights went.[61] Mill transformed the ryotwari system into an instrument for the radical transformation of Indian society through the means it afforded of the definition of individual rights.[62] He criticized the Permanent Settlement for giving the zemindar too much power over the cultivator,[63] and he recommended that the immediate cultivator be the proprietor.[64]

In his support of the ryotwari system, Mill was influenced by Ricardo. His discussion of taxes in *Elements of Political Economy* (1821), which was intended as a summary for those who wished to learn the essential doctrines of Ricardo's *Principles of Political Economy* (1817), was largely derived from Ricardo. But he went further than Ricardo on the feasibility and desirability of taxes on rent. His attempt to implement the radical conclusions he drew from Ricardo's interpretation of the rent doctrine in the Indian

[58] Mill, *History*, ed. Wilson, v. 348.

[59] Ibid. v. 340.

[60] The main proponents of the ryotwari system were Thomas Munro, who was the governor of Madras from 1820 to 1827, and Monstuart Elphinstone, who was governor of Bombay from 1819 to 1827. For the details of the ryotwari system and its background, see K. Ballhatchet, *Social Policy and Social Change in Western India 1817–1830* (Oxford: Oxford University Press, 1957), and T. H. Beaglehole, *Thomas Munro and the Development of Administration Policy in Madras 1792–1818: The Origins of 'the Madras System'* (Cambridge: Cambridge University Press, 1966). For its intellectual underpinnings, see Ranajit Guha, *A Rule of Property*.

[61] Eric Stokes, *The English Utilitarians and India* (1959; Oxford: Clarendon Press, 1963), 23.

[62] Ibid. 76.

[63] Mill, *History*, ed. Wilson, v. 346.

[64] Ibid. v. 347.

revenue system, has been called the 'single most important application of Ricardian economics in practice'.[65] If rent was pure surplus earned on intra-marginal land after the payment of wages and profits, then it could be fixed without affecting production or prices. The 'share of the rent of land, which may be taken to defray the expenses of the government, does not affect the industry of the country'. This is because the cultivation of the land depends upon the capitalist, 'to whom the appropriate motive is furnished, when he receives the ordinary profits of stock'. It is therefore a matter of 'perfect indifference' whether he 'pays the surplus, in the shape of rent, to an individual proprietor; or, in that of revenue, to a government collector'.[66] Where land is owned communally as in the early stages of society, it is a simple matter for the state to appropriate part of the annual produce as rent. Even where private property exists, there seems no difficulty in making the rent 'answerable for the whole of the public burdens'. This would only require 'a greater quantity of land to be a property of equal value'.[67] So European progress in the shape of private incomes from land was a retrograde step. What might have gone to meet community needs was annexed to private individuals. Mill wanted to see property in the hands of the greatest number; as Bentham put it in a letter to R. M. Roy, what Mill aimed at 'above all things is the giving stability and security to landed property in the hands of the greatest number throughout British India'.[68] This was in accordance with Mill's stress on the fundamental task of government as being to secure to all individuals the fruits of their labours, a task made difficult by the rapaciousness which was intrinsic to the nature of élites, and even more difficult by landed settlements such as the Permanent Settlement.[69] Mill proposed that the state should remain as the landlord and each peasant should hold his land directly from the state as its tenant. This advocacy of the nationalization of the soil struck at the liberal tradition for which the institution of private property was the foundation of progress and individual liberty.[70]

However, there was another aspect to Mill's support of the ryotwari system. This support constituted an attack on what

[65] Mill, *Economic Writings*, 197. [66] Ibid. 338. [67] Ibid. 339.

[68] *Works*, x. 590.

[69] On the rapacity of élites, see 'Essay on Government', suppl. to *Encyclopaedia Britannica* (London: J. Innes, *c*.1825), 9.

[70] Stokes, *English Utilitarians and India*, 87.

Bentham called the 'language of the Aristocratic School', in which '*property* and *virtue* are synonymous terms',[71] and for which '*property* is *probity*'.[72] John Barrell has argued that the increasing differentiation of British society in the eighteenth century in terms of occupation was seen to give rise to a number of problems. Among these was the danger of those whose living depended on their success in specific occupations placing their own interests before those of the nation as a whole. This raised the issue of how inherited notions of political unity could be adapted so as to represent what seemed to be an increasingly differentiated society as a unified one, and on what basis such a unity could be grasped.[73] It was in response to these problems that the notion of the gentleman as the natural leader of society was defined. It was by virtue of the possession of landed property that the class of landed gentry were the only group in society who could take a disinterested view of society, since they were not involved in a specific occupation which of necessity would have narrowed their political perspectives.[74] This body of ideas was re-expressed by Wordsworth, when in 1818 in 'Two Addresses to the Freeholders of Westmorland' he contrasted the pedigree and creed of Broughman, to those of Lord Lonsdale and his son, Lord Lowther, whose estates 'may be looked upon as a pledge for their conduct'.[75] As he put it, 'Men of large estates cannot but be men of wide concerns.'[76] It was also this body of ideas which Coleridge developed later, when he argued that property was the only permanent element in the polity which provided a safeguard against the worst excesses of the *laissez-faire* spirit of commerce.[77] Bentham's definition of the aptitudes necessary for political representatives in his *Plan of Parliamentary Reform*,[78] and the measures he stipulated which would guarantee these virtues in a reformed political system,[79] were a clear attack on this ideology. He pointedly remarked '*Opulence*, *indolence*, *intellectual weakness*, *cowardice*, *tyranny*—oh yes, these five are

[71] Bentham, *Plan of Parliamentary Reform* (London: R. Hunter, 1817), p. xix.

[72] Ibid. p. clxi.

[73] Barrell, *English Literature in History*, 15.

[74] Ibid. 32–3.

[75] William Wordsworth, 'Two Addresses to the Freeholders of Westmorland', in *The Prose Works of William Wordsworth*, ed. W. J. B. Owen and Jane Worthington Smyser (Oxford: Clarendon Press, 1974), iii. 175.

[76] Ibid. iii. 176.

[77] Coleridge, *On the Constitution of the Church and State*, in *Collected Works of Samuel Taylor Coleridge*, ed. John Colmer (Princeton, NJ: Princeton University Press, 1976), x. 24.

[78] Bentham, *Plan of Parliamentary Reform*, p. lxvi.

[79] Ibid. 5.

naturally in one.'[80] Mill agreed with this sentiment when in his 'Essay on Government', upon which he started work in 1820,[81] he argued that 'Intellectual powers are the offspring of labour,' and since 'hereditary Aristocracy are deprived of the strongest motives to labour', it follows they do not have the necessary intellectual strengths requisite for political leadership.[82] In fact, Mill's essay is an attack on the notion of the English gentleman as 'a favourable specimen of civilization'. He points to the behaviour of Englishmen in the West Indies as slave owners to prove that 'the ruling Few, would, if checks did not operate in the way of prevention, reduce the great mass of the people subject to their power, at least to the condition of negroes in the West Indies'.[83] He declared that it is false 'there is in the mind of a King, or in the minds of an Aristocracy, any point of saturation with the objects of desire'.[84] Similarly, in the *History* he rejected the argument that higher salaries lessen corruption among public servants: 'The prevalence of the idea that satiating the servants of the public with wealth is a secret for rendering them honest, only proves how little the art of government has borrowed as yet from the science of human nature.'[85] It was because of the insatiability of the desire for power that a political system had to be devised which would ensure representation of all the interests of the community, and which would undermine the operations of what Bentham called the sinister interest that led to 'universal interest crouching under the conjunct yoke' of the monarchy and aristocracy.[86] Mill's support of the ryotwari system therefore has to be seen as part of a wider attack on the equation of property with probity in the 'Aristocratic School', an equation which played an important part in the defining of the gentlemanly ideal, and in disguising the operations of the sinister interests of the ruling élite in the British empire as a whole.

A Wide and Ungoverned Imagination

However, it was Mill's psychological and aesthetic beliefs which were central to his attack on the fiction of Indian wealth. Mill

80 Ibid. p. cxxxvi.

81 Macvey Napier papers, Add. MS 34, 612, fo. 354, Mill to Napier, 10 Sept. 1819.

82 Mill, 'Essay on Government', 7.

83 Ibid. 12–14.

84 Ibid. 11.

85 Mill, *History*, ed. Wilson, iii. 291.

86 Bentham, *Plan of Parliamentary Reform*, p. xix.

argued that it was the susceptibility of the imagination to being misled by superficial appearances which led to the misrepresentation of India as wealthy. His distrust of the imagination is the unifying strand of his *History*. Mill sees the imagination as a faculty which needs to be controlled by the philosophic intelligence. In his 'Essay on Education', the only time when Mill credits the human mind with an ability to initiate trains of ideas is when the appetite is involved: 'the appetites of individuals have a greater power over the succession of ideas, as the thought of the object which the individual desires, leads him to the thought of that by which he may attain it.'[87] A man's appetite may lead him to pursue things inconsistent with 'the most effectual pursuit of happiness', so it is the purpose of education to inculcate temperance. The clearest example of the higher faculties being usurped by desires is when Mill considers the predicament of Englishmen in India, deprived of 'the salutary dread of the scrutinizing minds, and free pens, of an enlightened public'. In such circumstances, 'the understanding waits, an humble servant, upon the affections'.[88] The imagination is only too ready to wait upon dangerous appetites; it is subservient to the 'ingenuity of fear and desire'.[89] It was precisely this subservience which was responsible for English credulity regarding the 'Oriental rhetoric on the riches of India'. In 1810 Mill had criticized Sir William Jones's 'susceptible imagination' for being impressed by the 'idea of Eastern wonders'.[90] His attack on Jones in the *History* developed this theme, when he described 'the fond credulity with which the state of society among the Hindus was for a time regarded'.[91] The fiction of the cultural riches of India, evident in the exaggerated notions of Indian antiquity and the 'saving hypothesis' which was used as a sentimental defence against any attempts to reform the conservative bias of British rule in India, was thus also the result of the imagination's susceptibility to being misled by appearances.

Mill's attack on the fiction of India's economic riches in his *History* was an attempt to undermine this dangerous relationship between the imagination and desire. His conception of the historian and the writing of history was defined on the basis of this distrust

87 James Mill, 'Essay on Education', in *James Mill on Education*, ed. W. H. Burston (Cambridge: Cambridge University Press, 1969), 54.

88 Mill, *History*, ed. Wilson, 227.

89 Ibid. i. 239.

90 James Mill, 'Voyage aux Indies Orientales', *Edinburgh Review*, 15 (Jan. 1810), 369.

91 Mill, *History*, ed. Wilson, ii. 84.

of the imagination as a faculty easily led astray by desire. Whilst the Mughals in the earliest travel accounts 'exhibited that gorgeous exterior, that air of grandeur and power, which were well calculated to impose upon the imagination of an unphilosophical observer',[92] the purpose of the philosophical historian was not to 'display the obvious outside of things', but to convey 'just ideas of all the transactions, legislative, administrative, judicial, mercantile, military, which he is called upon to describe', using the 'most profound knowledge of the laws of human nature, which is the end, as well as the instrument, of everything'.[93] Mill argued that in Hindu records, 'the times over which the memory has any influence are rejected, and the imagination riots in those in which it is unrestrained'.[94] Such works mark 'the state of a rude and credulous people, whom the marvellous delights; who cannot estimate the use of a record of past events; and whose imagination the real occurrences of life are too familar to engage'.[95] Indian legends are the 'offspring of a wide and ungoverned imagination'.[96]

Mill makes clear his philosophy of language when he condemns Sanskrit for having too many words for the same object: 'The highest merit of language would consist in having one name for everything which required a name and no more than one. Redundancy is a defect in language, not less than deficiency.'[97] Mill's world is the world of measurable concrete objects; and language has to be held down to this world. In the 'Essay on Education' he defined intelligent trains of ideas as those which correspond to the 'sequences in nature'.[98] In *Analysis of the Phenomena of the Human Mind*, the marks of language are seen as a number of 'sensible objects', by which we can ensure any succession of ideas.[99] It is for reasons of economy that names are given to a cluster of sensations, rather than to each individual sensation. Since language has to be an accurate reflection of the world, Mill condemned the use of language in imaginative literature and especially in Indian literature, in which 'the real occurrences of life are too familiar'. Thus, the scale of utility upon which Mill based his assessment of

[92] Mill, *History*, ed. Wilson, ii. 109.
[93] Ibid. i, p. xvii.
[94] Ibid. i. 112.
[95] Ibid. i. 115–16.
[96] Ibid. i. 115.
[97] Ibid. i. 63–4.
[98] Mill, 'Essay on Education', 94.
[99] James Mill, *Analysis of the Phenomena of the Human Mind*, ed. J. S. Mill, 2 vols. (London: Longmans, Green, Reader, and Dyer, 1869), i. 132.

cultures was formulated partly on the basis of this distrust of the imagination, since it was the distortions of this faculty which prevented men from forming the accurate assessments of affairs upon which they could define means to achieve their interests. It was also this which led them to waste ingenuity on 'contemptible and mischievous objects'.[100] It is possible that Mill influenced one of his colleagues in the Examiner's Office, Thomas Love Peacock, whose essay on *The Four Ages of Poetry* (1820) resembled Mill's argument. Mill believed that the first step towards perfect history 'is the production of prose compositions, expressly destined to exhibit a record of real transactions'.[101] He condemned poetry as 'the language of the passions', and since 'men feel before they speculate', it is by poetry that 'the minds of rude men are the most powerfully activated'.[102] Peacock argued that poetry plays a less significant role in advanced than in primitive societies. He ridicules the notion of the poet seer and describes a poet in contemporary society as 'a semi-barbarian in a civilized community'. It is mainly on grounds of utility, in Mill's sense of the word as usefulness, that he is critical of poetry: 'in whatever degree poetry is cultivated, it must necessarily be to the neglect of some branch of useful study'. Poets address their 'minstrelsy' not to 'the thinking and studious, and scientific and philosophical part of the community, not to those whose minds are bent on the pursuit and promotion of permanently useful ends and aims', but to that 'much larger portion of the reading public, whose minds are not awakened to the desire of valuable knowledge, and who are indifferent to anything beyond being charmed, moved, excited, affected, and exalted'.[103]

Mill's distrust of the imagination was to a certain extent typical of political radicals, who were aware of how easily it could be manipulated by the rhetoric of the conservative ideology which sought to enhance the mystique of the Crown and of the status quo. Paine went so far as to describe the Crown as a 'thing in the imagination, the propriety of which is more than doubted, and the legality of which in a few years will be denied',[104] and he likened the whole paraphernalia of aristocracy with its titles and forms of

100 Ibid. ii. 105.

101 Mill, *History*, ed. Wilson, ii. 49.

102 Ibid. ii. 33.

103 *The Works of Thomas Love Peacock*, ed. Henry Cole (London: Richard Bentley and Sons, 1875), iii. 335–7.

104 Thomas Paine, *Rights of Man* (Harmondsworth: Penguin, 1984), 122.

address to what he called 'the fairy tribe' invented by the imagination.[105] Furthermore, his attack on Burke's rhetoric was cast in similar terms. The central problem with Burke's *Reflections* was that it was inspired by the 'rhapsody of his imagination',[106] which meant that he offered no reasons or evidence for his beliefs.[107] It was his uncontrolled imagination which was responsible for the superficial character of his book, which was a 'dramatic performance' in which many 'poetical liberties' were taken.[108] Hence he had no sympathy for the suffering of the masses in France; he was not affected by the 'reality of distress' but by the 'showy resemblance of it striking his imagination'. As Paine succinctly put it, 'He pities the plumage, but forgets the dying bird.'[109] Both Bentham and Mill were sensitive to the way in which the drama of public ceremonies captivated people's imaginations and made them contented, 'one would almost say happy, to be slaves'.[110] Ann Hone has argued that a central conviction of political radicals in this period was that truth had a natural superiority over error, once it was made evident. It was this conviction which was the basis of the emphasis on publication and pamphleteering.[111] But this conviction also rested on a distrust of the imagination. Bentham made this clear in his *Plan of Parliamentary Reform*: 'by speeches, imagination is fascinated,—passion in excess excited,—time for comprehensive conception and cool judgement denied:—substitute *writing*, no advantage can in any of these shapes be gained by any side to the injury of any other'.[112] This was also the foundation of their argument for publicity. One of the ways to ensure governments did not abuse their powers was to make their proceedings as public as possible, and by this Bentham meant frequent publication of reports of, for example, parliamentary or court proceedings in a clearly accessible language.[113] In this emphasis on the written word, Bentham and Mill were also arguing against another conservative view which had developed since the 1790s. Burke had blamed the French revolution on the diffusion of the ideas of the *philosophes*, who represented the sort of ethos of letters and the written word which Bentham and later Mill espoused. Burke was committed to a

105 Ibid. 81.

106 Ibid. 50. 107 Ibid. 64. 108 Ibid. 59. 109 Ibid. 51.

110 See introduction, n. 10.

111 J. Ann Hone, *For the Cause of Truth: Radicalism in London 1796–1821* (Oxford: Clarendon Press, 1982), 237.

112 Bentham, *Plan of Parliamentary Reform*, p. cv. 113 Ibid. 18–20.

common law order, backed by an unwritten constitution. Paine had attacked this, arguing that when a constitution cannot be produced in a written form, it was nonsense to talk of a constitution,[114] just as Bentham was to argue that common law as *lex non scripta* was hardly law at all. What Burke and later Wordsworth stressed was the importance of tradition and its roots in illiterate forms of cultural life. For both Burke and Wordsworth social welfare was dependent upon the continuity of literate culture with oral culture, and upon writing's subservience to speech.[115] This found expression in the 1798 and 1800 prefaces to the *Lyrical Ballads*, in which Wordsworth argued that poetic diction should be based 'on the real language of men in a state of vivid sensation', that is, on the language of men in 'humble and rustic life'. This language was 'more permanent, and a far more philosophical language', than any other hitherto used by poets.[116] It was the humble and rustic ranks who preserved the ethos of speech from the encroaching ethos of letters, an ethos which Wordsworth had himself succumbed to during his years of political radicalism. It was Wordsworth's discussion with Hazlitt in the spring of 1798 in which the latter stressed the value of the ethos of letters, which was the occasion for the lines in 'The Tables Turned' describing the 'meddling intellect' as distorting the 'beauteous forms of things'.[117]

Mill developed his attack on the imagination in his *Analysis of the Phenomena of the Human Mind* of 1828, which was a restatement of Hartleian psychology. Hartley had made clear in his *Observations on Man* that the pleasures of the imagination were given more weight in 'the Infancy of Knowledge' and 'in the early Ages of the World'.[118] Mill was therefore following Hartley in placing the imagination low in the hierarchy of mental activity. In particular, Mill attacked the 'appropriation of the name Imagination, to the trains [of ideas] of the poet', and declared, 'If imagination consists in bringing trains before the mind involving a number of new combinations, imagination is probably more the occupation

[114] Ibid. 71.

[115] James K. Chandler, *Wordsworth's Second Nature: A Study of the Poetry and Politics* (Chicago: University of Chicago Press, 1984), 160.

[116] William Wordsworth, *Poetical Works*, ed. T. Hutchinson and Ernest De Selincourt (1936; Oxford: Oxford University Press, 1981), 734–5.

[117] Chandler, *Wordsworth's Second Nature*, 150.

[118] David Hartley, *Observations on Man, His Frame, His Duty, and His Expectations*, 2 vols. (London: James Leake and Wm Frederick, 1749), i. 431.

of the philosopher than of the poet.'[119] He asserted that the succession of ideas in the poet's mind is governed by the same laws as those in the merchant's and lawyer's. The reason the poet's ideas receive 'a peculiar degree of attention' is because they are ideas of 'all that is most lovely and striking in the visible appearance of nature, and all that is most interesting in the actions and affections of human beings'.[120] The greatest difference lies in the lawyer's or merchant's train of ideas not being pleasurable in themselves, but directed to a particular end. In the poet, 'the train is its own end. It is all delightful, or the purpose is frustrate'.[121] By the standards of Mill's utilitarianism, this is to confuse means with ends in a particularly flagrant way, by making this confusion delightful. Bentham expresses a similar view, when he writes of a poet, 'whether in his character of historic fabulist or dramatic fabulist, putting or not putting the words of his discourse in metrical form' is full of 'insincerity', and 'neither for their object nor for their effect have anything but to amuse, unless it be in some cases to excite to action'.[122] In the end, Mill asserts that all men have imaginations, if by imagination is meant simply having trains of ideas. If by imagination is meant 'ideas which compose the train do not come together in the same combinations in which the sensations are received,' this is true 'in every train of any considerable length', so that the imagination of the practitioners of many 'vulgar arts' are equal to those of poets.[123] Mill also analyses the notions of the beautiful and the sublime in terms of the association of ideas;[124] he did not even consider it worth refuting Kant's notion of the sublime, which had greatly influenced such poets as Coleridge and Wordsworth.[125] It was also the increasing importance of the sublime as an aesthetic concept which, as Partha Mitter has shown, led to a reinterpretation of Indian art in the early nineteenth century, and a break from the tradition of viewing this art as monstrous.[126]

There is a wider significance to Mill's attack on the imagination in the *Analysis of the Phenomena of the Human Mind*. The *Analysis*

119 Mill, *The Human Mind*, i. 244.

120 Ibid. i. 242.

121 Ibid. i. 243.

122 C. K. Ogden, *Bentham's Theory of Fictions* (London: Kegan Paul and Co., 1932), 18.

123 Mill, *The Human Mind*, i. 244–5.

124 Ibid. ii. 230–7.

125 For a lucid exposition of Kant's influence on Coleridge and Wordsworth see Mary Warnock, *Imagination* (London: Faber & Faber, 1976), parts 1–3.

126 Partha Mitter, *Much Maligned Monsters: The History of European Reactions to Indian Art* (Oxford: Clarendon Press, 1977), 119–22.

was a restatement of Hartley's psychology. As John Stuart Mill argued, Mill's reputation of 'being the reviver and second founder of the Association Psychology' rested on the publication of this study.[127] The depiction of Mill's work as a revival of associationist psychology is apt because it was precisely this psychology which was rejected by Coleridge in his development of his views of the imagination, a development heavily influenced by Kantian epistemology as modified by Fichte and Schelling. Mary Warnock has shown that by 1803 Coleridge had abandoned Hartleian psychology for an active and creative role of the imagination.[128] This notion of the imagination drew on Kantian epistemology in which perception of the world of objects was not possible without first constituting that world by the schematism of our imagination.[129] In the *Critique of Pure Reason*, Kant argued that 'the order and regularity in appearances, which we entitle *nature*, we ourselves introduce'. This order would not be found 'had not we ourselves, or the nature of our mind, originally set them there'.[130] In particular, he argued that 'we must assume a pure transcendental synthesis of imagination as conditioning the very possibility of all experience'.[131] It was this epistemology according to which we constitute the world we observe by the schematism of the imagination which Mary Warnock has described as the 'Kantian Copernican revolution'.[132] It was also this epistemology which intensified Mill's distrust of the imagination. In a letter of 1817, he informed Francis Place that he had been reading Kant's *Critique of Pure Reason*. He declared, 'I see clearly enough what poor Kant is about—but it would require no little time to give an account of him.'[133] Indeed, in an earlier letter to Place he had given just such an account of 'the whole ground work of Kant's philosophy'.[134] In his 'Essay on Education' he made a dry comment about Kant's dissatisfaction with the 'humble origin' of happiness in 'simple sensations', and expressed his disagreement with the latter's view that 'there is something in human happiness, and in the human intellect, which soars high above this corporeal level'.[135] Mill was confident that 'Hartley's is the true scent', and

[127] Mill, *The Human Mind*, i, p. xi.

[128] Warnock, *Imagination*, 87.

[129] Ibid. 126.

[130] Immanuel Kant, *Critique of Pure Reason* (1787), trans. N. K. Smith (London: Macmillan, 1963), 147.

[131] Ibid. 133.

[132] Warnock, *Imagination*, 126.

[133] Francis Place papers, Add. MS 35, 152, fo. 220, Mill to Place, 8 Oct. 1816.

[134] Add. MS 35, 152, fo. 217, Place to Mill, 2 Oct. 1816.

[135] Mill, 'Essay on Education', 66.

that 'it will require no little persevering reflection to render the application of his theory perfectly familiar to one's mind in every part of the field of thought'.[136] He had declared his intention to embark on such a project the previous year when he argued that Hartley's doctrine 'might be put in a point of view so clear & striking, that metaphysics thereafter would not be very mysterious',[137] and he was to boast later 'If I had time to write a book I would make the human mind as plain as the road from Charing Cross to St. Paul's.'[138]

Mill's *Analysis of the Phenomena of the Human Mind* in 1828 was just such an attempt to make the workings of the human mind plain. It is clear, then, that by the time Mill had finished writing the *History*, he was not only contemplating a restatement of Hartley's psychology, but he was also conversant with Kantian epistemology. The *History* was thus an attack on views of the imagination as creative and active, and the role these views played in the fabrication of the fictions of India's economic and cultural riches. It was not just that Jones's susceptible imagination had been deceived in his beliefs about Indian history; he had actually expressed an anti-mimetic view of the imagination in his essay 'On the Arts, Commonly Called Imitative', in *Poems, Consisting Chiefly of Translations from the Asiatick Languages* (1772), which was the companion essay to his piece 'On the Poetry of Eastern Nations'. The views in this essay prefigured some of those in the Preface to the *Lyrical Ballads*. Jones argued that poetry 'was originally no more than a strong, and animated expression of the human passions, of *joy* and *grief*, *love* and *hate*, *admiration* and *anger*, sometimes pure and unmixed, sometimes variously modified and combined . . .'[139] He ventured a definition of poetry as 'some vehement passion . . . expressed in strong words, exactly measured, and pronounced, *in a common voice*, in just cadence, and with proper accents'.[140] Wordsworth also saw poetry as rooted in 'the spirit of the passions of men', and as 'the spontaneous overflow of powerful feelings'.[141] There are closer similarities between Jones and Words-

[136] Add. MS 35, 152, fo. 220.

[137] Add. MS 35, 152, fo. 162, Mill to Place, 6 Sept. 1815.

[138] Add. MS 35, 153, fo. 29, Mill to Place, 6 Dec. 1817 (in Place's hand).

[139] *The Works of Sir William Jones*, ed. A. M. Jones, 6 vols. (London: G. G. and J. Robinson, R. H. Evens, 1799), iv. 550. [140] Ibid. iv. 553.

[141] *Poetical Works*, 735.

worth on the subject of mimesis. Jones searches for a principle other than mimesis:

It shall be my endeavour in this paper to prove, that, though *poetry* and *musick* have, certainly, a power of *imitating* the manners of men, and several objects in nature, yet, that their greatest effect is not produced by *imitation*, but by a very different principle, which must be sought in the deepest recesses of the human mind.[142]

This principle is not just that poetry is the expression of the passions:

It seems to me, that, as those parts of *poetry*, *musick*, and *painting*, which relate to the passions, affect by *sympathy*, so those, which are merely descriptive, act by a kind of *substitution*: that is, by raising in our minds, affections, or sentiments, analogous to those which arise in us, when the respective objects in nature are presented to our senses . . . Thus will each artist gain his end not by *imitating* the works of nature, but by assuming her power, and causing the same effect upon the imagination, which her charms produce to the senses: this must be the chief object of a poet, a musician, and a painter . . .[143]

While defining imitation as a lower form of art, Jones also suggests that nothing can be added to 'Nature'. Discussing music, Jones asks, 'Since nature has given us a delightful harmony of her own, why should we destroy it by the additions of art?'[144] He also claims that 'the passions, which were given by nature, never spoke in an unnatural form'.[145] So by definition poetry and music are not mimetic, but express harmonies which are a part of 'Nature'; it is only painting which is mimetic. Wordsworth also writes that the poet 'will feel that there is no necessity to trick out or to elevate nature'.[146] He echoes Jones's view that poetry acts 'by a kind of substitution' to evoke passions in the absence of objects analogous to those evoked by the objects when present. Among the qualities of a poet, he lists:

a disposition to be affected more than other men by absent things as if they were present: an ability of conjuring up in himself passions which are indeed far from being the same as those produced by real events, yet (especially in those parts of the general sympathy which are pleasing and delightful) do more nearly resemble the passions produced by real events

142 *Works*, iv. 550.
143 Ibid. iv. 559–60.
144 Ibid. iv. 553–4.
145 Ibid. iv. 558.
146 *Poetical Works*, 737.

than anything which from the motions of their own minds merely, other men are accustomed to feel in themselves . . .[147]

Wordsworth is more positive than Jones about what the latter calls 'substitution'. The power of the imagination to produce images in the absence of objects is crucial to Wordsworth's own poetry and to his theory of it. When we see in the mind's eye, we concentrate upon those images which are meaningful, which we are able to form because of the significance of that which they represent. So, the feeling engendered by an image may be more powerful in the absence than in the presence of an object; poetry 'takes its origin from emotion recollected in tranquillity'.[148]

1817 was also the year of the publication of Coleridge's *Biographia Literaria*, in which an even more powerful conception of the imagination was defined, and one which had a political relevance. The *Biographia* rejected Hartleian associationist psychology and the radicalism of the poet's youth in order to argue for a theory of imagination which was based on Schelling's modification of Kant. This meant defining what Coleridge called the primary imagination as 'the living power and prime agent of all human perception', and its acts of creation as analogous to divine creation. Following on from this, he defined the secondary imagination as a faculty which dissolves in order to re-create, and as idealizing and unifying.[149] In 1812 Mill had vehemently attacked the very notion of an established Church.[150] The *Biographia*, on the other hand, used the notion of the secondary imagination to defend the established Church, as an institution whose cultural authority, which extended to such matters as setting the standards for the language of the community, consisted of diffusing the principles upon which to unify the nation. This was the only way to overcome sectarianism; and by sectarianism Coleridge was not only thinking of religious sectarianism, but the increasing class divisions of the post-war period as well. The philosophy of the *Biographia* was developed later in *On the Constitution of the Church and State* of 1829, which was provocatively anti-utilitarian in its approach to institutions.[151] It tried to redefine

[147] Ibid. 737.

[148] Ibid. 740.

[149] S. T. Colerige, *Biographia Literaria or Biographical Sketches of My Literary Life and Opinions* (1817), ed. G. Watson (London: J. M. Dent, 1975), 167.

[150] James Mill, 'Schools for All, in Preference to Schools for Churchmen only', in *James Mill on Education*, 120–92.

[151] See ch. 4.

and thereby salvage the cultural authority of the establishment after the disaster of Catholic Emancipation, in such a way as to make such incidents in the future have no bearing on its essential power. As Nigel Leask has argued, in Coleridge's thought the politics of the imagination became authoritarian, static, and class defined, and formed the basis of a view of cultural authority as transcendental.[152] Given the increasing sophistication of such ideas of the imagination employed for political ends, it is difficult not to believe that Mill was also not being provocative when he published his work on Hartleian associationist psychology in 1828, a work whose simplicity of style is only surpassed by the even more brutal simplicity of its ideas. Both Coleridge and Mill were trying to forge a new idiom for the middle classes. Coleridge's purpose was to transform the patriarchalist idiom of the *ancien régime* to fit new political realities, and thereby ensure that the middle classes would become a pillar of the establishment. This involved mediating and redefining German idealism for the establishment in an attempt to place its cultural authority to unify the nation on a new footing. Mill's 1817 'Essay on Government' was also an attempt to give a new language to the middle ranks, in order to prepare them for leadership in a reformed political system. Its premisses, its mode of argument, and its style could hardly be more different from the characteristics of Coleridge's writings in this period. In Macaulay's words, Mill not only affected a 'quakerly plainness' in his style, but he tried to deduce 'the science of government from the principles of human nature', which Macaulay considered 'utterly impossible' and a completely inappropriate mode of reasoning in political matters.[153] Jonathan Clark has argued that the patriarchalist idiom of the *ancien régime* was not open to criticism in the light of its own principles, or its sense of its own history,[154] but his contention that Mill's stance in the 'Essay on Government' is derived from the patriarchalist idiom of the *ancien régime* is misplaced. It was precisely because of the very features of the patriarchalist idiom which Clark stresses that Mill elaborated principles apparently

[152] Nigel Leask, *The Politics of the Imagination in Coleridge's Critical Thought* (Basingstoke: Macmillan, 1988), 143.

[153] T. B. Macaulay, 'Utilitarian Logic and Politics', *Edinburgh Review*, 49 (Mar. 1829), 161, 185.

[154] J. C. D. Clark, *English Society 1688–1832: Ideology, Social Structure and Political Practice during the Ancien Regime* (Cambridge: Cambridge University Press, 1985), 322.

rational and *ex nihilo* on which his argument in his 'Essay on Government' rests, which he forged to be of universal application. It was also because Mill had to stand outside the powerful idiom of the *ancien régime* that he attacked it by writing a *History of British India* and not a *History of Britain*. In India the ideology of the British establishment was writ large against an alien background, and it gave Mill the necessary distance to fashion the tools and principles with which to launch an attack on it.

R. A. Fenn has pointed out the role which an imitative principle plays in Mill's argument in his 'Essay on Government'.[155] This essay ended with a paean of praise to the middle classes, whom he argued would be the leaders in a reformed political system, since they had the requisite intellectual, moral, and economic qualities which would enable them to set the tone for society as a whole.[156] He felt sure that 'the opinions of that class of people, who are below the middle rank, are formed, and their minds directed by that intelligent and virtuous rank, who come the most immediately in contact with them', that is, the middle rank. It is the latter who are 'models for their imitation'.[157] It is an imitative principle which provides the links between classes in his projected polity, and which ensures that the lower orders would be the safe recipients of the right of franchise. Thus, Mill's notion of the imagination as imitative also played a role in his political theory, just as Coleridge's did in the *Biographia*. But to some extent it was also responsible for the differences between his conception of democracy and John Stuart Mill's conception of it. The elder Mill's model of society has been described as a classical economic model, in which the purpose of government is to harmonize the conflicting interests of individual agents pursuing their own ends.[158] In this conception of social life the political system is represented as a market, and the behaviour of voters and those for whom they vote is analogous to the behaviour of the buyers and sellers of goods. The individual voter is in a market for the policy that will maximize his utility, and the representatives are the delegates who seek to achieve this on behalf of their electors.[159] This non-dynamic theory of government contrasts

[155] Robert A. Fenn, *James Mill's Political Theory and Political Philosophy* (New York: Garland Publishing Inc., 1987), 94, 101.

[156] Mill, 'Essay on Government', 32.

[157] Ibid. 32.

[158] Alan Ryan, 'Two Concepts of Politics and Democracy: James and John Stuart Mill', in Martin Fleisher (ed.), *Machiavelli and the Nature of Political Thought* (London: Croom Helm, 1973), 82.

[159] Ibid. 88.

with the younger Mill's view, which Alan Ryan has called the participant or self-developmental account of social life.[160] In this view, the framework of social and political life should nurture such goals as the self-development and self-realization of individuals. It was in accordance with this view that in *Utilitarianism* (1861) J. S. Mill argued that it would be 'absurd that while, in estimating all other things, quality is considered as well as quantity, the estimation of pleasures should be supposed to depend on quantity alone'.[161] To a certain extent, this difference between the elder and younger Mill can be accounted for by the more positive view the latter had of Coleridge. In his 1840 essay on Coleridge, he wrote that 'Whoever could master the premises and combine the methods of both [Bentham and Coleridge], would possess the entire English philosophy of his age.'[162] In a sense, his view of political life was just such a combination, and that is why he put a much greater emphasis on self-development and self-expression than his father did. The elder Mill's distrust of any notion of the imagination as creative or expressive was part of a conception of human nature in political life which left less room for the achievement of the goals his son felt should be fostered.

There was yet a further reason for Mill's fear of such views of the imagination as defined by Coleridge. This was the role such an imagination could play in defining cultural and national identities. Bentham's and Mill's project was a universalist one, based on a unificatory epistemology. But in the late eighteenth and early nineteenth centuries there was a major trend tending to the opposite; cultures were increasingly being defined in relation to newly discovered literary, historical, and mythological material. It was also in this period that German biblical criticism was placing a new value on myth as not mere fable or unworthy fiction, but as an important way by which communities were imagined, and by which they constituted their own sense of the past in relation to which they defined themselves.[163] This new value placed on myth influenced Coleridge; it was one of his lifelong preoccupations to write mythological epic, which would be a unifying symbol for the com-

[160] Ibid. 78.

[161] J. S. Mill, *Utilitarianism*, ed. Mary Warnock (London: Fontana Press, 1985), 258–9.

[162] J. S. Mill, *Mill on Bentham and Coleridge*, ed. F. R. Leavis (Cambridge: Cambridge University Press, 1980), 102.

[163] See ch. 2.

munity in the process of self-construction.[164] Myths were not only unifying symbols; they were the product of that imagination which Coleridge had described as unifying and idealizing, and which he had used in the *Biographia* to restore a sense of national unity. In a letter he wrote to the then Tory Prime Minister, Lord Liverpool, in 1817, Coleridge had explicitly equated the predominance of what he called 'mechanic philosophy', under which he would have included utilitarianism, with the decay of the organic sense of a historical community. 'We are become', he wrote, 'like a Herd of Americans, a people without a *History*.'[165] It was also this new sense of the value of mythologies which Southey celebrated in his oriental epics. Mill's rhetoric was forthright in its denunciation of this positive view of mythology. Mill's distrust of the imagination explains why he was suspicious of patriotism, especially that species of patriotism which took pride in indigenous traditions and customs inherited from the past. Patriotism could be based on a process similar to that in writing poetry, especially in its 'panegyrical' origins. Peacock argued that the 'first rude songs of all nations appeared to be a sort of brief historical notices, in a strain of tumid hyperbole, of their exploits and possessions of a few pre-eminent individuals'.[166] Such panegyric involved a heroic view of the past incompatible with Mill's belief views on the relevance of the past to assessing contemporary cultures and their institutions. For Bentham, the disposition to reform could be seen as binding a democratic polity together, and replacing earlier notions of civic virtue and patriotism.[167] Indeed, it was consistent with Mill's and Bentham's views to see the concept of a 'nation' as a 'fabulous' and dangerous fiction, on a par with the notion of gods, dragons, and mythical countries, objects whose 'separate existence is capable of becoming a subject of belief',[168] not least because it was a threat to their unificatory epistemology.

[164] For a discussion of the influence of German biblical criticism on Coleridge, see Eleanor Shaffer, *'Kubla Khan' and the Fall of Jerusalem: The Mythological School in Biblical Criticism and Secular Literature 1770–1880* (Cambridge: Cambridge University Press, 1975), chs. 1–4.

[165] S. T. Coleridge, 'To Lord Liverpool', 28 July 1817, letter 1072 of *Collected Letters of Samuel Taylor Coleridge*, ed. E. L. Griggs, 6 vols. (Oxford: Clarendon Press, 1959), iv. 761.

[166] Peacock, *Four Ages of Poetry*, 325.

[167] Frederick Rosen, *Jeremy Bentham and Representative Democracy: A Study of the Constitutional Code* (Oxford: Clarendon Press, 1983), 23.

[168] Ogden, *Bentham's Fictions*, pp. xxxv–xxxvi. Benedict Anderson has argued that the nation is 'an imagined political community', and so nations can be

Mill's rejection of notions of the imagination as creative was in keeping with his conception of the mind as passive in his scheme of education. But there is a discrepancy between this view of the mind, and the conflicting view he also held in which reason is seen to mould the materials of the world, and to elaborate the principles upon which a new political order could be built. W. H. Burston has pointed out the inconsistency in Mill's philosophy between conceiving of man's ideal in teleological terms, and explaining his nature in the mechanistic terms of association psychology.[169] Mill's belief in history as a narrative of progress would have been more tenable if he had rejected associationist psychology and adopted Kantian epistemology. Jones had made a distinction between history, philosophy, and art. History is 'the observation and remembrance of *mere facts*, independently of *ratiocination*, which belongs to philosophy, or of *imitations* and *substitutions*, which are the province of art'.[170] Kant makes a somewhat similar distinction:

> If I abstract from all the content of knowledge, objectively regarded, then all knowledge, subjectively regarded, is either historical or rational. Historical knowledge is *cognitio ex datis*; rational knowledge is *cognitio ex principiis*.[171]

Kant resolved these differences in his philosophy of history. In 'What is Enlightenment?' (1784), Kant is sure of the inevitability of progress 'in general enlightenment', which is 'the proper destination' of human nature.[172] In the first two critiques, the progress of history is controlled by empirical forces alone, and the highest good is transcendent to our world.[173] In the 'Idea for a Universal History from a Cosmopolitan Point of View' (1784), history is seen as fulfilling a hidden scheme. The eighth thesis declares:

'distinguished not by their falsity/genuineness, but by the style in which they are imagined'. (*Imagined Communities: Reflections on the Origin and Spread of Nationalism* (London: Verso, 1983), 15.)

[169] *James Mill on Philosophy and Education*, ed. W. H. Burston (London: The Athlone Press, 1973), 187.

[170] Sir William Jones, 'On Asiatick History, Civil and Natural', *Asiatick Researches*, 4 (1794), 2.

[171] Kant, *Critique of Pure Reason*, 655.

[172] Immanuel Kant, 'What is Enlightenment?', in *On History*, ed. with an introduction by L. W. Beck (1963; Indianapolis: The Library of Liberal Arts, 1980), 7.

[173] Yirmiahu Yovel, *Kant and the Philosophy of History* (Princeton, NJ: Princeton University Press, 1980), 77, 72.

The history of mankind can be seen, in the large, as the realization of Nature's secret plan to bring forth a perfectly constituted state as the only condition in which the capacities of mankind can be fully developed, and also bring forth that external relation among nations which is perfectly adequate to this end.[174]

From the third critique onwards, however, the highest good becomes a historical goal, in which harmony will prevail between the systems of nature and morality.[175] For Kant, the history of reason has two main manifestations: one is the history of reason reshaping the world, and the other is the history of reason becoming known and explicated to itself. The first aspect of the history of reason is a practical process, whereby reason imprints itself upon the actual world, reshaping its empirical organization in the light of its own goals and interests. The second aspect is a theoretical process whereby human reason articulates its essential concepts, principles, and interests within a coherent system.[176] In 'The Architectonic of Pure Reason' Kant wrote that 'In accordance with reason's legislative prescriptions, our diverse modes of knowledge must not be permitted to be a mere rhapsody, but must form a system.' What is aimed at is '*architectonic* unity', where 'the scheme which originates from an idea, (in which reason propounds the ends *a priori*, and does not wait for them to be empirically given) serves as the basis'.[177] It is clear, then, that Kant's notion of history as progress was consistent with his epistemology as a whole. For those who adopted something akin to this epistemology, such as Southey,[178] there was less of a tension between the notion of reason moulding the world in a historical narrative of progress and their concept of the mind than in Mill's views.

The Grossest Images of Sensual Pleasure

Mill's distrust of the imagination was thus derived from Hartley's *Observations of Man* (1749), which placed the imagination low in the hierarchy of mental activity. But it was also reinforced by Mill's own puritanism. William Thomas has argued that Mill's strain of puritanism gave *The History of British India* its predominant

[174] Immanuel Kant, 'Idea for a Universal History from a Cosmopolitan Point of View', in *On History*, 21.

[175] Yovel, *Kant and History*, 72.

[176] Ibid. 6.

[177] Kant, *Critique of Pure Reason*, 653–4.

[178] See ch. 2.

tone.[179] This strain of puritanism was also detected by commentators in the early nineteenth century. In his attack on the philosophic radicals, Macaulay drew an explicit comparison between them and the Puritans when he claimed that 'Philosophical pride has done for them what spiritual pride did for the Puritans in a former age; it has generated in them an aversion for the fine arts, for elegant literature, and for the sentiments of chivalry.'[180] Similarly, in his critique of Mill's 'Essay on Government' he again noted their contempt for 'elegant literature'.[181] It was the combination of Mill's puritanism and his associationist psychology which was the basis of his distrust of the imagination.

Mill completed the divinity course at Edinburgh University in January 1797, and for a while was a Presbyterian preacher.[182] In 1805 he translated C. Viller's *The Spirit and Influence of the Reformation*, in which he takes the author to task for speaking of the Bible as mere scraps of the literature of distant ages: 'These books comprise the extraordinary code of laws communicated by a benevolent divinity to man.'[183] In his *Autobiography*, John Stuart Mill writes that his father taught him to take 'the strongest interest in the Reformation, as the great and decisive contest against priestly tyranny for liberty of thought'.[184] This view is evident in the 'Essay on Government' in which the elder Mill praised the Reformation as an example of how 'the power bestowed upon the people, of judging for themselves, has been productive of good effects, to a degree which has totally altered the condition of human nature, and exalted man to what may be called a different stage of existence'.[185] When he started his *History* in 1806, Mill was contributing to the Evangelical *Eclectic Review*.[186] Bain claims Mill became an atheist in 1808,[187] so it is possible that when Mill wrote the second book of his *History*, 'Of the Hindus', he was still a Christian. This is borne out by his contention that there are two sources of 'just and rational views of God', 'revelation' and 'sound reflection upon

179 William Thomas, *The Philosophic Radicals: Nine Studies in Theory and Practice 1817–1841* (Oxford: Clarendon Press, 1979), 101.

180 T. B. Macaulay, 'The Present Administration', *Edinburgh Review*, 46 (June–Oct. 1827), 261.

181 Macaulay, 'Utilitarian Logic and Politics', 160–1.

182 Alexander Bain, *James Mill: A Biography* (London: Longmans, Green, and Co., 1882), 21.

183 Cited by Bain, *Mill*, 52.

184 J. S. Mill, *Autobiography and Literary Essays*, ed. J. M. Robson and J. Stillinger, in *Collected Works of John Stuart Mill*, i (Toronto: University of Toronto Press, 1981), 45.

185 Mill, 'Essay on Government', 30.

186 Bain, *Mill*, 62.

187 Ibid. 79.

the frame and government of the universe'.[188] The sources he uses also indicate his allegiances. For example, he draws on the Serampore missionary William Ward's *A View of the History, Literature, and Religion of the Hindoos* (1811), which was one of the most notable works of the Baptist mission in India.[189] This work's missionary message and its harsh depiction of Hindu culture, reinforced Mill's own missionary zeal to redeem India from her own culture.

Ward's work was first published in 1811, but Mill frequently refers to the 1817 edition. This indicates that, even after the rejection of his faith, his connections with Protestant dissenters remained strong. He was one of the main contributors to the Quaker William Allen's *The Philanthropist* from 1810 onwards.[190] In 1809 he was involved in the formation of the Royal Lancastrian Society, afterwards called the British and Foreign School Society. His article on the Lancastrian dispute in the *Philanthropist* in 1812, 'Schools for All, in Preference to Schools for Churchmen Only', is less an attack on the Church of England's policy on education, than on its very right to exist. There were close similarities between Mill's ideas on education, and those of the Baptist mission at Serampore; both gave very little place to literature, art, and play.[191] They also emphasized the importance of 'useful' knowledge. Bentham's *Chrestomathia* (that is, 'conducive to useful learning') was published in 1817; it was written to set out the curriculum and teaching methods to be used in a new secondary day school for children of the 'middling and higher ranks in life'.[192] In a long footnote in his 'Essay on Education', Mill compared the curriculum of *Chrestomathia* with that of the Baptist missionary schools in India:

> We mention with extraordinary satisfaction, that an idea of education, hardly less extensive than what is here alluded to, has been adopted by that enlightened and indefatigable class of men, the Baptist Missionaries in India, for the population, poor as well as ignorant, of those extensive and populous regions.[193]

188 Mill, *History*, ed. Wilson, i. 226.

189 E. D. Potts, *British Baptist Missionaries in India 1793–1837: The History of Serampore and its Missions* (Cambridge: Cambridge University Press, 1967), 92.

190 Bain, *Mill*, 82.

191 J. S. Mill, *Autobiography*, 13, 39; M. A. Laird, *Missionaries and Education in Bengal 1793–1837* (Oxford: Clarendon Press, 1972), 264.

192 Jeremy Bentham, *Chrestomathia*, ed. M. J. Smith and W. H. Burston, in *The Collected Works of Jeremy Bentham* (Oxford: Clarendon Press, 1983), p. xi.

193 Mill, 'Essay on Education', 108–11.

Mill also continued to eulogize the Reformation. In *A Fragment on Mackintosh* (1835) Hobbes is compared to Luther as a great thinker,[194] and in an article towards the end of his life, he claimed that mankind would have been damned by the 'threefold cord' of Church, state, and the law, had it not been for printing and the Reformation.[195]

So Mill rejected his faith but retained its basic moral outlook.[196] In some ways, Mill wrote more as a dissenting Protestant than a utilitarian in his attack on Hindu culture. This is borne out by his attitude to the caste system. He does not consider the possible utility of the caste system in an Indian context, nor that in India it might ensure the greatest happiness of the greatest number. He considers Muslim society superior to Hindu society because of the absence of a caste system, 'that institution which stands a more effectual barrier against the welfare of human nature than any other institution which the working of caprice and of selfishness have ever produced'.[197] Wilson, by contrast, expressed a more positive and sophisticated view of the caste system:

> The multiplication of castes in India . . . is the work of the people, amongst the most degraded of whom, prevails, not the shame, but the 'pride' of caste. The lowest native is no outcaste, he has an acknowledged place in society; he is the member of a class; and he is invariably more retentive of the distinction than those above him. In depicturing [*sic*] the horrors of the system, European writers lose sight of the compensations.[198]

He argues that one of the lower castes in India may be 'less unhappy, than many of the paupers of the civilised communities of Europe, with which no man owns companionship or kindred'.[199] Mill's criticism of the caste system as inegalitarian was not based on utilitarian grounds. There is no necessary connection between utilitarianism and its creed of the greatest happiness of the greatest number, and democracy. For a part of his life Bentham was not a democrat. Bentham, James Mill, and John Stuart Mill produced

[194] James Mill, *A Fragment on Mackintosh* (London: Baldwin and Cradock, 1835), 19.

[195] James Mill, 'The State of the Nation', *London Review*, 1 (Apr.–July 1835), 8–9.

[196] James Mill, *The History of British India*, ed. William Thomas (Chicago: University of Chicago Press, 1975), p. xv.

[197] Mill, *History*, ed. Wilson, ii. 343.

[198] Ibid. i. 140.

[199] Ibid. i. 140.

three different accounts of democracy although they were all utilitarians. Also, although Bentham did give a high priority to equality as an end of utility, he made it clear that other ends such as security, subsistence, and abundance have higher status.[200] It was Mill who converted Bentham to the reform movement; but much of Bentham's work had been written during the Enlightenment, when he trusted in benevolent despotism to effect his reforms. His change of political views was only a change in the appropriate methods to achieve his aims. The basic idea of the reforms, and the final end to which they were devoted, the maximization of utility, did not change. Nor did the intellectual foundations and attitudes which make such an end appropriate.[201] Mill's strictures on the caste system as inegalitarian were more in the tradition of Protestant denunciation of the system as maintaining a priesthood apparently similar to the Roman Catholic clergy. Charles Grant's *Observations on the State of Society among Asiatic Subjects of Great Britain* had expressed this attitude. He condemned the caste system as an 'oppressive and insulting tyranny', which subjects the lower castes to 'perpetual abasement'. He argued that if 'the genius of a Newton should arise in that class, it could have no room to expand'.[202] He also considered the 'whole fabric' of Hinduism as 'the work of a crafty and imperious priesthood, who feigned a divine revelation and appointment, to invest their own order, in perpetuity, with the most absolute empire over the civil state of the Hindoos, as well as over their minds'.[203] If there is any genuine knowledge among the Hindus, it is 'monopolized and concealed by the Brahmins' and it 'spread little light among the great body of the people'.[204] Mill cites Grant's *Observations* to substantiate his view that the 'priesthood is generally found to usurp the greatest authority, in the lowest state of society'. It is 'only in rude and ignorant times that men are so overwhelmed with the power of superstition as to pay unbounded veneration and obedience to those who artfully clothe themselves with the terrors of religion'.[205] Mill draws a comparison with the Roman Catholic clergy: 'It was in the dark ages that the Romish priesthood usurped so many privileges.'[206] Thus, Mill's view of the

200 Rosen, *Bentham and Representative Democracy*, 200, 217.

201 Ross Harrison, *Bentham* (London: Routledge & Kegan Paul, 1983), 8–9.

202 C. Grant, 'Observations on the State of Society among Asiatic Subjects of Great Britain . . .', *Parliamentary Papers*, 10 (1812–13), paper 282, pp. 44–5.

203 Ibid. 45.

204 Ibid. 75.

205 Mill, *History*, ed. Wilson, i. 128.

206 Ibid. i. 128.

caste system as perpetuating a priesthood and its monopolies was influenced less by utilitarianism than by a tradition of Protestant denunciation of caste, clearly represented by Grant's *Observations*.

The terms Mill uses to describe the imagination and its products suggest a threatening, unrestrained Eros which challenges reason's supremacy. Both Bentham and Mill exhibit the urge to tame ungoverned production. For Bentham, the principle of utility, which 'neither requires nor admits of any other regulator than itself',[207] provides the standard by which to reduce a body of customary law into one of statutory law, and to survey the 'trackless wild' of the field of legislation, restraining 'the licentiousness of interpretation' in law.[208] He talks of punishment as 'an *artificial* consequence annexed' by political authority to an offensive act, with the view to cutting short the production of events 'similar to the obnoxious part of its natural consequences, in other instances'.[209] Mill's *History* could not have been written without the 'exercise of discrimination, that is, of criticism in a chaotic mass'.[210] Referring to the confused state of law in India he declares classification to be 'the groundwork of all accurate thought', and then proceeds to classify Hindu law himself, in a way carrying out Bentham's boast of being able to produce a useful code out of the Koran.[211] It was this attempt to tame trackless wilds which gave the *History* its predominant tone. But Mill's conception of utility differed considerably from Bentham's. Mill gave Bentham's theories a 'puritanical twist'.[212] For Bentham, the term 'utility' denoted anything which led to pleasurable consequences.[213] For Mill, the term 'utility' denoted usefulness, as he made clear in his *History* when he elaborated a scale of measurement to assess cultures.[214] Mill could not accept Bentham's hedonism. John Stuart Mill describes his father's position as Epicurean, 'in as much as it was utilitarian, taking as the exclusive test of right and wrong, the tendency of actions to produce pleasure or pain'. But he was also a Cynic, in that he had 'scarcely any belief in pleasure', and 'deemed very few of them

207 Bentham, *Principles of Morals*, 58.

208 Jeremy Bentham, *Corrigenda for Of Laws in General*, 232.

209 Bentham, *Principles of Morals*, 157.

210 Mill, *History*, ed. Wilson, i, p. xvii.

211 Jeremy Bentham, 'On Time and Place', *The Works of Jeremy Bentham*, ed. J. Bowring (Edinburgh: Wm Tait, 1843), i. 191.

212 Thomas, *Philosophic Radicals*, 12.

213 Harrison, *Bentham*, 170.

214 See ch. 4.

worth the price which, at least in the present state of society, must be paid for them'. He also considered 'the greatest number of miscarriages in life . . . to be attributable to the overvaluing of pleasures'. For Mill, temperance was the 'central point of educational precept'.[215] As R. A. Fenn has pointed out, the elder Mill's ideal of mastering the greatest number of felicitous associations and of rising above mere short-term pleasure through the practising of temperance looks forward to his son's stress on the importance of quality, and not just quantity, in assessing the weight which should be given to various pleasures.[216]

However, Mill sought not just to break with the patriarchalist idiom of the *ancien régime*, but also with the tradition of what we can call infidel radicalism. Jones's work on comparative mythology in the *Asiatick Researches*, the periodical published by the Asiatic Society of Bengal, could be seen as part of the tradition of comparativism represented by such writers as Volney, Dupuis, Sir William Drummond, Erasmus Darwin, and Richard Payne Knight, all of whom drew parallels between Christianity and heathen mythologies in order to refute Christianity's claims to a unique revelation. There was also a significant interest in such works in fertility rites and cults, with a corresponding celebration of sexuality in opposition to what were seen as the ascetic tendencies of contemporary Christian mores.[217] As late as 1822, Coleridge's son, Hartley Coleridge, in an article for the *London Magazine* entitled 'On the Poetical Use of the Heathen Mythology', attacked the sceptical use which this sort of comparative mythology was being put to, and defended the exclusive claims of Christianity and Christian culture itself.[218] Jones's hymns to Hindu deities, most of which had been written in 1785, had not only emphasized the parallels between the mythologies of different cultures, but were also characterized by an imagery of fertility which was part of the celebration of the notion of sakti. In another of Jones's poems, *The Enchanted Fruit; Or, The Hindu Wife: An Antediluvian Tale*, there is an explicit association between a liberating celebration of sexuality and matriarchy.[219] It depicts the Hindu golden age as governed by the 'grand rule' that 'WHAT PLEASETH, HATH NO LAW

[215] J. S. Mill, *Autobiography*, 50.

[216] Fenn, *James Mill*, 50.

[217] Marilyn Butler, *Romantics, Rebels and Reactionaries: English Literature and its Background 1760–1830* (Oxford: Oxford University Press, 1981), 78, 130.

[218] Hartley Coleridge, 'On the Poetical Use of the Heathen Mythology', *London Magazine*, 5 (Feb. 1822), 113–20.

[219] *Works*, vi. 181.

FORBIDDEN', and it compares this age with the contemporary epoch 'bound by vile unnatural laws', named after the goddess Kali, a goddess 'By some base woman-hater fram'd'.[220] Matriarchy was not only associated with India; Thomas Taylor, the Neoplatonist, wrote a poem, 'The Dream', published in 1798, which celebrated the Goddess Diana as part of what he called the 'vivific series', of which other goddesses such as Isis were also manifestations.[221] This 'vivific series' was close to the sakti which Jones celebrated in his hymns. So Jones's Orient was also the *locus* of a fecundity which was threatening to Mill's instrumental rationality. Furthermore, they celebrated a mythological and religious system which was characterized by the 'grossest images of sensual pleasure'. Mill argued that it was 'by no means unnatural for the religion of a rude people to unite opposite qualities, to preach the most harsh austerities, and at the same time to encourage the loosest morality'.[222] On the assumption that laws are 'proofs of the manners of a people', he concludes from an examination of Hindu law on adultery, which 'includes every unlawful species of sexual indulgence, from the least, to the most injurious, or offensive', that it indicates 'one of the most depraved states of the sexual appetite'.[223] In the *History of British India*, the imagination was often depicted in terms of a threatening Eros. The celebration of sexuality through non-Christian myths was seen as not only part of this Eros, but also as a positive comment on certain forms of religious experience. Utilitarianism was very much a secular philosophy, and at least in Mill's formulation of it, there could be no place for such experience.

But Mill was not just attacking infidel radicalism; he was also reacting against the libertine tradition of radicalism. This tradition consisted of hostility to religious authority, and a belief in hedonistic morality, with an emphasis on instinctual sexuality.[224] John Wilkes's *Essay on Woman* was part of this tradition, and it continued into the 1890s with Oscar Wilde. Its literature was often anti-establishment and obscene; it highlighted the sexual crimes and hypocrisies of the establishment. This literature reached its height in 1820–1 with the Queen Caroline affair.[225] But there was

220 Ibid. vi. 180–1.

221 *Monthly Magazine and British Register for 1797*, 4 (1798), 375–6.

222 Mill, *History*, ed. Wilson, i. 294.

223 Ibid. i. 186.

224 Ian McCalman, 'Unrespectable Radicalism: Infidels and Pornography in Early Nineteenth-Century London', *Past and Present*, 104 (1984), 99.

225 Ibid. 84.

also another, more serious angle to this tradition of unrespectable radicalism. Some of the London booksellers and publishers in the post-war period such as George Cannon and John Benjamin Brookes dealt not only in pornography; they also pirated copies of notorious poets such as Byron and Shelley.[226] Their purpose was to attack the imposition of a code of conduct by the Church and ruling élite. Some of Bentham's work could be seen to be part of this tradition. In a manuscript of 1817 entitled 'Sextus', Bentham defended the principle of utility against asceticism. He argued that sexual pleasure received more hostility from religious morality because it was greater than any other pleasures, and more importantly, because unlike any other pleasure, it was within the equal reach of the poor and rich.[227] He also claimed that the 'religious terrors' on which asceticism rests were derived from the writings of St Paul and not from those of Jesus,[228] an argument which he later developed in *Not Paul but Jesus*. So Bentham's hedonism could be seen as part of this tradition of sexual radicalism. Mill was perhaps more sensitive to the growing influence of the evangelicals on the moral tone of the age, a hegemony which they established out of all proportions to their numbers.[229] As a result, he was also more anxious to present political radicalism as respectable, and this could only be achieved if it distanced itself from the libertine tradition of radicalism. It was Mill and not Bentham who contributed partly to radicalism's absorption of an ethic of respectability and self-improvement during the 1820s and 1830s.

But the similarities between Mill's puritanism and evangelicalism must not be overestimated. Boyd Hilton has shown how the tradition of 'devotional' economics of Christian and evangelical writers attacked the secular political economy of such figures as Ricardo and the Mills.[230] The premisses of this kind of 'soteriological economics' ran counter to Bentham's hedonism; what was important was not the pursuit of pleasure, but the sacrifice of earthly pleasure for the sake of an everlasting and final reward.[231] For such thinkers the economy was an arena of spiritual trial, which is why they did not reject the discipline of political economy as a mode of enquiry,[232]

[226] Ibid. 99.

[227] Bentham MS, University College London, Box 161, fo. 8.

[228] Ibid. fo. 1.

[229] Boyd Hilton, *The Age of Atonement: The Influence of Evangelicalism on Social and Economic Thought, 1795–1865* (Oxford: Clarendon Press, 1988), 219.

[230] Ibid. 6–7. [231] Ibid. 33. [232] Ibid. 36.

as Southey seemed to be doing when he referred to it as a 'pseudo-science'.[233] What was distinctively modern about utilitarianism was that it was a secular idiom. It tried to formulate a whole new vocabulary to describe polities. In order to do this, it had to attack and replace non-secular ways of depicting and defending societies, ways which had been redefined and strengthened in this period of revitalized conservatism during which religion set the terms for loyal patriotism. R. A. Fenn has pointed out that Mill favoured systematic, all encompassing approaches, but he has not suggested any reasons why this should be so.[234] As already indicated, as early as 1780 Bentham had described himself as a system-maker and system-builder.[235] For utilitarianism to succeed as the 'militant faith' which Mill's *History* transformed it into,[236] it had to offer the same assurances and certainties that religious idioms could; hence Mill's writings favour systematic, all-encompassing approaches with a pseudo-deductive style of argument which stresses the certainty of conclusions derived from unassailable premisses. Furthermore, it was only in this way that he could formulate the unificatory epistemology for the project of censorial jurisprudence, which would enable him to formulate a programme of reform not just for Britain but for British India as well.

There are other more specific reasons for his system building. The movement for radical reform in the early nineteenth century was divided. This was partly due to the mixed social composition of the radical movement which reflected the change in the population of London because of immigration from all over the British isles.[237] There were also disagreements over whether or not constitutional means should be used to further the cause of reform. This was the case after the Ministry of All Talents, which came to power in 1806. This was the only government in the main Whig tradition between 1783 and 1827, but it achieved little in the way of reform.[238] Between 1812 and 1816 there was no central aspiration or direction to metropolitan radicalism, and disagreements over strategies

[233] Robert Southey, 'On Emigration', in *Essays, Moral and Political*, 2 vols. (London: John Murray, 1832), ii. 210.

[234] Fenn, *James Mill*, 1.

[235] See ch. 4.

[236] Duncan Forbes, 'James Mill and India', *Cambridge Journal*, 5 (Oct. 1951–Sept. 1952), 31.

[237] Hone, *For the Cause of Truth*, 3.

[238] Clive Emsley, *British Society and the French Wars 1793–1815* (London: Macmillan, 1979), 129.

increased in 1816 when there was mounting distress after a bad harvest, especially after the violence at the Spa Fields meeting of 2 December. Cobbett and Hunt supported direct action; Burdett wanted to work within the constitution. Both Cobbett and Hunt were viewed with suspicion by Francis Place, Bentham and Mill, as dangerous mob orators who had done much damage to the prospects of reform.[239] Even the Gagging Acts and repressive legislation of 1817 did not renew radical solidarity.[240] The new parliamentary session which opened on 14 January 1819 reinforced the isolated position of the radical MPs, and relations between Whigs and radicals were as strained as ever, with the pamphlet war between the two clarifying neither radical nor Whig political theory.[241] Nor did the Peterloo massacre of 16 August 1817 or the Six Acts introduced on 29 November help to heal these divisions.[242] Ann Hone concludes that divisiveness and dissension were the notable features of radicalism.[243] This is part of the reason why Bentham in his *Plan of Parliamentary Reform* of 1817 and James Mill in his 'Essay on Government' argued for radical reform on the basis of clear systematic principles. It was hoped these clear principles would bridge the gap between the different classes of reformers and heal their divisions by showing clearly as the subtitle of Bentham's *Plan* put it, the 'Necessity of Radical, and the Inadequacy of Moderate, Reform'.[244] This would also give the radical movement a well-defined goal and a sense of direction, and above all, a clearly articulated theory which both the Whigs and Tories lacked. Indeed, Bentham was at pains to show how there was a 'General coincidence of interests' between the latter two in their opposition to radical reform, which explained the 'tacit *co-operation*' between them.[245]

The differences between Bentham's and Mill's idiom and that of other radicals are also evident in the criticisms Bentham made of the doctrine of natural rights. In 1809 he criticized Major John Cartwright's definition of political liberty as 'a sacred right of nature' by describing such a concept as a 'mere lawyer-like fiction

239 Hone, *For the Cause of Truth*, 220, 260–7.
240 Ibid. 273.
241 Ibid. 293.
242 Ibid. 305.
243 Ibid. 318.
244 For an account of the development and content of moderate reform, see J. R. Dinwiddy, '"The Patriotic Linen-Draper": Robert Waithman and the Revival of Radicalism in the City of London, 1795–1818', *Bulletin of the Institute of Historical Research*, 46 (May 1973), 72–4.
245 Bentham, *Plan of Parliamentary Reform*, pp. cccvi, cccix.

invented for a mask to the fallacy called Petitio Principii'.[246] In a manuscript of 1810–11 entitled *Fallacies*, he considered in detail the doctrine of the rights of man. There are three main objections he makes to it. First, he considers it a vague generality which, unlike the principle of utility, 'disdains experience, inquiry, argument'. Secondly, it offers no method to resolve conflicts; on the contrary, 'on every difference of will or opinion [it] excites man to the use of force,' nor can it provide any reason for 'restraining any man from doing any thing that he pleases'. Thirdly, it 'consists in the allegation of a *right* as having existence not under and in virtue of but in opposition to the existing law', whereas it is the purpose of legislation to confer and define such rights within a broad political and social framework.[247] As J. R. Dinwiddy has argued, it is the incisiveness and modernity of the ideas in such writings which provides a striking contrast between Bentham's political theorizing and that of most constitutional theorizing of the time.[248]

Another reason for Bentham's and Mill's all-encompassing approaches and model-building was that the popular demand for reform had always fluctuated with economic conditions. For example, demands increased during the crisis of the post-war period, but when conditions improved in London from 1820 to 1826 these demands subsided.[249] The demands for reform were primarily demands for economical reform, as the increasing importance of the ideology of free trade espoused by the middle classes reflected. This attacked such mercantilist practices as the East India Company's monopoly of trade, and also the Orders in Council of 1807, which had prohibited seaborne trade with France and her allies by neutrals. Parliamentary reform was not central to this doctrine of free trade.[250] Bentham and Mill wanted to base their programmes for reform on more permanent principles, and political relationships, rather than economic ones, remained central to their analysis of society. As far as they were concerned there were good reasons for radical and systematic reform which were independent of the flux of economic conditions. Again in this they were different from most radical propagandists who rarely used

246 Bentham MS, University College London, Box 125, fo. 141, p. 11.

247 Bentham MS, University College London, Box 105, fos. 16–19.

248 J. R. Dinwiddy, 'Bentham's Transition to Political Radicalism 1809–10', *Journal of the History of Ideas*, 36 (Oct.–Dec. 1975), 700.

249 Hone, *For the Cause of Truth*, 356.

250 Emsley, *The French Wars*, 177.

abstract theorizing and often used current situations and events to support arguments for the necessity of political change.[251]

The Gains of a Higher Character

The systematic and all-encompassing character of Mill's thought must not obscure its contradictions and tensions. Some of these have already been discussed. Furthermore, the *History* itself seems to suffer a loss of nerve in dealing with British India. This is evident in its abrupt ending:

> With regard to subsequent events, the official papers, and other sources of information, are not sufficiently at command. Here, therefore, it is necessary that, for the present, this *History* should close.[252]

There is no attempt to draw any overall conclusion. Mill's anti-imperialist stance was part of a general liberal denunciation of the empire, which, being conducted on mercantilist principles, offended liberal values. The doctrine of free trade, utilitarian demands for inexpensive government, and economists' stress on 'productive', non-governmental expenditure, led to the view that colonies were a corrupting financial burden.[253] None the less, the philosophical radicals were ambivalent about imperialism. After the 1830s many classical writers and philosophic radicals supported the movement for extending the empire. This movement embodied a vision of a new type of society which would be a fulfilment of liberal values rather than an aberration from them.[254] Bentham wavered in his anti-colonial stance, although his publication of 'Emancipate Your Colonies!' in 1830 suggested that he had returned to this stance.[255] But he was still ambivalent. As we have seen, he also made an exception to the applicability of his argument in the case of India.[256] Even before the support for the extension of empire in the 1830s, Mill's *History* expressed this ambivalence clearly. It is divided between an attack on India as a financial burden, and as perpetuating bad government in Britain, and a vision of embodying liberal values in a new society. The *History* remains indecisive in its

251 Hone, *For the Cause of Truth*, 326–7.

252 Mill, *History*, ed. Wilson, vi. 479.

253 Donald Winch, *Classical Political Economy and Colonies* (London: London School of Economics and Political Science, 1965), 144.

254 Ibid. 144.

255 Ibid. 38.

256 See ch. 4.

attitude, hence the lack of any overall conclusion. It is Wilson, rather than Mill, who is positive about the British role in India.

Wilson argues that it is too narrow to see British rule in India simply in economic terms:

> The gain of a higher character, the moral and political power derived from India by England, is a much more real, and important, and honourable benefit, than all the pounds, shillings, and pence that have ever been, or ever will be conveyed from the pockets of the people of India to those of the people of Great Britain.[257]

Wilson sees it as the duty 'imposed upon us by the supremacy of our power' to establish 'UNIVERSAL TRANQUILITY UNDER THE GUARANTEE AND SUPREMACY OF THE BRITISH GOVERNMENT'.[258] He condemns the policy of non-interference in the affairs of native states as a form of moral cowardice: 'However mischievous the consequences, and although engendering within their respective dominions tumult, anarchy, and civil war, non-interference was to be the policy which was to be substituted for that of a benevolent and powerful protector.'[259] This was a variant of the notion that the only way to atone for the original sin of acquiring India was to fulfil the duty imposed by that acquisition.[260] Wilson seems to be close to Charles Grant's view that 'we cannot renounce them [the Indians] without guilt, though we may also contract great guilt in the government of them'.[261] Towards the end of the *History*, Wilson again stresses the 'evils which are inseparable from the . . . unnatural rule of foreign masters differing in origin, language, civilization, and religion'.[262] The sympathy these rulers have with India does not arise from 'an identity of interests or reciprocity of feeling'. Since they 'have no permanent stake in the country, no personal pride in its embellishment, no personal profit in its improvement', India can never be home to them. Their sympathy with Indians arises only from 'a sense of duty'.[263] Wilson was expressing an attitude which Hutchins has described as 'the Victorian cult of conduct', which was akin to the notion of 'the White Man's Burden'. Pain and discomfort were felt to be useful in character

257 Mill, *History*, ed. Wilson, vi. 472.

258 Ibid. viii. 412.

259 Ibid. ix. 253–4.

260 Francis Hutchins, *The Illusion of Permanence: British Imperialism in India* (Princeton, NJ: Princeton University Press, 1967), 5.

261 Grant, 'Observations', 23.

262 Mill, *History*, ed. Wilson, ix. 394.

263 Ibid. ix. 394.

building. India became valued not for its pleasures of promise but because it was possible to be unhappy there. It was only in adversities that one discovered one's duty.[264] To a certain extent this is implicit in Mill's and Jones's work. Wilson felt he had some affinity with Mill, which is why he wrote a continuation of Mill's *History* and not an entirely new work. But it is Wilson who makes this explicit, and so justifies British rule by the idea of the moral responsibility of the British in India.

To a certain extent, Mill's loss of confidence in his *History* points to the limited influence which utilitarianism had on British India. Bentham described Lord William Bentinck's appointment as governor-general of India in 1828 as heralding 'the golden age of British India'.[265] In 1833 a commission was established to frame a body of codified law for the whole of British India (the Law Commission under Macaulay).[266] This act embodied the principles of centralized authority and uniformity expressed in James Mill in his evidence before the Parliamentary Committee in 1832, although it did not follow his recommendations exactly.[267] It was Mill who recommended Macaulay to the directors of the East India Company for the post of legal member of the governor-general's council, and who defined that post. In the course of his evidence, Mill stressed the need for an Indian legislative council whose business should consist of studying what laws were required, and then framing them. These laws would apply throughout British India, and would replace the previous system of separate 'regulations' made by the governors-general of the three presidencies of Madras, Bombay, and Bengal.[268] Mill had great confidence in this experiment in India. In a letter of 27 August 1834, he wrote, 'India will be the first country on earth to boast a system of law and judicature as near perfection as the circumstances of the people would admit.'[269] Behind these innovations lie the ideas of legislative process embodied in Bentham's *Codification Proposal and Constitutional*

[264] Hutchins, *The Illusion of Permanence*, 28.

[265] Bentham MS, University College London, 'To Lord William Bentinck', 19 Nov. 1829, Box 10, fo. 179 (partly in copyist's hand).

[266] Eric Stokes, *The English Utilitarians and India* (Oxford: Clarendon Press, 1963), 173.

[267] John Clive, *Thomas Babington Macaulay: The Shaping of the Historian* (London: Secker & Warburg, 1973), 312. [268] Ibid. 311.

[269] James Mill, *Selected Economic Writings*, ed. D. Winch (Edinburgh: Oliver and Boyd, 1966), 19.

Code.[270] The cast of the Penal Code drafted by Macaulay in 1835 and enacted in 1860 as the Criminal Law of India, was derived from Bentham, as 'a code of law drawn not from existing practice or from foreign law systems, but created *ex nihilo* by the disinterested philosophic intelligence'.[271] The actual drafting of the Penal Code reflected Bentham's influence in the use of improvements he advocated;[272] and Macaulay adopted Bentham's nomenclature and classfication of offences in *An Introduction to the Principles of Morals and Legislation*. Thus, Governor-General Bentinck's remark to Mill, 'I am going to British India, but I shall not be Governor-General; it is you who will be Governor-General,' and Bentham's that 'Mill will be the living executive—I shall be the dead legislature of British India,' were apparently not idle rhetoric.[273]

But this influence must not be exaggerated. Although the penal code was drafted in 1835 it was not enacted as the criminal law of India until 1860. This timelag indicates an important point about British India. And this was that by many British rule in India was seen to be a failure by the time of the 1857 rebellion. For example, British capitalism in India was a relative failure. India had not become a rich colony of plantation and conversion as some had thought in the 1820s. Little money was put into the economy and profits were quickly repatriated because of the uncertain trading environment.[274] India had also been written off as an indigenous plantation economy in which peasants produced crops under state control for flourishing export markets. Despite its size India was a relatively inefficient producer of agricultural raw materials with only a weak foothold in foreign markets. The British never gained sufficient control over peasant producers to extract cash crops as a form of tribute.[275] The structure of landholding as it had emerged from the pre-colonial period and been consolidated by British administrators and revenue courts meant profits were monopolized by rural money lenders and landlords. The Indian authorities approached matters of agrarian reform with the greatest of caution.[276]

[270] Stokes, *English Utilitarians and India*, 163.

[271] Ibid. 224–5.

[272] Ibid. 230.

[273] Forbes, 'Mill and India', 25. The former remark was reported in a letter to Colonel Young from Bentham, 28 Dec. 1827, in *Works*, x. 576–8.

[274] C. A. Bayly, *Indian Society and the Making of the British Empire* (Cambridge: Cambridge University Press, 1988), 202.

[275] Ibid. 202.

[276] Ibid. 203.

The societies of the Indian subcontinent proved to be much more flexible than had been supposed, and survived and consolidated themselves.[277] Furthermore, the British in India often pretended to have power which in reality they did not possess. B. S. Cohn has stressed the importance of studying these levels of power[278] and Anil Seal has pointed out the extent to which British rule in India depended upon local power élites.[279] This has also been the view of R. E. Frykenburg, who has argued that the structure of the colonial state was dependent on local and traditional power.[280] Thus the so-called age of reform of the 1830s was limited. It was not until the 1860s that programme of reform for public works, Anglicization, and the law really got under way. Before this period utilitarianism had a limited effect on British India. It failed to achieve its purpose of becoming the imperial ideology of British rule, and failed to give British rule a consistency of purpose which would replace the conflicting aims of a body which was merchant, ruler, and land revenue farmer.

[277] C. A. Bayly, *Indian Society and the Making of the British Empire*, 205.

[278] B. S. Cohn, *An Anthropologist among the Historians and Other Essays* (Delhi: Oxford University Press, 1987), 485.

[279] Anil Seal, 'Imperialism and Nationalism in India', in J. Gallagher and A. Seal, *Locality, Province and Nation: Essays on Indian Politics, 1870–1940* (Cambridge: Cambridge University Press, 1973), 9. See also J. Rosselli, *Lord William Bentinck: The Making of a Liberal Imperialist 1774–1839* (London: Chatto and Windus for Sussex University Press, 1974), 298.

[280] See 'Village Strength in South India', in R. E. Frykenburg (ed.), *Land Control and Social Structure in Indian History* (Madison, Wis.: University of Wisconsin Press, 1969), 243–4; also 'Company Circari in the Carnatic, *c.*1799–1859: The Inner Logic of Political Systems in India', in R. G. Fox (ed.), *Realm and Region in Traditional India* (Delhi: Vikas, 1977), 117–64.

CONCLUSION: MILL'S *HISTORY* AS A 'CLASSIC IN THE HISTORY OF PHILISTINISM'[1]

This study has suggested that the emergence of utilitarianism and the conservative ideology which it attacked in the early nineteenth century was closely involved with the British imperial experience in India. It is difficult to make a distinction between colonial and domestic issues when considering the nature of ideology in this period. Indeed, it was crucial to the emergence of utilitarianism as a rhetoric of reform to ignore any such distinction. In doing so it elaborated an idiom in which to compare and contrast cultures, as well as to criticize them; this enabled it to throw some light on the problem of what constituted consistency between one's political views in Britain and one's political views in British India. It is this, and the whole character of the body of ideas of which it was a part, which distinguishes the liberal imperialism of James Mill from that of such figures as Jones. Furthermore, an important part of Mill's critique of the revitalized conservatism of his time was an attack on the relationship between notions of the imagination, which he considered epistemologically unsound and politically dangerous, and the creation of an Orient in the work of Jones and his colleagues. This dimension of Mill's *History* has been somewhat neglected. For example, even Ronald Inden, whilst he points out in his analysis of the *History* as a 'hegemonic' text that Mill equated India with an imagination which was threatening in its fecundity,[2] omits to mention that the *History* was first and foremost an attack on the ruling British ideology of the time. It was in India that this ideology was writ large against an alien background. So whilst the *History* did equate India with a threatening imagination, it was more importantly an attempted critique of a politics of the imagination, which underpinned the conservative ideology which

1 William Thomas, *Mill* (Oxford: Oxford University Press, 1985), 68.

2 R. Inden, *Imagining India* (Oxford: Basil Blackwell, 1990), 44–5, 49.

was the target of his attack,[3] and which resulted in what Mill believed were distorted views on India and the British role there. These politics were also intimately involved with the defining and construction of cultural identities, a concern which was intensified by the impact of the French Revolution.

In its analysis of texts which can be seen to form part of an orientalism, this study has tended to disagree with some aspects of Edward Said's thesis.[4] Perhaps the major problem thrown up by Said's work is what one scholar has called 'Orientalism in Reverse',[5] but for the purposes of this study, it is important to consider briefly whether Foucault's and Said's arguments about the relationship between power and knowledge can help or hinder us in understanding the nature of British rule in India in this period. The extent to which scholars have pointed out the British reliance on local networks of power has already been pointed out.[6] Imperial power, in India at least, was of a much more fragile nature than the sort of imperial power depicted in Said's *Orientalism*. In the late eighteenth and early nineteenth centuries British rule in India was hardly imbued with a singular idiom or purpose. The status of the Company as merchant, ruler, and revenue farmer was much debated about. Its relations with Parliament, the Board of Control, and the Court of Directors were complex and sometimes acrimonious. In a persuasive essay on the recruitment and training of East India Company servants, B. S. Cohn has argued that Haileybury helped to define a distinctive ethos for the Company's servants, which, together with the fact that most of them were drawn from what he calls the old service families, made for an eighteenth-century fossil culture.[7] It was the anomalous nature of the East India Company which its radical critics emphasized. Furthermore, as Christopher Bayly has

[3] The classic account of the literature of the so-called 'Age of Revolution' from the 1790s to the 1830s as a literature of reaction remains Marilyn Butler's *Romantics, Rebels, and Reactionaries: English Literature and its Background 1760–1830* (Oxford: Oxford University Press, 1981).

[4] See introduction. For some wider attempts at criticizing Said, see the review symposium of *Orientalism* in the *Journal of Asian Studies*, 39 (May 1980). For a brilliant critique of Foucault which in some ways applies to Said as well, since he relies on Foucault for his methodology, see Charles Taylor, 'Foucault on Freedom and Truth', *Political Theory*, 12 (May 1984), 152–83.

[5] Sadik Jalal al-'Azm, 'Orientalism and Orientalism in Reverse', *Khamsin: Journal of Revolutionary Socialists of the Middle East*, 8 (1981), 5–26.

[6] See ch. 5.

[7] B. S. Cohn, 'The Recruitment and Training of British Civil Servants in India, 1600–1860', in *An Anthropologist among the Historians and Other Essays* (Delhi: Oxford University Press, 1987), 500–33.

pointed out, the East India Company's rule came to be seen as a dismal failure before 1857. Many of the professed objectives of British rule were not achieved, and disorder was endemic up to 1857.[8] Documents such as the 'Fifth Report from the Select Committee on the Affairs of the East India Company' (1812) reflect the experimental and cautious nature of British rule at the time. It also reflected a sensitivity to the complexities of local polities and the Company's relation to them,[9] as well as an awareness of the fragile nature of Company rule.[10] The report was also adamant that the civil administration of justice should respect the views and interests of the 'subsisting manners and usages of the people'.[11] If there was a dominant concern of British rule in this period, it was to appropriate and legitimize itself through indigenous idioms.[12] This does not seem to fit into Said's rather monolithic conception of the irresistibility of imperial power. There were threads of continuity between the successor states to Mughal power in eighteenth-century India and British rule in this period. To a certain extent, the East India Company was pushing to its conclusion the logic of the political economy of its precursors.[13] In other words, the basis for many of the features of East India Company rule were already laid in the preceding period, and British rule was not a startling imposition or break from the past. The Mughal emperor continued to be a source of authority long after the decline of effective Mughal imperial power, and the British, like other regional powers, showed scrupulous regard for this authority.[14] Finally, the extent to which the indigenous societies of the subcontinent survived, adapted, and consolidated themselves throughout this period also points to the complexity of the interactions between these societies and British rule in India, and to the way in which Indian groups were active agents, and not passive bystanders and victims in their creation as colonial subjects.[15]

[8] C. A. Bayly, *Indian Society and the Making of the British Empire* (Cambridge: Cambridge University Press, 1988), 200–6.

[9] *Parliamentary Papers*, 7 (1812), 20.

[10] Ibid. 70, 70–4.

[11] Ibid. 13.

[12] See e.g. Jorg Fisch, *Cheap Lives and Dear Limbs: The British Transformation of the Bengal Criminal Law 1769–1817* (Wiesbaden: Franz Steiner Verlag, 1983), which examines the complex motives dictating the British administration of Islamic law in their territories.

[13] C. A. Bayly, *Imperial Meridian: The British Empire and the World, 1780–1830* (London: Longman, 1989), 60.

[14] See ch. 1.

[15] Bayly, *Indian Society and the Making of the British Empire*, 5, 38, 45–78, 206.

However, although this study runs counter to some aspects of Said's thesis, it can be seen to reinforce his argument on another level, in so far as whilst Mill attacked the Orient of Jones's imagination and the epistemology underpinning it, his *History of British India* was still unable to view India in terms other than as part of a strategy for attacking British society itself; India was important only in so far as it played a part in a larger political and epistemological venture whose purpose was to fashion a critique of the ruling British ideology of the time. But it is also important to point out the self-reinforcing nature of Said's argument and the all-encompassing notion of power which it relies on in its analysis of the strategies of orientalism. By distancing oneself from the circularity of Said's argument, and replacing his all-embracing notion of power with a more limited notion of power, it might be possible to bring out even more forcefully the subtlety and profundity of various forms of orientalism, whilst paying heed to their conflicting strands and complexities. Said's argument is self-reinforcing in so far as it does not make clear whether a sound understanding of another culture is possible, and what such an understanding would consist of if it were possible. In this way he is able to criticize orientalists on two opposed counts. If the Orient is made familiar, if its foreignness is translated, and so as Said puts it, 'its meanings decoded, its hostility tamed',[16] the orientalist stands condemned. If the Orient, rather than becoming familiar, is seen as unfamiliar and unknown, the orientalist again stands condemned. Said aims to unmask and dispel illusion, and yet he does not specify what to replace this illusion with. This reflects an important feature of Foucault's philosophy, whose analyses seem to be an unmasking of power, but at the same time argue that the idea of liberating truth is an illusion. The regime relativity of truth implies that we can never attack our own episteme by appealing to any principle or set of principles, because these would constitute another truth regime.[17] It is in opposition to Foucault's notion of power that

[16] Edward Said, *Orientalism* (London: Routledge & Kegan Paul, 1978), 103.

[17] Michel Foucault, *Power/Knowledge: Selected Interviews and Other Writings, 1972–1977*, ed. Colin Gordon (Brighton: Harvester Press, 1980), 131–3; see also 'Questions of Method: An Interview with Michel Foucault', in Kenneth Baynes *et al.*, (eds.), *After Philosophy: End or Transformation?* (Cambridge, Mass.: MIT Press, 1987), 108–15. It also remains a puzzle as to how we are to stand outside our episteme in order to shape an analysis of its systems of power if our location in this episteme is, as Foucault implies, inescapable.

Charles Taylor argues for seeing power as imposed constraint, thereby relating it to some sense of purposeful human agency, and to some idea of the possibilities of liberation.[18] As it is, the circularity of Said's argument and its all-encompassing notion of power in some ways actually impedes our understanding of orientalist discourses and their relationships to power and knowledge so as to obscure both the scope and weight of these texts, and the nature of imperial power in such a context as early nineteenth-century British India. By operating with a more limited notion of power, one would also be able to address the problems which Sadik Jalal al-'Azm raises about orientalism in reverse by analysing how both indigenous and orientalist idioms actually shaped and moulded each other in a variety of ambiguous relationships.[19]

Such an approach would enable us to evaluate the intricacies of texts not simply as part of the kind of orientalism mapped out by Said, but also in terms other than those which form the parameters of his rather monolithic definition of orientalist discourse. Indeed, both Bentham's and Mill's attempts to articulate an idiom in which cultures could be compared and contrasted, as well as criticized, could suggest some ways in which the central problems raised by Said about the nature of cross-cultural understanding in general[20] might be approached. It is also important not to assess the intellectual endeavour embodied in Mill's utilitarianism simply on the basis of its lack of real influence on policy in British India, and to thereby dismiss it, in Bernard Williams's phrase, as 'Government House utilitarianism'.[21] In his powerful argument for the integrity of a patriotic history, Ranajit Guha has stressed the need to challenge Mill's annexation of Indian history as a portion of British history.[22] In doing so, he has discussed Bankimchandra's notion that a true history of Bengal could only be a representation of its past by Bengalis themselves.[23] But in his discussion of ethnocentri-

18 'Foucault on Freedom and Truth', 173–4.

19 Indira Chowdhury Sengupta has analysed this in relation to 19th-century Bengali historiography in 'History as an Empowering Discourse in Nineteenth Century Bengal', a paper delivered at the Fifth Annual Conference of the British Association of South Asian Studies, Mar. 1991, SOAS, Univ. of London.

20 Said, *Orientalism*, 24, 327.

21 Bernard Williams, *Ethics and the Limits of Philosophy* (London: Fontana Press, 1985), 108.

22 Ranajit Guha, *An Indian Historiography of India: A Nineteenth-Century Agenda and its Implications* (Calcutta: K. P. Bagchi, 1988), 50.

23 Ibid. 57.

city and understanding, Charles Taylor has pointed out the dangers of accepting self-descriptions uncritically in the effort to understand the agents of another culture. Making sense of agents does require that we understand their self-descriptions; but we can only make sense of them if we grasp both how they see things and what is wrong and self-contradictory in their self-descriptions. This may be the starting point of understanding another culture. Simply recovering self-descriptions casts no light on events, precisely because the relevant language of self-description may be confused and contradictory.[24] Challenging these languages of self-description would also involve challenging our own; the one cannot be questioned without questioning the other. Taylor cites Montesquieu as 'an excellent example of an illuminating theory in comparative politics' which uses a 'language of perspicuous contrast'.[25] It is misleading to represent James Mill as simply annexing Indian history as a portion of British history. Mill's purpose was to attack the powerfully dominant ideology of British society at the time and his *History* used British India as a matrix in which to do so. In its attack it defined a secular language in which cultures could be compared and contrasted, as well as criticized. Both Bentham and Mill made it abundantly clear that criticizing another culture meant criticizing one's own. Mill at least offered the possibility of some sort of liberating critique, that is a critique which affords the possibility of changing the way we define ourselves in order to change our practices for the better. For such a possibility to exist, sometimes it is necessary to give little weight to the past. The relationship between our past and present selves is in any case far from unproblematic.[26] If Mill's *History* was an exercise in philistinism, it was also an exercise in disenchantment, but this disenchantment was necessary in order to cut through the bolstering of constraining identities with which a set of aesthetic attitudes was in profound collusion.

[24] Charles Taylor, *Social Theory as Practice* (Delhi: Oxford University Press, 1983), 28–30.

[25] Ibid. 38–9.

[26] Derek Parfit has a thought-provoking analysis of these problems in *Reasons and Persons* (Oxford: Oxford University Press, 1986), part 3.

Bibliography

PRIMARY WORKS

Sir William Jones

The Works of Sir William Jones, ed. A. M. Jones, 6 vols. (London: G. G. and J. Robinson, R. H. Evens [*sic*], 1799).

'A Discourse on the Institution of a Society, for Inquiring into the History, Civil and Natural, the Antiquities, Arts, Sciences, and Literature of Asia', *Asiatick Researches*, 1 (1788), pp. ix–xvi.

'On the Gods of Greece, Italy and India', *Asiatick Researches*, 1 (1788), 221–75.

'A Conversation with Abram, an Abyssinian, Concerning the City of Gwender and the Sources of Nile', *Asiatick Researches*, 1 (1788), 383–8.

'The Second Anniversary Discourse', *Asiatick Researches*, 1 (1788), 405–14.

'On the Hindu's [*sic*]', *Asiatick Researches*, 1 (1788), 414–32.

'On the Arabs', *Asiatick Researches*, 2 (1790), 1–17.

'On the Tartars', *Asiatick Researches*, 2 (1790), 19–41.

'On the Persians', *Asiatick Researches*, 2 (1790), 43–66.

'The Design of a Treatise on the Plants of India', *Asiatick Researches*, 2 (1790), 345–52.

'On the Musical Modes of the Hindus: Written in 1784, and since much Enlarged', *Asiatick Researches*, 3 (1792), 165–83.

'On the Mystical Poetry of the Persians and Hindus', *Asiatick Researches*, 3 (1792), 165–83.

'On the Origin and Families of Nations', *Asiatick Researches*, 3 (1792), 479–92.

'Asiatick History, Civil and Natural', *Asiatick Researches*, 4 (1794), 1–17.

'On the Philosophy of the Asiaticks', *Asiatick Researches*, 4 (1794), 165–80.

The Letters of Sir William Jones, ed. G. Cannon, 2 vols. (Oxford: Clarendon Press, 1970).

TEIGNMOUTH, Baron (John Shore), *Memoirs of the Life, Writings, and Correspondence of Sir William Jones* (London: J. Brettell and John Hatchard, 1804).

Robert Southey

The Correspondence of Robert Southey with Caroline Bowles, ed. Edward Dowden (London: Longmans, Green & Co., 1881).

New Letters of Robert Southey, ed. Kenneth Curry, 2 vols. (New York and London: Columbia University Press, 1965).

The Life and Correspondence of Robert Southey, ed. Revd. Charles Cuthbert Southey, 6 vols. (London: Longman, Brown, Green & Longmans, 1849).

'Baptist Missionary Society', *Annual Review for 1802*, 1 (1803), 207–18.

'*Asiatick Researches*', *Annual Review for 1803*, 2 (1804), 898–908.

'Edward Davies' *Celtic Researches*', *Annual Review for 1804*, 3 (1805), 634–44.

'James Bruce's *Travels to Discover the Source of the Nile*', *Annual Review for 1805*, 4 (1806), 2–16.

'Moore's *Epistles, Odes, and other Poems*', *Annual Review for 1806*, 5 (1807), 498–9.

'Sharon Turner's *History of the Anglo-Saxons*', *Annual Review for 1807*, 6 (1808), 219–26.

'*Asiatick Researches*', *Annual Review for 1807*, 6 (1808), 643–54.

'Baptist Missionary Society', *Quarterly Review*, 1 (Feb. and May 1809), 193–226.

'Lives of Nelson', *Quarterly Review*, 3 (Feb. 1810), 218–62.

'On the Evangelical Sects', *Quarterly Review*, 4 (May 1810), 480–514.

'Sir George Stewart Mackenzie's *Travels in the Island of Iceland, during the Summer of the year 1810,* and William Jackson Hooker's *Journal of a Tour in Iceland, in the Summer of 1809*', *Quarterly Review*, 7 (Mar. 1812), 48–92.

'Forbes' *Oriental Memoirs*', *Quarterly Review*, 12 (Oct. 1814), 180–227.

'*Travels of Ali Bey in Morocco, Tripoli, Cyprus, Egypt, Arabia, Spain, and Turkey between the Years 1803 and 1807*', *Quarterly Review*, 15 (July 1816), 299–345.

'Henry Koster's *Travels in Brazil*', *Quarterly Review*, 15 (July 1816), 344–87.

'Life of Cromwell', *Quarterly Review*, 25 (July 1825), 279–347.

'Dr. Sayers' *Works*', *Quarterly Review*, 35 (Jan. 1827), 175–220.

'Political and Moral State of Portugal', *Quarterly Review*, 41 (July 1829), 184–226.

'George Head's *Forest Scenes and Incidents in the Wilds of North America*', *Quarterly Review*, 42 (Jan. 1830), 80–105.

'Moral and Political State of the British Empire', *Quarterly Review*, 44 (Jan. 1831), 261–317.

'Moore's *The Life and Death of Lord Edward Fitzgerald*', *Quarterly Review*, 46 (Nov. 1831), 213–63.

Thalaba the Destroyer (1801), in *The Poetical Works of Robert Southey, Collected by Himself*, 10 vols. (London: Longman, Orme, Brown, Greene, and Longmans, 1840), vol. iv.

Madoc (1805), in *The Poetical Works of Robert Southey, Collected by Himself* (London: Longman, Orme, Brown, Green and Longmans, 1840), vol. v.

The Curse of Kehama (1810), in *The Poetical Works of Robert Southey, Collected by Himself* (London: Longman, Orme, Brown, Green, and Longmans, 1840), vol. viii.

'The Poet's Pilgrimage to Waterloo', in *The Poetical Works of Robert Southey, Collected by Himself* (London: Longman, Orme, Brown, Green, and Longmans, 1840), vol. x.

History of Brazil, 3 vols. (London: Longman, Orme, Brown, Green, and Longmans, 1810–19).

The Byrth, Lyf, and Actes of Kyng Arthur; of his Noble Knyghtes of the Rounde Table, Theyr Merveyllous Conquestes and Adventures, introduction and notes by Southey, 2 vols. (London: Longman, Hurst, Rees, Orme, and Brown, 1817).

Sir Thomas More: Or, Colloquies on the Progress and Prospects of Society, 2 vols. (London: John Murray, 1829).

Essays, Moral and Political, 2 vols. (London: John Murray, 1832).

Oliver Newman: A New-England Tale (Unfinished): With Other Poetical Remains, ed. Herbert Hill (London: Longman, Brown, Green, and Longmans, 1845).

Journal of a Tour in Scotland in 1819, ed. C. H. Herford (London: John Murray, 1929).

Southey's Common-Place Book, ed. John Wood Warter, 4 vols. (London: Longmans, 1849).

Selections from the Letters of Robert Southey, ed. John Wood Warter, 4 vols. (London: Longman, Brown, Green, and Longmans, 1856).

Thomas Moore

The Poetical Works of Thomas Moore, ed. Thomas Moore, 10 vols. (London: Longman, Orme, Brown, Green, and Longmans, 1840–1).

Memoirs, Journal, and Correspondence of Thomas Moore, ed. Lord John Russell, 8 vols. (London: Longman, Brown, Green, and Longmans, 1853).

Prose and Verse Humorous, Satirical, and Sentimental, by Thomas Moore, with Suppressed passages from the Memoirs of Lord Byron, chiefly from the Author's Manuscript and all hitherto Inedited [*sic*] *and Uncollected*, ed. R. H. Shepherd (London: Chatto and Windus, 1878).

The Letters of Thomas Moore, ed. Wilfred S. Dowden, 2 vols. (Oxford: Clarendon Press, 1964).

The Journal of Thomas Moore, ed. Wilfred S. Dowden, 3 vols. (Newark: University of Delaware Press, 1983–6).

Letter to the Roman Catholics of Dublin (London: J. Carpenter, 1810).

Lalla Rookh: An Oriental Romance (London: Longman, Hurst, Rees, Orme, and Brown, 1817).

Fables for the Holy Alliance (London: Longman, Hurst, Rees, Orme, and Brown, 1823).

Memoirs of Captain Rock, the Celebrated Irish Chieftain. Written by Himself (London: Longman, Hurst, Rees, Orme, Brown, and Green, 1824).

'Ode to the Sublime Porte', *The Times*, 3 Nov. 1826.

'State of Protestantism in Germany', *Edinburgh Review*, 54 (Sept. 1831), 238–55.

Travels of an Irish Gentleman in Search of a Religion. By the Editor of 'Captain Rock's Memoirs', 2 vols. (London: Longman, Rees, Orme, Brown, Green, and Longman, 1833).

'Henry O'Brien's *The Round Towers of Ireland*', *Edinburgh Review*, 59 (Apr. 1834), 143–54.

The History of Ireland, 3 vols. (London: Longman, 1838–46).

Jeremy Bentham

Bentham Papers, University College, London.

Bentham Papers, British Library.

Of Laws in General, in *The Collected Works of Jeremy Bentham*, ed. H. L. A. Hart (London: The Athlone Press, 1970).

An Introduction to the Principles of Morals and Legislation (1789), in *The Collected Works of Jeremy Bentham*, ed. J. H. Burns and H. L. A. Hart (London: The Athlone Press, 1970).

Chrestomathia, in *The Collected Works of Jeremy Bentham*, ed. M. J. Smith and W. H. Burston (Oxford: Clarendon Press, 1983).

Plan of Parliamentary Reform, in the Form of a Catechism, with Reasons for Each Article, Shewing the Necessity of Radical, and the Inadequacy of Moderate, Reform (London: R. Hunter, 1817).

'Emancipate Your Colonies! Jeremy Bentham to the National Convention of France, January 1793. An Unpublished Argument' (London: R. Hunter, 1838).

'Essay on the Influence of Time and Place in Matters of Legislation', in *The Works of Jeremy Bentham*, ed. John Bowring (Edinburgh: William Tait; London: Simpkin, Marshall, & Co., 1843), i. 171–94.

Panopticon; or, the Inspection-House: Containing the Idea of a New Principle of Construction Applicable to any Sort of Establishment, in which Persons of any description are to be kept under Inspection (1791), in *The Works of Jeremy Bentham*, ed. John Bowring (Edinburgh: William Tait; London: Simpkin, Marshall, & Co., 1843), vol. iv.

James Mill

Francis Place papers, British Library.

Macvey Napier papers, British Library.

'Malthus' *Essay on the Principle of Population*', *Literary Journal*, 2 (Dec. 1803), 577–87.

'Horne Tooke's *Diversions of Purley*', *Literary Journal of Domestic and Foreign Literature*, 1 (1806), 1–16.

'C. J. Fox's *A History of the early Part of the Reign of James the Second*', *Annual Review for 1808*, 7 (1809), 99–114.

'De Guignes' Voyage à Pekin', *Edinburgh Review*, 14 (July 1809), 407–29.

'Voyage aux Indies Orientale', *Edinburgh Review*, 15 (Jan. 1810), 363–84.

'Affairs of India', *Edinburgh Review*, 16 (Apr. 1810), 127–57.

'Malcolm's *Sketch of the Political History of India*', *Edinburgh Review*, 20 (1812), 38–54.

'Charles Stewart's *History of Bengal*', *Eclectic Review*, 1 (1814), 140–58.
'Dugald Stewart's *Elements of the Philosophy of the Human Mind*', *British Review*, 6 (1815), 170–200.
'Southey's *Book of the Church*', *Westminster Review*, 3 (Jan. 1825), 167–212.
'Ecclesiastical Establishments', *Westminster Review*, 5 (Apr. 1826), 504–48.
'Formation of Opinions', *Westminster Review*, 6 (May–July 1826), 1–23.
'The State of the Nation', *Westminster Review*, 6 (May–July 1826), 249–78.
'The State of the Nation', *London Review*, 1 (Apr.–July 1835), 1–24.
'The Church, and its Reform', *London Review*, 1 (Apr.–July 1835), 257–95.
'The Article Colony', reprinted from the Supplement to the *Encyclopaedia Britannica* (London: J. Innes, *c.*1820).
Essays on Government, Jurisprudence, Liberty of the Press, and Law of Nations. Written for the Supplement to the Encyclopaedia Britannica (London: J. Innes, *c.*1825).
A Fragment on Mackintosh (London: Baldwin and Cradock, 1835).
The History of British India (1817), 5th edn. with Notes and Continuation by H. H. Wilson, 10 vols. (London: James Madden, Piper, Stephenson, and Spence, 1858).
The History of British India, ed. William Thomas (Chicago: University of Chicago Press, 1975).
Analysis of the Phenomena of the Human Mind (1828); new edn. with Notes Illustrative and Critical by Alexander Bain, Andrew Findlater, and George Grote; ed. with Additional Notes by John Stuart Mill, 2 vols. (London: Longmans, Green, Reader, and Dyer, 1869).
James Mill: Selected Economic Writings, ed. Donald Winch (Edinburgh: published for the Scottish Economic Society by Oliver and Boyd, 1966).
James Mill on Education, ed. W. H. Burston (Cambridge: Cambridge University Press, 1969).

OTHER WORKS CONSULTED

AARSLEFF, HANS, *The Study of Language in England 1780–1860* (1967; Minneapolis: University of Minnesota Press, 1983).
ABDEL-MALEK, ANWAR, 'Orientalism in Crisis', *Diogenes*, 44 (1963), 103–40.
ABRAMS, M. H., *Natural Supernaturalism: Tradition and Revolution in Romantic Literature* (New York: W. H. Norton & Co., 1980).
—— *The Correspondent Breeze: Essays on English Romanticism* (New York: W. H. Norton & Co., 1984).
ADAMS, P. G., *Travel Literature and the Evolution of the Novel* (Lexington, Ky.: University Press of Kentucky, 1983).
AHMED, AKBAR S., *Millenium and Charisma among Pathans: A Critical Essay in Social Anthropology* (London: Routledge and Kegan Paul, 1976).

—— *Toward Islamic Anthropology: Definition, Dogma, and Directions* (Lahore: Vanguard, 1987).

AKENSIDE, MARK, *The Pleasures of Imagination: A Poem* (London: R. Dodsley, 1744).

AL-'AZM, SADIK JALAL, 'Orientalism and Orientalism in Reverse', *Khamsin, Journal of Revolutionary Socialists of the Middle East*, 8 (1981), 5–26.

ANDERSON, BENEDICT, *Imagined Communities: Reflections on the Origin and Spread of Nationalism* (London: Verso, 1983).

ANTIPPAS, ANDY P., 'Four New Southey Letters', *Wordsworth Circle*, 5 (Spring 1974), 91–6.

ARBERRY, A. J., 'New Light on Sir William Jones', *Bulletin of the School of African and Oriental Studies*, 11 (1943–6), 673–85.

—— 'Persian Jones', *Asiatick Review*, 40 (Apr. 1944), 186–96.

—— *Asiatic Jones: The Life and Influence of Sir William Jones* (London: Longman, 1946).

ARNOLD, MATTHEW, *The Complete Prose Works of Matthew Arnold*, ed. R. H. Super, 11 vols. (Ann Arbor, Mich.: University of Michigan Press, 1962).

—— *Matthew Arnold on Education*, ed. Gillian Sutherland (London: Penguin, 1973).

ASAD, TALAL (ed.), *Anthropology and the Colonial Encounter* (London: Ithaca Press, 1973).

—— with DIXON, JOHN, 'Translating Europe's Others', in Francis Barker (ed.), *Europe and its Others*, 2 vols. (Colchester: University of Essex Press, 1985), 170–7.

The Asiatick Miscellany: Consisting of Original Productions, Fugitive Pieces, Translations, Imitations, and Extracts, from Curious Publications, 2 vols. (Calcutta: Daniel Stuart, 1785).

BAIN, ALEXANDER, *James Mill: A Biography* (London: Longmans, Green, & Co., 1882).

BALDICK, CHRIS, *The Social Mission of English Criticism 1848–1932* (Oxford: Clarendon Press, 1983).

BALLHATCHET, K., 'The Home Government and Bentinck's Educational Policy', *Cambridge Historical Journal*, 10 (1950–2), 224–9.

—— *Social Policy and Social Change in Western India 1817–1830* (London: Oxford University Press, 1957).

—— *Race, Sex and Class under the Raj: Imperial Attitudes and Policies and their Critics, 1793–1905* (London: Weidenfeld and Nicholson, 1980).

BARKER, FRANCIS, *et al.* (eds.) *1789: Reading Writing Revolution* (Colchester: University of Essex Press, 1982).

—— *Europe and its Others*, 2 vols. (Colchester: University of Essex Press, 1985).

BARRELL, J., *English Literature in History 1730–80: An Equal, Wide Survey* (London: Hutchinson, 1983).

BAYLY, C. A., *Indian Society and the Making of the British Empire* (Cambridge: Cambridge University Press, 1988).

—— *Imperial Meridian: The British Empire and the World 1780–1830* (London: Longman, 1989).

BAYNES, KENNETH, *et al.* (eds.), *After Philosophy: End or Transformation?* (Cambridge, Mass.: MIT Press, 1987).

BEAGLEHOLE, T. H., *Thomas Munro and the Development of Administration Policy in Madras 1792–1818: The Origin of 'the Madras System'* (Cambridge: Cambridge University Press, 1966).

BEARCE, G. D., *British Attitudes towards India, 1784–1858* (Oxford: Oxford University Press, 1961).

BECK, L. W. (ed.), *On History: Immanuel Kant* (Indianapolis: The Library of Liberal Arts, 1963).

BECKETT, J. C., *A Short History of Ireland* (1952; London: Hutchinson University Library, 1971).

—— *The Anglo-Irish Tradition* (London: Faber and Faber, 1976).

BERNAL, MARTIN, 'Black Athena Denied: The Tyranny of Germany over Greece and the Rejection of the Afroasiatic Roots of Europe: 1780–1980', *Comparative Criticism*, 8 (1986), 3–69.

BERNHARDT-KABISCH, ERNEST, 'Southey in the Tropics: *A Tale of Paraguay* and the Problem of Romantic Faith', *Wordsworth Circle*, 5 (Spring 1974), 97–104.

BEST, G. F. A., 'The Protestant Constitution and its Supporters, 1800–1829', *Transactions of the Royal Historical Society*, 5th series 8 (1958), 105–27.

BEYER, WERNER W., *The Enchanted Forest* (Oxford: Basil Blackwell, 1963).

BONFANTE, GIULIANO, 'Ideas on the Kinship of the European Languages from 1200 to 1800', *Journal of World History*, 1 (July 1953), 679–99.

BOWERSOCK, G. W. *et al.* (eds.), *Edward Gibbon and the Decline and Fall of the Roman Empire* (Cambridge, Mass.: Harvard University Press, 1977).

BRAMSTED, E. K., and MELHUISH, K. J. (eds.), *Western Liberalism: A History in Documents from Locke to Croce* (London: Longmans, 1978).

BRASTED, H. V., 'Irish Models and the Indian National Congress, 1870–1922', *Journal of South Asian Studies, NS* 8 (June–Dec. 1985), 24–45.

BRINTON, CRANE, *The Political Ideas of the English Romanticists* (1926; University of Michigan Press, 1966).

BROWN, WALLACE CABLE, 'Thomas Moore and English Interest in the East', *Studies in Philology*, 34 (1937), 576–88.

—— 'Robert Southey and English Interest in the Near East', *English Literary History*, 5 (1938), 218–24.

BRYANT, JACOB, *A New System; or, An Analysis of Ancient Mythology: Wherein an Attempt is Made to Divest Tradition of Fable; and to reduce the Truth to its Original Purity*, 3 vols. (1774; London: T. Payne, 1775).

BURKE, EDMUND, *Reflections on the Revolution in France and on the Proceedings in Certain Societies in London Relative to that Event* (1790; ed. with an introduction by Conor Cruise O'Brien (London: Penguin, 1984).

—— *An Appeal from the New to the Old Whigs, in Consequence of some Late Discussions in Parliament, Relative to the Reflections on the French Revolution* (London: J. Stocdall, 1791).

—— *The Writings and Speeches of Edmund Burke: India: Madras and Bengal*, ed. P. J. Marshall (Oxford: Clarendon Press, 1981), vol. v.

BURSTON, W. H., *James Mill on Philosophy and Education* (London: The Athlone Press, 1973).

BUTLER, MARILYN, *Romantics, Rebels & Reactionaries: English Literature and its Background 1760–1830* (Oxford: Oxford University Press, 1981).

—— 'Revising the Canon', *The Times Literary Supplement*, (4–10 Dec. 1987), 1349, 1359–60.

CANARY, ROBERT H., and KOZICKI, HENRY, *Literary Form and Historical Understanding* (Madison, Wis.: University of Wisconsin Press, 1978).

CANNON, G., 'A New, Probable Source for "Kubla Khan"', *College English*, 17 (Dec. 1955), 136–42.

—— 'Sir William Jones and Edmund Burke', *Modern Philology*, 54 (1956–7), 165–86.

—— 'The Literary Place of Sir William Jones, 1746–94', *Journal of the Asiatic Society*, 11 (1960), 47–61.

—— 'Five New Letters by Sir William Jones', *Philological Quarterly*, 51 (1972), 951–5.

—— 'Foundations of Oriental and Comparative Studies: The Correspondence of Sir William Jones', *Comparative Criticism*, 3 (1981), 157–96.

—— 'The Construction of the European Image of the Orient: A Bicentenary Re-appraisal of Sir William Jones as Poet and Translator', *Comparative Criticism*, 8 (1986), 167–88.

—— *Oriental Jones: A Biography of Sir William Jones (1746–1794)* (New York: Asia Publishing House, 1964).

CANNON, J., *Parliamentary Reform 1640–1832* (Cambridge: Cambridge University Press, 1973).

CARNALL, GEOFFREY, *Robert Southey and His Age: The Development of a Conservative Mind* (Oxford: Clarendon Press, 1960).

CHADWICK, HENRY, *The Early Church* (London: Pelican, 1967).

CHANDLER, J. K., *Wordsworth's Second Nature: A Study of the Poetry and Politics* (Chicago: Chicago University Press, 1984).

CHATTERJEE, PARTHA, *Nationalist Thought and the Colonial World: A Derivative Discourse?* (London: Zed Books, 1978).

CLARK, J. C. D., *English Society 1688–1832: Ideology, Social Structure and Political Practice during the Ancien Regime* (Cambridge: Cambridge University Press, 1985).

CLAYTON, P. A., *The Rediscovery of Ancient Egypt: Artists and Travellers in the Nineteenth Century* (London: Thames and Hudson, 1982).

CLIVE, JOHN, *Thomas Babington Macaulay: The Shaping of the Historian* (London: Secker and Warburg, 1973).

COBBAN, ALFRED, *Edmund Burke and the Revolt against the Eighteenth Century: A Study of the Political and Social Thinking of Burke, Wordsworth, Coleridge and Southey* (1929; London: George Allen and Unwin, 1960).

COHEN, RALPH, 'History and Genre', *New Literary History*, 17 (Winter 1986), 203–18.

COHN, B. S., *An Anthropologist among the Historians and Other Essays* (Delhi: Oxford University Press, 1987).

Coleman, B., *Conservatism and the Conservative Party in Nineteenth-Century Britain* (London: Edward Arnold, 1988).

Coleridge, Hartley, 'On the Poetical Use of the Heathen Mythology', *London Magazine*, 5 (Feb. 1822), 113–20.

Coleridge, S. T., *The Collected Letters of Samuel Taylor Coleridge*, ed. E. L. Griggs, 6 vols. (Oxford: Clarendon Press, 1959), vol. iv.

—— *Biographia Literaria or Biographical Sketches of My Literary Life and Opinions* (1817), ed. George Watson (London: J. M. Dent, 1975).

—— *The Collected Works of Samuel Taylor Coleridge*, ed. John Colmer (Princeton, NJ: Princeton University Press, 1976), vol. x.

—— 'Mr. Southey and Wat Tyler I', *Essays on his Times*, ed. David V. Erdman, 3 vols. in *The Collected Works of S. T. Coleridge*, ed. Kathleen Coburn (London: Routledge and Kegan Paul, 1978), ii. 449–54.

—— 'Mr. Southey and Wat Tyler II', *Essays on his Times*, ed. David V. Erdman, 3 vols. (London: Routledge and Kegan Paul, 1978), ii. 454–60.

—— 'Mr. Southey and Wat Tyler IV: Apostacy and Renegadism', *Essays on his Times*, ed. David V. Erdman, 3 vols. (London: Routledge and Kegan Paul, 1978), ii. 473–8.

Colley, L., 'The Apotheosis of George III: Loyalty, Royalty, and the British Nation 1760–1820', *Past and Present*, 102 (1984), 94–129.

Collins, William, *The Poems of Thomas Gray, William Collins, Oliver Goldsmith*, ed. Roger Lonsdale (London: Longmans, 1980).

Conant, P., *The Oriental Tale in England in the Eighteenth Century* (1908; New York: Octagon Books, 1967).

Copley, A. R. H., 'Projection, Displacement and Distortion in Nineteenth Century Moral Imperialism: A Re-examination of Charles Grant and James Mill', *Calcutta Historical Journal*, 7 (1953), 1–26.

Critical Review, 59 (1785), 19–21, review of William Jones, 'A Discourse on the Institution of a Society', and 'A Hymn to Camdeo'.

Cronin, Richard, *Imagining India* (London: Macmillan Press, 1989).

Culler, A. Dwight, 'Monodrama and the Dramatic Monologue', *Publication of the Modern Language Association of America*, 90 (May 1975), 366–85.

Cunningham, V., *Everywhere Spoken Against: Dissent in the Victorian Novel* (Oxford: Clarendon Press, 1977).

Curry, Kenneth, 'Southey's Contributions to *The Quarterly Review*', *Wordsworth Circle*, 6 (Autumn 1975), 261–72.

—— *Southey* (London: Routledge and Kegan Paul, 1975).

Cutts, Elmer, 'The Background of Macaulay's Minute', *The American Historical Review*, 58 (Oct. 1952–July 1953), 824–53.

Dalby, Michael, 'Nocturnal Labors in the Light of Day', *The Journal of Asian Studies*, 39 (May 1980), 485–93.

Davy, Humphry, *Fragmentary Remains, Literary and Scientific, of Sir Humphrey Davy*, ed. John Davy (London: John Churchill, 1858).

De Meester, Marie E., *Oriental Influence in the English Literature of the Nineteenth Century* (Heidelberg, 1915).

De Quincey, Thomas, 'Idea of a Universal History on a Cosmo-politan Plan by Immanuel Kant', *London Magazine*, 10 (Oct. 1824), 385–93.

DERRETT, J. D. M., *Religion, Law and the State in India* (London: Faber and Faber, 1968).

DINWIDDY, J. R., '"The Patriotic Linen-Draper": Robert Waithman and the Revival of Radicalism in the City of London 1795–1818', *Bulletin of the Institute of Historical Research*, 46 (May 1973), 72–94.

—— 'Bentham's Transition to Political Radicalism 1809–10', *Journal of the History of Ideas*, 36 (Oct.–Dec. 1975), 683–700.

DIRKS, N. B., *The Hollow Crown: Ethnohistory of an Indian Kingdom* (Cambridge: Cambridge University Press, 1987).

DREW, J., *India and the Romantic Imagination* (Delhi: Oxford University Press, 1987).

DUMONT, LOUIS, *Homo Hierarchichus: The Caste System and its Implications* (Chicago: University of Chicago Press, 1980).

DYSON, K. K., *A Various Universe: A Study of the Journals and Memoirs of British Men and Women in the Indian Subcontinent 1765–1856* (Oxford: Oxford University Press, 1978).

EAGLETON, TERRY, *Literary Theory: An Introduction* (Oxford: Basil Blackwell, 1983).

EMBREE, A. T., *Charles Grant and British Rule in India* (London: George Allen and Unwin, 1962).

—— *Imagining India: Essays on Indian History*, ed. by Mark Juergensmeyer (Delhi: Oxford University Press, 1990).

EMSLEY, CLIVE, *British Society and the French Wars 1793–1815* (London: Macmillan Press, 1979).

FAIRCHILD, H. N., *The Noble Savage: A Study in Romantic Naturalism* (New York: Columbia University Press, 1928).

FARQUHAR, J. N., *Modern Religious Movements in India* (New York: Macmillan & Co., 1915).

FENN, R. A., *James Mill's Political Theory and Political Philosophy* (New York: Garland Publishing Inc., 1987).

FERGUSON, ADAM, *An Essay on the History of Civil Society* (1766; London: T. Cadell, 1773).

'Fifth Report from the Select Committee on the Affairs of the East India Company', *Parliamentary Papers*, 7 (1812).

FISCH, JORG, *Cheap Lives and Dear Limbs: The British Transformation of the Bengal Criminal Law 1769–1817* (Wiesbaden: Franz Steiner Verlag, 1983).

FORBES, DUNCAN, 'James Mill and India', *Cambridge Journal*, 5 (Oct. 1951–Sept. 1952), 19–33.

FORBES, JAMES, *Reflections on the Character of the Hindoos and on the Importance of Converting them to Christianity. Being the Preface to, and Conclusion of, a Series of Oriental Letters, Which Will Shortly be Published* (London: White and Cochrane, 1810).

—— *Oriental Memoirs: Selected and Abridged from a Series of Familiar Letters Written during Seventeen Years Residence in India: Including Observations on Parts of Africa and South America, and a Narrative of Occurrences in Four India Voyages* (London: White, Cochrane, & Co., 1813).

FOUCAULT, MICHEL, *The Order of Things: An Archaeology of the Human Sciences* (1966; London: Tavistock Publications, 1970).

—— *The Archaeology of Knowledge* (1969; London: Tavistock Publications, 1972).

—— *Power/Knowledge: Selected Interviews and Other Writings, 1972–1977*, ed. by Colin Gordon (Brighton: The Harvester Press, 1980).

FRYKENBURG, R. E. (ed.), *Land Control and Social Structure in Indian History* (Madison, Wis.: University of Wisconsin Press, 1969).

—— 'Company Circari in the Carnatic, *c.* 1799–1859: The Inner Logic of Political Systems in India', in R. G. Fox (ed.), *Realm and Region in Traditional India* (Delhi: Vikas, 1977), 117–64.

GAINES, BARRY, 'The Editions of Malory in the Early Nineteenth Century', *The Papers of the Bibliographical Society of America*, 68 (1974), 1–17.

GALLAGHER, J., and SEAL, ANIL, *Locality, Province and Nation: Essays on Indian Politics, 1870–1940* (Cambridge: Cambridge University Press, 1973).

GASKILL, HOWARD, '"Ossian" Macpherson: Towards a Rehabilitation', *Comparative Criticism*, 8 (1986), 113–46.

GEDDES, ALEXANDER, *Prospectus of a New Translation of the Holy Bible* (Glasgow: printed for the author, 1786).

—— *The Holy Bible; or, The Books Accounted Sacred by Jews and Christians; Otherwise Called the Books of the Old and New Covenants: Faithfully Translated from Corrected Texts of the Originals* (London: printed for the author by J. Davis, 1792).

GELLNER, ERNEST, 'In Defence of Orientalism', *Sociology*, 14 (May 1980), 295–9.

—— *Nations And Nationalism* (1983; Oxford: Basil Blackwell, 1984).

—— *Relativism and the Social Sciences* (Cambridge: Cambridge University Press, 1985).

GIBBON, EDWARD, *The History of the Decline and Fall of the Roman Empire* (1776–88), ed. William Smith, 8 vols. (London: John Murray, 1862).

GIDDENS, ANTHONY, *Profiles and Critiques in Social Theory* (London: Macmillan, 1982).

GILLEY, SHERIDAN, 'Nationality and Liberty, Protestant and Catholic: Robert Southey's Book of the Church', in Stuart Mews (ed.), *Religion and National Identity* (Oxford: Basil Blackwell, 1982), 409–32.

GODECHOT, JACQUES, *The Counter-Revolution: Doctrine and Action, 1789–1804* (London: Routledge and Kegan Paul, 1961).

GOLDSMITH, OLIVER, *The Poems of Thomas Gray, William Collins, Oliver Goldsmith*, ed. Roger Lonsdale (London: Longmans, 1980).

GOSSMAN, ANN, '"Harmonious Jones" and Milton's Invocations', *Notes and Queries*, 199 (1954), 527–29.

GRANT, C., 'Observations on the State of Society among Asiatic Subjects of Great Britain, particularly with respect to Morals; and on the means of improving it. Written chiefly in the year 1792', *Parliamentary Papers*, 10 (1812–13), paper 282.

GRAY, THOMAS, *The Poems of Thomas Gray, William Collins, Oliver Goldsmith*, ed. Roger Lonsdale (London: Longmans, 1980).
GREENBERG, MICHAEL, *British Trade and the Opening of China 1800–42* (1951; New York: Monthly Review Press, 1979).
GUHA, RANAJIT, *A Rule of Property for Bengal: An Essay on the Idea of Permanent Settlement* (New Delhi: Orient Longman, 1982).
—— 'On some Aspects of the Historiography of Colonial India', *Subaltern Studies*, 1 (Delhi: Oxford University Press, 1982), 1–8.
—— 'The Prose of Counter-Insurgency', *Subaltern Studies*, 2 (Delhi: Oxford University Press, 1983), 1–40.
—— *An Indian Historiography of India: A Nineteenth-Century Agenda and its Implications* (Calcutta: K. P. Bagchi, 1988).
—— *Selected Subaltern Studies* (New York: Oxford University Press, 1988).
—— 'Dominance without Hegemony and its Historiography', *Subaltern Studies*, 6 (Delhi: Oxford University Press, 1989), 276–329.
GUPTA, K. P. S., *The Christian Missionaries in Bengal 1793–1833* (Calcutta: Firma K. L. Mukhopadhyay, 1971).
HARRIS, ROY, *The Language Makers* (London: Duckworth, 1980).
HARRISON, ROSS, *Bentham* (London: Routledge and Kegan Paul, 1983).
HARTLEY, DAVID, *Observations on Man, His Frame, His Duty, and His Expectations*, 2 vols. (London: James Leake and Wm. Frederick, 1749).
HAZLITT, W., *The Spirit of the Age; or, Contemporary Portraits* (1825), in *The Complete Works of William Hazlitt*, ed. P. P. Howe (London: J. M. Dent, 1932), vol. xi.
HEBER, REGINALD, 'Southey's *History of Brazil*', *Quarterly Review*, 4 (Nov. 1810), 434–74.
HECHTER, M., *Internal Colonialism: The Celtic Fringe in British National Development* (London: Routledge and Kegan Paul, 1975).
HEGEL, G. W. F., *Lectures on the Philosophy of World History*, trans. H. B. Nisbet, with an introduction by Duncan Forbes (Cambridge: Cambridge University Press, 1975).
HENNIG, JOHN, 'Thomas Moore as Theologian', *Irish Monthly*, 75 (1947), 114–24.
HERBERT, BEDA, 'Thomas Moore, Apologist', *Irish Monthly*, 80 (1952), 48–52.
HEWITT, R. M., 'Harmonious Jones', *Essays and Studies*, 28 (1942), 42–59.
HEXTER, T. H., 'The Protestant Revival and the Catholic Question in England 1778–1829', *Journal of Modern History*, 8 (Mar.–Dec. 1936), 297–319.
HILL, GEOFFREY, 'A Short History of British India', in *Tenebrae* (London: André Deutsch, 1978).
HILLIKER, J. F., 'English Utilitarians and Indian Education', *Journal of General Education*, 27 (Apr. 1975–Jan. 1976), 103–10.
HILTON, BOYD, *The Age of Atonement: The Influence of Evangelicalism on Social and Economic Thought, 1795–1865* (Oxford: Clarendon Press, 1988).

HJEJLE, B., 'The Social Policy of the East India Company with Regard to Sati, Slavery, Thagi, and Infanticide, 1772–1858' (D.Phil thesis, Oxford, 1958).

HOFFPAUIR, RICHARD, 'The Thematic Structure of Southey's Epic Poetry', *Wordsworth Circle*, 6 (Autumn 1975), 240–8.

HOLLIS, MARTIN, and LUKES, STEVEN, *Rationality and Relativism* (1982; Oxford: Basil Blackwell, 1983).

HONE, J. ANN, *For the Cause of Truth: Radicalism in London 1796–1821* (Oxford: Clarendon Press, 1982).

HUME, L. J., 'Bentham's Panopticon: An Administrative History—1', *Historical Studies*, 15 (Oct. 1973), 703–21.

—— 'Bentham's Panopticon: An Administrative History—2', *Historical Studies*, 16 (Apr. 1974), 36–54.

—— 'The Political Function of Bentham's Theory of Fictions', *Bentham Newsletter*, 3 (Dec. 1979), 18–27.

HUMPHREYS, R. A., *Robert Southey and his History of Brazil* (London: The Hispanic and Luso-Brazilian Council, 1978).

HUTCHINS, FRANCIS G., *The Illusion of Permanence: British Imperialism in India* (Princeton, NJ: Princeton University Press, 1967).

INDEN, RONALD, 'Orientalist Constructions of India', *Modern Asian Studies*, 20 (July 1986), 401–46.

—— *Imagining India* (Oxford: Basil Blackwell, 1990).

INGHAM, K., *Reformers in India 1793–1833: An Account of the Work of Christian Missionaries on Behalf of Social Reform* (Cambridge: Cambridge University Press, 1956).

IYER, R. (ed.), *The Glass Curtain between Asia and Europe: A Symposium on the Historical Encounters and the Changing Attitudes of the Peoples of the East and the West* (London: Oxford University Press, 1965).

—— 'Utilitarianism and All That (The Political Theory of British Imperialism in India)', *South Asian Affairs*, 8 (1960), 9–71.

JARRETT-KERR, MARTIN, 'Indian Religion in English Literature 1675–1967', *Essays and Studies*, 37 (1984), 87–103.

JEFFERSON, ANNE, and ROBEY, DAVID, *Modern Literary Theory: A Comparative Introduction* (London: Batford, 1982).

JEFFREY, FRANCIS, 'Southey's *Thalaba*', *Edinburgh Review*, 1 (Oct. 1802), 63–83.

—— 'Southey's *The Curse of Kehama*', *Edinburgh Review*, 17 (Feb. 1811), 429–65.

—— 'Moore's *Lalla Rookh*', *Edinburgh Review*, 18 (1817), 1–35.

JOHNSTON, H. J. M., *British Emigration Policy 1815–30* (Oxford: Clarendon Press, 1972).

JORDAN, HOOVER H., *Bolt Upright: The Life of Thomas Moore*, 2 vols. (Salzburg: Salzburg Studies in English Literature, 1975).

KANT, IMMANUEL, *The Critique of Judgement*, trans. J. C. Meredith (Oxford: Clarendon Press, 1952).

—— *Critique of Pure Reason* (1787), trans. N. K. Smith (London: Macmillan, 1963).

KAPP, ROBERT A., 'Introduction to Review Symposium of Edward Said's Orientalism', *Journal of Asian Studies*, 39 (May 1980), 481–4.

KATZ, JONATHAN, 'Indian Musicological Literature and its Context', *Purusartha*, 7 (1983), 37–75.

KEJARIWAL, O. P., *The Asiatic Society of Bengal and the Discovery of India's Past 1784–1838* (Delhi: Oxford University Press, 1988).

KENNEDY, WILLIAM F., *Humanist Versus Economist: The Economic Thought of Samuel Taylor Coleridge*, University of California Publications in Economics, 17 (Berkeley, Calif.: University of California Press, 1958).

KING, R. W., 'A Note on Shelley, Gibbon, Voltaire, and Southey', *Modern Language Review*, 51 (1956), 225–7.

KOEBNER, R., 'Despot and Despotism: Vicissitudes of a Political Term', *Journal of the Warburg and Courtauld Institutes*, 14 (1951), 275–302.

KOPF, DAVID, 'Hermeneutics versus History', *Journal of Asian Studies*, 39 (May 1980), 495–506.

—— *British Orientalism and the Bengal Renaissance: The Dynamics of Indian Modernization 1773–1835* (Berkeley, Calif.: University of California Press, 1969).

LA CAPRA, DOMINICK, *Rethinking Intellectual History: Texts, Contexts, Language* (Ithaca, NY: Cornell University Press, 1983).

—— *History and Criticism* (Ithaca, NY: Cornell University Press, 1985).

LAIRD, M. A., *Missionaries and Education in Bengal 1793–1837* (Oxford: Clarendon Press, 1972).

LAITINEN, KAI, *Literature of Finland: An Outline* (Helsinki: Otava, 1985).

LAURIE, W. F. B. (ed.), *Sketches of Some Distinguished Anglo-Indians*, 2 vols. (London: W. H. Allen & Co., 1888).

LEASK, NIGEL, *The Politics of the Imagination in Coleridge's Critical Thought* (Basingstoke: Macmillan, 1988).

LECKIE, G. F., *An Historical Survey of the Foreign Affairs of Great Britain* (London: J. Bell, 1808).

LEERSEN, JOSEPH, 'On the Edge of Europe: Ireland in Search of Oriental Roots, 1650–1850', *Comparative Criticism*, 8 (1986), 91–112.

LEVIN, DAVID, *History as Romantic Art: Bancroft, Prescott, Motley, and Parkman* (Stanford, Calif.: Stanford University Press, 1959).

LIVELY, JACK, and REES, JOHN (eds.), *Utilitarian Logic and Politics: James Mill's 'Essay on Government', Macaulay's Critique and the Ensuing Debate* (Oxford: Clarendon Press, 1978).

LLOYD-JONES, HUGH, *et al.* (eds.), *History and Imagination: Essays in honour of H. R. Trevor Roper* (London: Duckworth & Co., 1981).

LOWTH, R., *Lectures on the Sacred Poetry of the Hebrews: Translated from the Latin of the Right Rev. Robert Lowth, D.D., to which are added, the Principal Notes of Professor Michaelis, and Notes by the Translator and Others* (London: J. Johnson, 1787).

LURKER, MANFRED, *The Gods and Symbols of Ancient Egypt: An Illustrated Dictionary* (London: Thames and Hudson, 1980).

MACAULAY, THOMAS BABINGTON, *The Works of Lord Macaulay*, 12 vols. (London: The Albany Edition, 1898).

—— *Macaulay's Essays on Lord Clive and Warren Hastings*, ed. John Lord (London, n.d.).

—— 'The Present Administration', *Edinburgh Review*, 46 (June–Oct. 1827), 245–67.

—— 'Utilitarian Logic and Politics', *Edinburgh Review* 49 (Mar. 1829), 159–89.

—— 'Southey's *Colloquies*', *Edinburgh Review*, 50 (Jan. 1830), 528–65.

McCalman, Ian, 'Unrespectable Radicalism: Infidels and Pornography in Early Nineteenth Century London', *Past and Present*, 104 (1984), 74–110.

McCormack, W. J., *Ascendancy and Tradition in Anglo-Irish History from 1789 to 1939* (Oxford: Clarendon Press, 1985).

Machin, G. I. T., *The Catholic Question in English Politics 1820 to 1830* (Oxford: Clarendon Press, 1964).

Maine, Henry Sumner, *The Effects of Observation of India on Modern European Thought* (London: John Murray, 1875).

Marshall, P. J., *The Impeachment of Warren Hastings* (Oxford: Oxford University Press, 1965).

—— *The British Discovery of Hinduism in the Eighteenth Century* (Cambridge: Cambridge University Press, 1970).

—— *Bengal: The British Bridgehead. Eastern India 1740–1828* (Cambridge: Cambridge University Press, 1987).

—— 'Empire and Authority in the later Eighteenth Century', *Journal of Imperial and Commonwealth History*, 15 (Jan. 1987), 105–22.

—— 'The Whites of British India: A Failed Colonial Society?', paper delivered at the Institute of Commonwealth Studies, University of London, 12 Nov. 1988.

Marshman, J. C., *The Life and Times of Carey, Marshman, and Ward: Embracing the History of the Serampore Mission*, 2 vols. (London: Longman & Co., 1859).

Martyn, Henry, *Journals and Letters of the Rev. Henry Martyn, B.D.*, ed. Revd. S. Wilberforce, 2 vols. (London: Thames Ditton, 1837).

Masters, Alfred, 'The Influence of Sir William Jones upon Sanskrit Studies', *Bulletin of the School of Oriental and African Studies*, 11 (1943–6), 798–806.

Mazlish, Bruce, 'James Mill and the Utilitarians', *Daedalus*, 97 (1968), 1036–59.

Mill, John Stuart, *Essays on Ethics, Religion, and Society*, textual editor John M. Robson, introductions by F. E. L. Priestley and D. P. Dryer, in *Collected Works of John Stuart Mill* (Toronto: University of Toronto Press, 1969), vol. x.

—— *A System of Logic Ratiocinative and Inductive: Being a Connected View of the Principles of Evidence and the Methods of Scientific Investigation*, textual editor John M. Robson, introduction by R. F. McRae, *Collected Works of John Stuart Mill* (Toronto: University of Toronto Press, 1973), vols. vii–viii.

—— *Essays on Politics and Society*, textual editor John M. Robson, introduction by Alexander Brady, in *Collected Works of John Stuart Mill* (Toronto: University of Toronto Press, 1977), vols. xviii–xix.

—— *On Bentham and Coleridge*, ed. F. R. Leavis (Cambridge: Cambridge University Press, 1980).

—— *Autobiography and Literary Essays*, ed. John M. Robson and Jack Stillinger in *Collected Works of John Stuart Mill*, vol. i (Toronto: University of Toronto Press, 1981).

—— *Utilitarianism*, ed. Mary Warnock (London: Fontana Press, 1985).

—— *Writings on India*, ed. J. M. Robson, Martin Moir, and Zawahir Moir, in *Collected Works of John Stuart Mill* (Toronto: University of Toronto Press, 1990), vol. xxx.

MINEAR, RICHARD H., 'Orientalism and the Study of Japan', *Journal of Asian Studies*, 39 (May 1980), 507–17.

MIRSKY, N. D., 'Mixed Marriages in Anglo-Indian and Indo-Anglian Fiction', (M.Litt. thesis, Oxford, 1985).

MITTER, PARTHA, *Much Maligned Monsters: History of European Reactions to Indian Art* (Oxford: Clarendon Press, 1977).

MOIR, MARTIN, 'The Examiner's Office: The Emergence of an Administrative Elite in East India House (1804–58)', *India Office Library and Records: Report for the Year 1977*.

MOORE, R. J., 'John Stuart Mill at East India House', *Historical Studies*, 20 (Oct. 1983), 497–519.

MOORE-GILBERT, B. J., *Kipling and Orientalism* (London: Croom Helm, 1986).

'Moore's *Captain Rock*', *Westminster Review*, 1 (Jan.–Apr. 1824), 492.

'Moore's *Fables for the Holy Alliance*', *Westminster Review*, 1 (Jan.–Apr. 1824), 18–26.

'Moore's *Lalla Rookh*', *British Review*, 10 (1817), 30–54.

'Moore's *Lalla Rookh*', *Critical Review*, 5 (1817), 560–81.

'Moore's *Letters and Journals of Lord Byron, with Notices of his Life*', *Westminster Review*, 12 (Jan.–Apr. 1830), 270–304.

MORGAN, PETER F., 'Southey: A Critical Spectrum', *Wordsworth Circle*, 5 (Spring 1974), 71–5.

MORGAN, PRYS, *A New History of Wales: The Eighteenth Century Renaissance* (Llandybie: Christopher Davies, 1981).

MOUSSA-MAHMOUD, F., *Sir William Jones and the Romantics* (Cairo: Anglo-Egyptian Bookshop, 1962).

MUKHERJEE, S. N., *Sir William Jones: A Study in Eighteenth-Century British Attitudes to India* (Cambridge: Cambridge University Press, 1968).

NANDY, ASHIS, *The Intimate Enemy: Loss and Recovery of Self under Colonialism* (1983; Delhi: Oxford University Press, 1988).

NISBET, ROBERT, *Conservatism: Dream and Reality* (Milton Keynes: Open University Press, 1986).

NIZAMI, F. H., 'Madrasahs, Scholars, and Saints: Muslim Response to the British Presence in Delhi and the Upper Doab 1803–1857' (D.Phil thesis, Oxford, 1983).

OBER, WARREN U., '"Mohammed": The Outline of a Proposed Poem by Coleridge', *Notes and Queries*, 203 (Jan.–Dec. 1958), 448.

OGDEN, C. V., *Bentham's Theory of Fictions* (London: Kegan Paul & Co., 1932).

—— 'The State of Nature and the Decline of Lockian Political Theory in England 1760–1800', *American Historical Review*, 46 (1940–1), 21–44.

O'HALLORAN, CLARE, 'Irish Re-creations of the Gaelic Past: The Challenge of Macpherson's Ossian', *Past and Present*, 124 (Aug. 1989), 69–95.

OWEN, ROGER, and SUTCLIFFE, BOB (eds.), *Studies in the Theory of Imperialism* (1972; London: Longmans, 1980).

PADEL, FELIX, 'British Rule and the Konds of Orissa: A Study of Tribal Administration and its Legitimating Discourse' (D.Phil thesis, Oxford, 1987).

PAINE, T., *Rights of Man* (1791; Harmondsworth: Penguin, 1984).

PARFIT, DEREK, *Reasons and Persons* (Oxford: Oxford University Press, 1986).

PEACOCK, T. L., 'Moore's *The Epicurean*', *Westminster Review*, 8 (Apr.–July 1827), 351–84.

—— *The Four Ages of Poetry*, in *The Works of T. L. Peacock*, ed. H. Cole (London: Richard Bentley & Sons, 1875), iii. 324–38.

PHILIPS, C. H. (ed.), *Historical Writing on the Peoples of Asia: Historians of India, Pakistan, and Ceylon* (1961; Oxford: Oxford University Press, 1962).

PINTO, V. DE SOLA, 'Sir William Jones and English Literature', *Bulletin of the School of Oriental and African Studies*, 11 (1943–6), 686–98.

PLAMENATZ, JOHN, *The English Utilitarians* (Oxford: Basil Blackwell, 1966).

POSTEMA, GERALD J., *Bentham and the Common Law Tradition* (1986; Oxford: Clarendon Press, 1989).

POTTS, E. D., *British Baptist Missionaries in India 1793–1837. The History of Serampore and its Missions* (Cambridge: Cambridge University Press, 1967).

PRICE, RICHARD, *A Discourse on the Love of our Country* (London: T. Cadell, 1789).

PROUDFIT, CHARLES L., 'Southey and Landor: A Literary Friendship', *Wordsworth Circle*, 5 (Spring 1974), 105–12.

PUSEY, E. P., *An Historical Enquiry into the Probable Causes of the Rationalist Character Lately Predominant in the Theology of Germany*, 2 vols. (London: C. and J. Rivington, 1828).

RAWSON, CLAUDE, 'Dining out in Paris and London', *The Times Literary Supplement*, 6 Sept. 1985, 963–4.

RAYCHAUDHURI, TAPAN, *Europe Reconsidered: Perceptions of the West in Nineteenth Century Bengal* (Delhi: Oxford University Press, 1988).

ROBINS, R. H., *A Short History of Linguistics* (London: Longman, 1979).

ROELLINGER, FRANCIS X., Jr., 'Mill on Education', *Journal of General Education*, 6 (Oct. 1951–July 1952), 246–59.

ROGERSON, J., *Old Testament Criticism in Nineteenth Century England and Germany* (London: SPCK, 1984).

ROSE, H. J., *The State of the Protestant Religion in Germany: in a Series of Discourses Preached before the University of Cambridge* (J. Deighton & Sons, 1825).

ROSEN, FREDERICK, *Jeremy Bentham and Representative Democracy: A Study of the Constitutional Code* (Oxford: Clarendon Press, 1983).

ROSSELLI, JOHN, *Lord William Bentinck: The Making of a Liberal Imperialist 1774–1839* (London: Chatto and Windus for Sussex University Press, 1974).

RUDE, GEORGE, *The Crowd in the French Revolution* (1959; Oxford: Oxford University Press, 1967).

RUNYAN, WILLIAM RONALD, 'Bob Southey's Diabolical Doggerel: Its Influence on Shelley and Byron', *Wordsworth Circle*, 6 (Autumn 1975), 249–54.

RYAN, ALAN, 'Two Concepts of Politics and Democracy: James and John Stuart Mill', in Martin Fleisher (ed.), *Machiavelli and the Nature of Political Thought* (London: Croom Helm, 1973).

—— *J.S. Mill* (London: Routledge and Kegan Paul, 1974).

SAID, EDWARD, *Orientalism* (London: Routledge and Kegan Paul, 1978).

—— *The World, the Text, and the Critic* (1983; London: Faber and Faber, 1984).

SALISBURY, Lord, 'Disintegration', *Quarterly Review*, 156 (July–Oct. 1883), 559–95.

SCHNEIDER, ELISABETH, *Coleridge, Opium and Kubla Khan* (Chicago: University of Chicago Press, 1953).

SCHOPENHAUER, ARTHUR, *The World as Will and Representation*, 2 vols. trans. E. F. J. Payne (New York: Dover Publications, 1969).

SCHWAB, RAYMOND, *The Oriental Renaissance: Europe's Rediscovery of India and the East, 1680–1880* (1950); trans. Gene Patterson-Black and Victor Reinking (New York: Columbia University Press, 1984).

SCRUTON, ROGER, *Thinkers of the New Left* (London: Longman, 1985).

SEAL, ANIL, *The Emergence of Indian Nationalism: Competition and Collaboration in the Later Nineteenth Century* (Cambridge: Cambridge University Press, 1968).

SEDLAR, JEAN W., *India and the Greek World: A Study in the Transmission of Culture* (Totowa, NJ: Rowan and Littlefield, 1980).

SENGUPTA, INDIRA CHOWDHURY, 'History as an Empowering Discourse in Nineteenth Century Bengal', paper delivered at the Fifth Annual Conference of the British Association of South Asian Studies, Mar. 1991, SOAS, Univ. of London.

SHAFFER, E. S., 'Rhetoric, "Orientalism" and Comparative Method', *Comparative Criticism*, 3 (1981), pp. xi–xxii.

—— *'Kubla Khan' and the Fall of Jerusalem: The Mythological School in Biblical Criticism and Secular Literature 1770–1880* (Cambridge: Cambridge University Press, 1975).

SHELLEY, MARY, *Frankenstein* (1818; Harmondsworth: Penguin, 1968).

SHORE, JOHN, 'Respecting the Permanent Settlement of the Lands in the Bengal Provinces', 18 June 1789, in *Parliamentary Papers*, 7 (1812), 182.

SIMMONS, JACK, *Southey* (London: Collins, 1945).

SINGH, BHUPAL, *A Survey of Anglo-Indian Fiction* (London: Oxford University Press, 1934).

SINGH, IQBAL, *Rammohun Roy: A Biographical Inquiry into the Making of Modern India* (London: Asia Publishing House, 1958).

SIRKIN, G., and SIRKIN, N. R., 'Of Raising Myths for Fun and Profit', *Columbia Forum*, 11 (Autumn 1968), 33–5.

—— —— 'The Battle of Indian Education: Macaulay's Opening Salvo Newly Discovered', *Victorian Studies*, 14 (June 1971), 407–28.

—— —— 'John Stuart Mill and Disutilitarianism in Indian Education', *Journal of General Education*, 24 (Apr. 1972–Jan. 1973), 231–65.

SMART, BARRY, *Michel Foucault* (Milton Keynes: Open University, Key Sociologists series, 1985).

SMITH, BYRON PORTER, *Islam in English Literature* (Beirut: American Press, 1939).

SMITH, OLIVIA, *The Politics of Language 1791–1819* (Oxford: Clarendon Press, 1984).

SOUSA-LEAO, J. DE, 'Southey and Brazil', *Modern Language Review*, 38 (1943), 181–91.

SPEAR, PERCIVAL, *The Oxford History of Modern India 1740–1975* (Delhi: Oxford University Press, 1978).

STAFFORD, WILLIAM, 'Religion and the Doctrine of Nationalism in England at the Time of the French Revolution and Napoleonic Wars', in Stuart Mews (ed.), *Religion and National Identity* (Oxford: Basil Blackwell, 1982), 381–95.

STANTON, MICHAEL N., 'Southey and the Art of Autobiography', *Wordsworth Circle*, 5 (Spring 1974), 113–19.

STOKES, ERIC, *The English Utilitarians and India* (1959; Oxford: Clarendon Press, 1963).

—— *The Peasant and the Raj: Studies in Agrarian Society and Peasant Rebellion in Colonial India* (Cambridge: Cambridge University Press, 1978).

—— 'Bureaucracy and Ideology: Britain and India in the Nineteenth Century', *Transactions of the Royal Historical Society*, 5th Series, 30 (1980), 131–56.

STORCH, R. F., 'The Politics of the Imagination', *Studies in Romanticism*, 21 (Autumn 1982), 448–56.

STREET, BRIAN, 'Orientalist Discourses in the Anthropology of Iran, Afghanistan, and Pakistan', in Richard Fardon (ed.), *Localising Strategies* (Edinburgh: Edinburgh University Press, 1989), 240–59.

TAWNEY, R. H., *Religion and the Rise of Capitalism* (1926; London: Penguin, 1961).

TAYLOR, CHARLES, *Social Theory as Practice* (Delhi: Oxford University Press, 1983).

—— 'Foucault on Freedom and Truth', *Political Theory*, 12 (May 1984), 152–83.

TAYLOR, THOMAS, 'The Dream: An Imitation of the Beginning of the Eleventh Book of Apuleius', *Monthly Magazine and British Register for 1797*, 4 (1798), 375–6.

THAPAR, ROMILA, 'Interpretations of Ancient Indian History', *History and Theory*, 7 (1968), 318–35.

—— 'Imagined Religious Communities? Ancient History and the Modern Search for a Hindu Identity', *Modern Asian Studies*, 23 (1989), 209–31.

—— MUKHIA, HARBANS, and CHANDRA, BIPAN, *Communalism and the Writing of Indian History* (New Delhi: People's Publishing House, 1977).

THOMAS, WILLIAM, *The Philosophic Radicals: Nine Studies in Theory and Practice 1817–1841* (Oxford: Clarendon Press, 1979).

—— *Mill* (Oxford: Oxford University Press, 1985).

TODD, F. M., *Politics and the Poet: A Study of Wordsworth* (London: Methuen, 1957).

TREVELYAN, CHARLES E., *On the Education of the People of India* (London: Longman, Orme, Brown, Green, and Longmans, 1838).

VENTURI, FRANCO, 'Oriental Despotism', *Journal of the History of Ideas*, 24 (Jan.–Mar. 1963), 133–42.

VERELST, H., *A View of the Rise, Progress, and Present State of the English Government in Bengal, Including a Reply to the Misrepresentations of Mr. Bolts, and other writers* (London: printed for J. Nourse, Brotherton, and Sewell, G. Robinson, T. Evans, 1772).

VESEY-FITZGERALD, S. G., 'Sir William Jones, the Jurist', *Bulletin of the School of Oriental and African Studies*, 11 (1943–6), 807–17.

VISWANATHAN, GAURI, *Masks of Conquest: Literary Study and British Rule in India* (London: Faber and Faber, 1990).

VOLNEY, CONSTANTINE FRANÇOIS DE, *The Ruins: or, A Survey of the Revolutions of Empires, to which is Added, the Law of Nature, by the same Author* (London: H. D. Symonds, 1801).

WALLACE, ANTHONY F., 'Revitalization Movements', *American Anthropologist*, 58 (Apr. 1956), 261–81.

WARNOCK, MARY, *Imagination* (London: Faber and Faber, 1976).

WASHBROOK, D. A., 'Law, State and Agrarian Society in Colonial India', *Modern Asian Studies*, 15 (1981), 649–721.

WEBER, MAX, *The Protestant Ethic and the Spirit of Capitalism*, trans. Talcott Parsons (London: Allen and Unwin, 1930).

WELLECK, RENÉ, *Immanuel Kant in England 1793–1838* (Princeton, NJ: Princeton University Press, 1931).

WESSELING, H. L. (ed.), *Expansion and Reaction: Essays on European Expansion and Reaction in Asia and Africa* (Leiden: Leiden University Press, 1978).

WHITE, HAYDEN, *Metahistory: The Historical Imagination in Nineteenth-Century Europe* (Baltimore: Johns Hopkins University Press, 1973).

—— 'The Narrativization of Real Events', *Critical Inquiry*, 7 (Summer 1981), 793–8.

—— 'The Politics of Historical Interpretation', *Critical Inquiry*, 9 (Sept. 1982), 113–37.

WILKINS, CHARLES (trans.), *The Bhagavad-Geeta* (London: C. Nourse, 1785).

WILLIAMS, BERNARD, *Ethics and the Limits of Philosophy* (London: Fontana Press, 1985).

WILLIAMS, GWYN A., 'Welsh Indians: The Madoc Legend and the First Welsh Radicalism', *History Workshop*, 1 (Spring 1976), 136–54.

—— *Madoc: The Making of a Myth* (Oxford: Oxford University Press, 1987).

WILLIAMS, RAYMOND, *Culture and Society 1780–1950* (1958; Harmondsworth: Penguin Books, 1979).

WILLIFORD, MIRIAM, 'Bentham on the Rights of Women', *Journal of the History of Ideas*, 36 (Jan.–Mar. 1975), 167–76.

WILSON, BRYAN R. (ed.), *Rationality* (1970; Oxford: Basil Blackwell, 1985).

WILSON, H. H., 'Education of the Natives of India', *Asiatic Journal*, 19 (Jan.–Apr. 1836), 1–16.

WINCH, DONALD, 'Classical Economics and the Case for Colonization', *Economica*, NS 30 (1963), 387–99.

—— *Classical Political Economy and Colonies* (London: London School of Economics and Political Science, 1965).

WITTFOGEL, K., *Oriental Despotism: A Comparative Study of Total Power* (New Haven, Conn.: Yale University Press, 1957).

WORDSWORTH, WILLIAM, 'Two Addresses to the Freeholders of Westmorland', in *The Prose Works of William Wordsworth*, ed. W. J. B. Owen and Jane Worthingtin Smyser (Oxford: Clarendon Press, 1974), vol. iii.

—— *Poetical Works*, ed. T. Hutchinson and E. de Selincourt (Oxford: Oxford University Press, 1981).

WRIGHT, HERBERT G., 'Southey's Relations with Finland and Scandinavia', *Modern Language Review*, 27 (Jan. 1932), 149–67.

—— 'Three Aspects of Southey', *Review of English Studies*, 9 (1933), 37–46.

YOVEL, YIRMIAHU, *Kant and the Philosophy of History* (Princeton, NJ: Princeton University Press, 1980).

ZALL, P. M., 'The Gothic Voice of Father Bear', *Wordsworth Circle*, 5 (Spring 1974), 120–8.

ZASTOUPIL, LYNN, 'J. S. Mill and India', *Victorian Studies*, 32 (Autumn 1988), 31–54.

Index

Printed in the United Kingdom
by Lightning Source UK Ltd.
103713UKS00001B/51

9 780198 117865